Inside a U.S. Embassy

Praise for the 2nd edition of *Inside a U.S. Embassy*

"An anthology of brief essays and personal testimonies penned by experienced professionals. . . . includes profiles . . . typical days . . . and amazing glimpses of the Foreign Service in action during moments of crisis. A fascinating revelation of the tireless men and women who labor to represent America abroad."

—*Midwest Book Review*

"I'm fascinated by the contents. I think that not only members of the Committee but all Americans will be deeply interested in this."

—Richard Lugar, R-Ind.
Senate Foreign Relations Committee

"I am absolutely a fan of this book. What makes it so interesting is that it's about individuals and what they do, and it's about how they support the United States in an active way."

—Ambassador Marc Grossman
Career Ambassador and Former Under Secretary of State for Political Affairs

"Every day in hundreds of places around the world, thousands of your fellow Americans are at work in direct support of you and your interests. From helping Americans in trouble, to formulating American foreign policy, to talking to foreign leaders about cooperation in hundreds of different areas from trade to technology to preventing nuclear war, these people make a difference. This book tells the fascinating inside story of how it all works."

—Ambassador Thomas R. Pickering
Boeing Company Senior Vice President for International Relations and
Former Under Secretary of State for Political Affairs

"*Inside a U.S. Embassy* is required reading for the first week of my university seminar on practical diplomacy. My students are amazed at the variety and uniqueness of Foreign Service work described in the book's first-hand accounts. I wouldn't teach the course without it."

—Ambassador Genta Hawkins Holmes
Former Diplomat in Residence, University of California, Davis

"*Inside a U.S. Embassy* sits on my desk and I recommend it to all interested in the Foreign Service."

—Ambassador Karl F. Inderfurth
Professorial Lecturer at George Washington University's Elliott School of
International Affairs and Former Assistant Secretary of State for South
Asian Affairs

"Readers will find an up-to-date, compelling, interesting, accurate and highly readable depiction of the Foreign Service and its vital role in service to our nation. The profiles and the stories all show the rich diversity of our people, in terms of both their varied backgrounds and the wide range of services they perform."

—Ambassador Ruth A. Davis
Distinguished Adviser for International Affairs at Howard University and
Former Director General of the Foreign Service

Inside a U.S. Embassy

DIPLOMACY AT WORK

Shawn Dorman, EDITOR

Foreign Service Books

A division of the American Foreign Service Association

Washington, D.C.

Foreign Service Books
American Foreign Service Association
2101 E Street N.W.
Washington DC 20037
(202) 338-4045; (800) 704-2372
www.afsa.org

Copyright © 2011 by FSBooks/American Foreign Service Association

All rights reserved.

First Edition, 1995, Karen Krebsbach (Editor)
Second Edition, 2003, Shawn Dorman (Editor)
Second Edition, Revised and Updated, 2005, Shawn Dorman (Editor)
Third Edition, 2011, Shawn Dorman (Editor)

ISBN 978-0-9649488-4-6

Library of Congress Control Number: 2011901135

Source for profile section maps: The World Factbook, 2010

Third Edition, Second Printing, September 2012

Printed in the United States by United Book Press on
acid-free Sustainable Forestry Initiative Certified paper.

Dedicated to the Men and Women
of the U.S. Foreign Service

Inside a U.S. Embassy
Diplomacy at Work

THIRD EDITION, 2011

Shawn Dorman, Editor and Project Director
Ian Houston, AFSA Executive Director and Book Project Adviser
Susan Maitra and Steve Honley, Associate Editors
Kathleen Dyson, Designer

Very special thanks to all the Foreign Service authors who shared their experiences for this book.

With warmest appreciation to the AFSA interns who helped out on the book project: Danielle Derbes, Laura Caton, Jennifer Thompson, Mark Hay, Ariana Austin, and Betsy Swift. Thank you to the AFSA Governing Board and to the members of the Inside Embassy Advisory Committee: John Naland, Ian Houston, Steve Kashkett, James Yorke, Susan Maitra, Rachel Friedland, Deborah Graze, Joe Bruns, Francesca Kelly, Austin Tracy, Yvette Malcioln, and Francisco Zamora. For expert proofing, many thanks go to Patricia Linderman and James Yorke. Special thanks to Kelly Adams-Smith for her support, and for writing. Much appreciation to the State Department's Office of Recruitment, Examination, and Employment, for making good use of the book from the very beginning. Thanks go to Potomac Books Publisher Sam Dorrance for his guidance, and to AFSA Executive Director Ian Houston, AFSA Treasurer Andrew Winter, and attorney Eric Rayman, for helping FSBooks become "real." And finally, deepest appreciation to *Foreign Service Journal* Editor Steve Honley, for always saying yes to another look, and to *FSJ* Senior Editor Susan Maitra for her wise counsel, endless patience, and support for the project.

Cover Photos: Front cover, from left: USAID Egypt Mission Director Hilda Arellano at a water project by the Nile River; Provincial Reconstruction Team Leader Jim DeHart in Panjshir, Afghanistan; Foreign Agricultural Service Attaché Holly Higgins with villagers in Lucknow, India; Deputy Chief of Mission Dan Picutta, EAP Assistant Secretary Chris Hill, Climate Change Special Envoy Todd Stern, and Acting State Spokesperson Robert Wood at a meeting with Chinese officials in Beijing. Back cover, from left: Ambassador Charles Ray at a USAID/World Health Organization event in Zimbabwe; Consular Officer Carolyn Dubrovsky at work in Kathmandu; Consulate Tijuana Foreign Service National Edgar Zamudio in Haiti for earthquake relief work.

Foreign Service Books
A division of the American Foreign Service Association
Washington, D.C.

Contents

PART II
Foreign Service Work and Life: Embassy, Employee, Family

PART III
A Day in the Life of the Foreign Service: One-Day Journals . . . 119

PART IV
The Foreign Service in Action: Tales from the Field 173

Why This Book?

By Shawn Dorman

Many Americans do not know what the Foreign Service is or understand what goes on inside a U.S. embassy. Yet the work done at our embassies and consulates around the world by the people who make up the Foreign Service is vitally important to America—our security, our economy, and our democracy. Every day, consular officers help stranded Americans get home. Every day, economic and commercial officers assist U.S. businesses to compete overseas. During times of upheaval, political officers are the ones on the front lines around the world keeping Washington informed about the real situation. U.S. diplomats negotiate the international agreements that end the wars, keep the peace, and protect and promote U.S. interests. Foreign Service diplomats and specialists are truly the unsung heroes of American foreign policy.

This book will give you an up-close and personal look into the work and lives of the people who make up the United States Foreign Service. The people you will meet work at big embassies as well as tiny consulates, in Asia, Africa, Europe, Latin America, and the Middle East. They are ambassadors and they are entry-level officers (and everything in between). They are development professionals, press officers, security agents, and computer experts. They are a diverse group, but they all share the same mission—to serve their country.

In the *Profiles* section, meet Foreign Service staff serving in almost every type of position in a typical U.S. embassy, and gain a sense of the vital role played by each member of an embassy team. In the *Day in the Life* section, take a rare hour-by-hour look at what Foreign Service employees actually do on the job, from Port-au-Prince to Vladivostok and beyond. The *Tales from the Field* section will give you a sense of the extraordinary, as the Foreign Service meets the challenges of today's complex world.

A new section for this third edition covers life and work in the Foreign Service, illustrating that it is not just a job, but a way of life. Beginning with the embassy country team, see how all the pieces of an embassy fit together; how a career is shaped; and how spouses, partners, and children navigate this unique lifestyle. Among other voices, hear from a Foreign Service National what it's like to work with Americans, from a spouse on working in the embassy, and from two young adults on growing up in the Foreign Service.

Input from our readers led us to write another new section, on joining the Foreign Service. Part V offers straightforward step-by-step guides to the complex hiring processes for State Department officers and specialists, the U.S. Agency for International Development (USAID), and the other foreign affairs agencies.

What Is the Foreign Service?

By John K. Naland and Susan Johnson

The 14,000 men and women of the Foreign Service represent the government and people of the United States. At more than 265 diplomatic and consular posts, the U.S. Foreign Service safeguards national security and manages America's relationships with the rest of the world. America's diplomacy began in the eighteenth century with Benjamin Franklin, Thomas Jefferson, John Adams, and others who were dispatched abroad by our young nation to promote its vital interests. Thanks to their skilled diplomacy, the warring colonies received vital French help—help that finally turned the tide of the revolution. In the years that followed, separate diplomatic and consular services evolved, each primarily staffed by short-term appointees who changed en masse after each new president took office.

Efforts to replace this inefficient "spoils system" gathered steam following a 1906 order by President Theodore Roosevelt that began to depoliticize the consular service and a 1909 order by President William Howard Taft to modernize the diplomatic service. Then, responding to America's increasing foreign involvement during and after World War I, U.S. Representative John Jacob Rogers, R-Mass., spearheaded the unification of the diplomatic and consular services into a single corps of professionals recruited and promoted on the basis of merit. The Foreign Service Act of 1924, known as the Rogers Act, established a career Foreign Service composed of professionals who possess keen understanding of the affairs, cultures, and languages of other countries and who are available to serve in assignments throughout the world as ordered. The Rogers Act of 1924 evolved into the Foreign Service Act of 1980, which set the framework of today's Foreign Service.

At any given time, two-thirds of Foreign Service personnel are stationed abroad staffing our embassies and consulates—serving one- to three-year tours—and one-third are working in the United States, mostly in Washington, D.C. Overseas, they are assisted by 37,000 locally employed staff. Domestically, they work beside Civil Service colleagues who provide continuity and expertise in functions such as legal, consular, and financial affairs. Foreign Service members work for five federal agencies: the Department of State, the U.S. Agency for International Development, the Department of Commerce's Foreign Commercial Service, the Department of Agriculture's Foreign Agricultural Service, and the International Broadcasting Bureau (primarily at the Voice of America). Foreign Service members also serve tours on congressional staffs and at other federal agencies, including the National Security Council, the Office of the U.S. Trade Representative, and the Department of Defense.

The Foreign Service is a career like no other. It is much more than a job; it is a uniquely demanding and rewarding way of life. As representatives of the United States to foreign governments, Foreign Service members have a direct impact on people's lives and participate in the making of history. They travel the globe, experiencing foreign cultures as no tourist can. They work alongside highly talented colleagues, face the unexpected every day, and find themselves in situations that push their ingenuity and creativity to the limit.

But a Foreign Service career also imposes significant demands. Typically, Foreign Service members spend two-thirds of their careers overseas, often in unhealthy or otherwise difficult locations. They live for extended periods of time far from parents, siblings, and old friends, and sometimes without familiar amenities or access to modern medical facilities. Due to international terrorism, Foreign Service members face physical danger almost everywhere they serve.

Most Foreign Service veterans, however, have found that the rewards of representing our nation far outweigh the personal burdens. Diplomacy is an instrument of national power, essential for maintaining effective international relationships, and a principal means through which the U.S. defends its interests, responds to crises, and achieves its international goals. The Foreign Service is a proud profession, safeguarding American interests by: managing diplomatic relations with other countries and international institutions; promoting peace and stability in regions of vital interest; bringing nations together to address global challenges; promoting democracy and human rights around the world; opening markets abroad to create jobs at home; helping developing nations establish stable economic environments; helping ensure that American businesspeople have a level playing field on which to compete for foreign investment and trade; protecting U.S. borders and helping legitimate foreign travelers enter the United States; and assisting U.S. citizens who travel or live abroad.

The American Foreign Service Association, established in 1924—the same year as the Foreign Service itself—is both a professional association and the collective bargaining representative for all active and retired Foreign Service professionals, more than 28,000 people. It negotiates the regulations affecting employees' careers, advocates Foreign Service issues before Congress, and communicates its professional concerns to the news media and general public. AFSA works to make the Foreign Service a better supported, more respected, and more satisfying place to spend a career and raise a family. These goals, in turn, serve to make the Foreign Service a more effective agent of U.S. international leadership.

Susan Johnson is AFSA president, and John Naland served as AFSA president from 2001 to 2003 and 2007 to 2009.

U.S. PRESENCE IN THE WORLD IN 2011

AFGHANISTAN
Kabul (E)

ALBANIA
Tirana (E)

ALGERIA
Algiers (E)

ANDORRA
Andorra La Vella (–)

ANGOLA
Luanda (E)

**ANTIGUA &
BARBUDA
ST. JOHNS** (–)

ARGENTINA
Buenos Aires (E)

ARMENIA
Yerevan (E)

AUSTRALIA
Canberra (E)
Melbourne (CG)
Perth (CG)
Sydney (CG)

AUSTRIA
Vienna (E)(M)

AZERBAIJAN
Baku (E)

BAHAMAS
Nassau (E)

BAHRAIN
Manama (E)

BANGLADESH
Dhaka (E)

**BARBADOS &
EAST CARIBBEAN**
Bridgetown (E)

BELARUS
Minsk (E)

BELGIUM
Brussels (E)(M)

BELIZE
Belmopan (E)

BENIN
Cotonou (E)

BERMUDA
Hamilton (CG)

BHUTAN
Thimpu (–)

BOLIVIA
La Paz (E)

**BOSNIA &
HERZEGOVINA**
Sarajevo (E)

BOTSWANA
Gaborone (E)

BRAZIL
Brasília (E)
Rio de Janeiro (CG)
São Paulo (CG)
Recife (C)

BRUNEI
Bandar Seri Begawan (E)

BULGARIA
Sofia (E)

BURKINA FASO
Ouagadougou (E)

BURMA
Rangoon (E)

BURUNDI
Bujumbura (E)

CAMBODIA
Phnom Penh (E)

CAMEROON
Yaounde (E)

CANADA
Ottawa (E)
Calgary (CG)
Halifax (CG)
Montreal (CG)(M)
Quebec City (CG)
Toronto (CG)
Vancouver (CG)
Winnipeg (C)

CAPE VERDE
Praia (E)

**CENTRAL
AFRICAN
REPUBLIC**
Bangui (E)

CHAD
N'Djamena (E)

CHILE
Santiago (E)

CHINA
Beijing (E)
Chengdu (CG)
Guangzhou (CG)
Hong Kong and Macau (CG)
Shanghai (CG)
Shenyang (CG)
Wuhan (CG)

COLOMBIA
Bogotá (E)

COMOROS
Moroni (–)

**CONGO,
DEMOCRATIC
REPUBLIC OF THE**
Kinshasa (E)

**CONGO, REPUBLIC
OF THE**
Brazzaville (E)

COSTA RICA
San Jose (E)

COTE D'IVOIRE
Abidjan (E)

CROATIA
Zagreb (E)

CUBA
Havana (IS)

CYPRUS
Nicosia (E)

CZECH REPUBLIC
Prague (E)

DENMARK
Copenhagen (E)

**DJIBOUTI,
REPUBLIC OF**
Djibouti (E)

**DOMINICAN
REPUBLIC**
Santo Domingo (E)

ECUADOR
Quito (E)
Guayaquil (CG)

EGYPT
Cairo (E)
Alexandria (APP)

EL SALVADOR
San Salvador (E)

**EQUATORIAL
GUINEA**
Malabo (E)

ERITREA
Asmara (E)

ESTONIA
Tallinn (E)

ETHIOPIA
Addis Ababa (E)(M)

FIJI
Suva (E)

FINLAND
Helsinki (E)

FRANCE
Paris (E)(M)
Marseille (CG)
Strasbourg (CG)
Bordeaux (APP)
Lyon (APP)
Rennes (APP)
Toulouse (APP)

GABON
Libreville (E)

GAMBIA, THE
Banjul (E)

GEORGIA
Tbilisi (E)

GERMANY
Berlin (E)
Dusseldorf (CG)
Frankfurt (CG)
Hamburg (CG)
Leipzig (CG)
Munich (CG)

GHANA
Accra (E)

GREECE
Athens (E)
Thessaloniki (CG)

GRENADA
St. George's (–)

GUATEMALA
Guatemala City (E)

GUINEA
Conakry (E)

GUINEA-BISSAU
Bissau (–)

GUYANA
Georgetown (E)

HAITI
Port-au-Prince (E)

HOLY SEE
Vatican City (E)

HONDURAS
Tegucigalpa (E)

HUNGARY
Budapest (E)

ICELAND
Reykjavik (E)

INDIA
New Delhi (E)
Chennai (CG)
Hyderabad (CG)
Kolkata (CG)
Mumbai (CG)

INDONESIA
Jakarta (E)
Surabaya (CG)
Medan (APP)

IRAN
Tehran (–)

IRAQ
Baghdad (E)

IRELAND
Dublin (E)

ISRAEL
Tel Aviv (E)
Jerusalem (CG)

ITALY
Rome (E)(M)
Florence (CG)
Milan (CG)
Naples (CG)

JAMAICA
Kingston (E)

JAPAN
Tokyo (E)
Naha, Okinawa (CG)
Osaka/Kobe (CG)
Sapporo (CG)
Fukuoka (C)
Nagoya (C)

JORDAN
Amman (E)

KAZAKHSTAN
Astana (E)
Almaty (CG)

KENYA
Nairobi (E)(M)

KIRBATI
Tarawa (–)

KOREA, NORTH
P'yongyang (–)

KOREA, SOUTH
Seoul (E)
Busan (APP)

KOSOVO
Pristina (E)

KUWAIT
Kuwait City (E)

KYRGYZ REPUBLIC
Bishkek (E)

LAOS
Vientiane (E)

LATVIA
Riga (E)

LEBANON
Beirut (E)

LESOTHO
Maseru (E)

LIBERIA
Monrovia (E)

LIBYA
Tripoli (E)

LIECHTENSTEIN
Vaduz (–)

LITHUANIA
Vilnius (E)

LUXEMBOURG
Luxembourg City (E)

MACEDONIA
Skopje (E)

MADAGASCAR
Antananarivo (E)

MALAWI
Lilongwe (E)

MALAYSIA
Kuala Lumpur (E)

MALDIVES
Male (–)

MALI
Bamako (E)

MALTA
Valletta (E)

MARSHALL ISLANDS, REPUBLIC OF
Majuro (E)

MAURITANIA
Nouakchott (E)

MAURITIUS
Port Louis (E)

MEXICO
Mexico City (E)
Ciudad Juarez (CG)
Guadalajara (CG)
Hermosillo (CG)
Matamoros (CG)
Monterrey (CG)
Nuevo Laredo (CG)
Tijuana (CG)
Merida (C)
Nogales (C)

MICRONESIA, FEDERATED STATES OF
Kolonia (E)

MOLDOVA
Chisinau (E)

MONACO
Monaco (–)

MONGOLIA
Ulaanbaatar (E)

MONTENEGRO
Podgorica (E)

MOROCCO
Rabat (E)
Casablanca (CG)

MOZAMBIQUE
Maputo (E)

NAMIBIA
Windhoek (E)

NAURU
Yaren (–)

NEPAL
Kathmandu (E)

NETHERLANDS
The Hague (E)(M)
Amsterdam (CG)

NETHERLANDS ANTILLES
Curaçao (CG)

NEW ZEALAND
Wellington (E)
Auckland (CG)

NICARAGUA
Managua (E)

NIGER
Niamey (E)

NIGERIA
Abuja (E)

NORWAY
Oslo (E)

OMAN
Muscat (E)

PAKISTAN
Islamabad (E)
Karachi (CG)
Lahore (CG)
Peshawar (CG)

PALAU, REPUBLIC OF
Koror (E)

PANAMA
Panama City (E)

PARAGUAY
Asuncion (E)

PAPUA NEW GUINEA
Port Moresby (E)

PERU
Lima (E)

PHILIPPINES
Manila (E)

POLAND
Warsaw (E)
Krakow (CG)

PORTUGAL
Lisbon (E)
Ponta Delgada, Azores (C)

QATAR
Doha (E)

ROMANIA
Bucharest (E)

RUSSIA
Moscow (E)
St. Petersburg (CG)
Vladivostok (CG)
Yekaterinburg (CG)

RWANDA
Kigali (E)

SAINT KITTS AND NEVIS
Basseterre (–)

SAINT LUCIA
Castries (–)

SAINT VINCENT AND THE GRENADINES
Kingstown (–)

SAMOA
Apia (E)

SAN MARINO
San Marino (–)

SAO TOME AND PRINCIPE
Sao Tome (–)

SAUDI ARABIA
Riyadh (E)
Dhahran (CG)
Jeddah (CG)

SENEGAL
Dakar (E)

SERBIA
Belgrade (E)

SEYCHELLES
Victoria (–)

SIERRA LEONE
Freetown (E)

SINGAPORE (E)

SLOVAKIA
Bratislava (E)

SLOVENIA
Ljubljana (E)

SOLOMON ISLANDS
Honiara (–)

SOMALIA
Mogadishu (–)

SOUTH AFRICA
Pretoria (E)
Cape Town (CG)
Durban (CG)
Johannesburg (CG)

SPAIN
Madrid (E)
Barcelona (CG)

SRI LANKA
Colombo (E)

SUDAN
Khartoum (E)
Juba (CG)

SURINAME
Paramaribo (E)

SWAZILAND
Mbabane (E)

SWEDEN
Stockholm (E)

SWITZERLAND
Bern (E)
Geneva (M)

SYRIA
Damascus (E)

TAIWAN
Taipei (American Institute)

TAJIKISTAN
Dushanbe (E)

TANZANIA
Dar es Salaam (E)

THAILAND
Bangkok (E)
Chiang Mai (CG)

TIMOR-LESTE
Dili (E)

TOGO
Lome (E)

TONGA
Nuku'alofa (–)

TRINIDAD & TOBAGO
Port of Spain (E)

TUNISIA
Tunis (E)

TURKEY
Ankara (E)
Istanbul (CG)
Adana (C)

TURKMENISTAN
Ashgabat (E)

TUVALU
Funafuti (–)

UGANDA
Kampala (E)

UKRAINE
Kyiv (E)

UNITED ARAB EMIRATES
Abu Dhabi (E)
Dubai (CG)

UNITED KINGDOM
London, England (E)
Belfast, Northern Ireland (CG)
Edinburgh, Scotland (CG)

UNITED STATES OF AMERICA
New York (M)
Washington (M)

URUGUAY
Montevideo (E)

UZBEKISTAN
Tashkent (E)

VANUATU
Port Villa (–)

VENEZUELA
Caracas (E)

VIETNAM
Hanoi (E)
Ho Chi Minh City (CG)

YEMEN
Sana'a (E)

ZAMBIA
Lusaka (E)

ZIMBABWE
Harare (E)

LEGEND

Embassy (E)

Consulate General (CG)

Consulate (C)

Mission to an International Organization (M)

Interest Section (IS)

American Presence Post (APP)

No U.S. Presence (–)

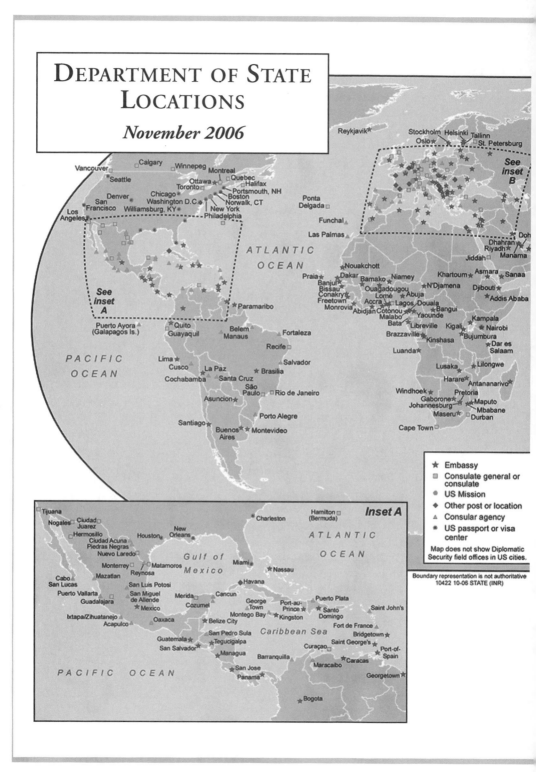

DEPARTMENT OF STATE LOCATIONS
November 2006

Reykjavik

Stockholm Helsinki Tallinn
Oslo St. Petersburg

See inset B

Vancouver   Calgary   Winnepeg   Montreal
Seattle   Ottawa   Quebec
                 Toronto   Halifax
Denver   Chicago   Portsmouth, NH
San   Washington D.C.   Boston
Francisco   Williamsburg, KY   Norwalk, CT
Los   New York
Angeles   Philadelphia

Ponta Delgada

Funchal

Las Palmas

ATLANTIC OCEAN

Dhahran
Riyadh   Manama
Jiddah

Nouakchott   Khartoum   Asmara   Sanaa
Praia   Dakar   Bamako   Niamey
Banjul   Ouagadougou   N'Djamena   Djibouti
Bissau   Conakry   Lomé   Abuja   Addis Ababa
Freetown   Accra   Lagos   Douala
Monrovia   Abidjan Cotonou   Bangui
           Malabo   Yaounde   Kampala
           Bata   Libreville   Kigali   Nairobi
           Brazzaville   Kinshasa   Bujumbura
                                      Dar es Salaam
Luanda

See inset A

Puerto Ayora (Galapagos Is.)   Quito   Belem   Fortaleza
                 Guayaquil   Manaus

Recife

Paramaribo

PACIFIC OCEAN

Lima   Salvador
Cusco   La Paz   Brasilia
Cochabamba   Santa Cruz
            São Paulo   Rio de Janeiro
Asuncion

Lusaka   Lilongwe
Harare   Antananarivo
Windhoek   Pretoria
Gaborone   Maputo
Johannesburg   Mbabane
Maseru   Durban

Cape Town

Porto Alegre

Santiago   Buenos Aires   Montevideo

★ Embassy
▢ Consulate general or consulate
● US Mission
◆ Other post or location
▲ Consular agency
✳ US passport or visa center

Map does not show Diplomatic Security field offices in US cities.

Boundary representation is not authoritative
10422 10-06 STATE (INR)

Inset A

Tijuana
Nogales   Ciudad Juarez   Charleston   Hamilton (Bermuda)
     Hermosillo   New
     Ciudad Acuna   Houston   Orleans   ATLANTIC OCEAN
     Piedras Negras
     Nuevo Laredo   Miami
Monterrey   Matamoros   Nassau
Cabo   Mazatlan   Reynosa
San Lucas
Puerto Vallarta   San Luis Potosi   Havana
Guadalajara   San Miguel   Cancun
          de Allende   Merida   Puerto Plata
          Mexico   Cozumel   George   Port-au-   Santo   Saint John's
Ixtapa/Zihuatanejo   Town   Prince   Domingo
   Acapulco   Oaxaca   Belize City   Montego Bay   Kingston
                                            Fort de France
                     San Pedro Sula   Caribbean Sea   Bridgetown
          Guatemala   Curaçao   Saint George's   Port-of-Spain
          San Salvador   Tegucigalpa
                 Managua   Barranquilla   Caracas
PACIFIC OCEAN   San Jose   Maracaibo   Georgetown
                 Panama
                       Bogota

Gulf of Mexico

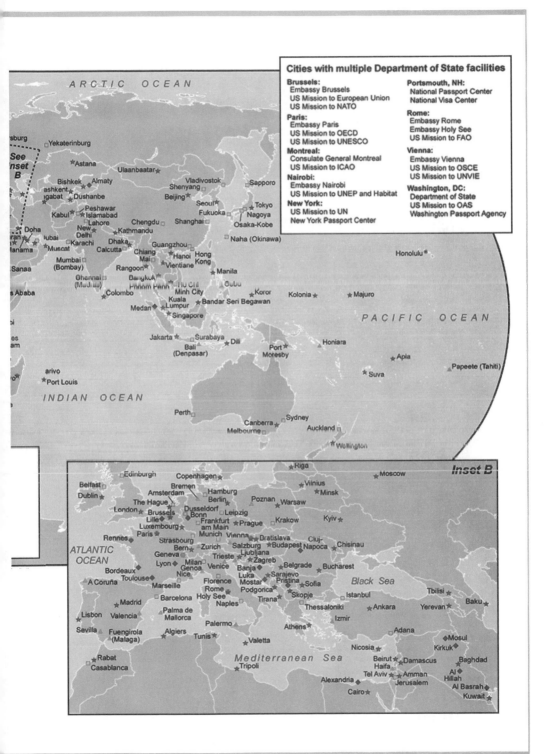

Cities with multiple Department of State facilities

Brussels:
Embassy Brussels
US Mission to European Union
US Mission to NATO

Paris:
Embassy Paris
US Mission to OECD
US Mission to UNESCO

Montreal:
Consulate General Montreal
US Mission to ICAO

Nairobi:
Embassy Nairobi
US Mission to UNEP and Habitat

New York:
US Mission to UN
New York Passport Center

Portsmouth, NH:
National Passport Center
National Visa Center

Rome:
Embassy Rome
Embassy Holy See
US Mission to FAO

Vienna:
Embassy Vienna
US Mission to OSCE
US Mission to UNVIE

Washington, DC:
Department of State
US Mission to OAS
Washington Passport Agency

FOREIGN AFFAIRS AGENCIES INSIDE U.S. EMBASSIES

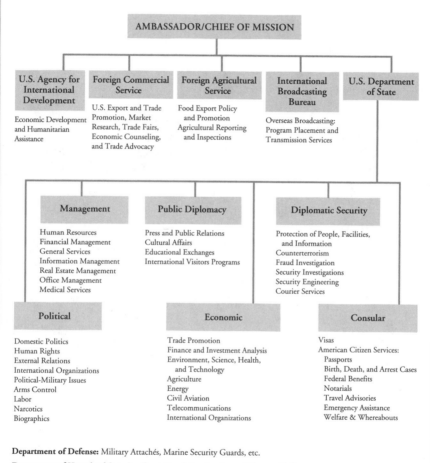

Department of Defense: Military Attachés, Marine Security Guards, etc.

Department of Homeland Security: Coast Guard, Immigration and Customs Enforcement, Customs and Border Protection, Citizenship and Immigration Services, Secret Service, Transportation Security Administration

Others: Central Intelligence Agency, Federal Bureau of Investigation, Peace Corps, Internal Revenue Service, Center for Disease Control and Prevention, Drug Enforcement Agency, Environmental Protection Agency, Federal Aviation Administration, Library of Congress, Depatent of the Treasury, U.S. Trade Representative

PART I
Profiles: Who Works in an Embassy?

By Shawn Dorman

Owned and operated by the U.S. Department of State, American embassies located in capitals around the world serve as headquarters for the U.S. federal government overseas. Each embassy is led by an ambassador who is the personal representative of the U.S. president and reports to the Secretary of State. The ambassador leads the country team, which brings together all the federal agencies with representatives in the country. It takes a whole team to run an embassy, and ambassadors are backed up by professionals handling everything from press briefings to security, and from keeping the lights on to visiting Americans in foreign jails. U.S. diplomats negotiate the agreements that build the U.S. relationship with the rest of the world.

Without a deputy chief of mission, the ambassador could easily become overwhelmed with day-to-day management tasks. Without an office management specialist as gatekeeper, the ambassador might find herself meeting with the foreign minister's staff assistant when she should be meeting the president. The information management staff ensures that the embassy's links to Washington and the rest of the world do not come to a screeching halt. Political and economic officers advise the ambassador on key people and issues; they warn of potential political unrest and seek out opportunities for U.S. companies. Consular officers assist Americans in trouble, facilitate legal travel and protect U.S. borders. Without the Locally Employed Staff, institutional memory would be lost every two or three years as American diplomats rotate in and out.

Every person working in an embassy plays a vital role, and the following profiles illustrate those roles. The people profiled work in embassies and consulates in every region of the world where the U.S. has representation. The largest U.S. embassies have more than a thousand employees, while some of the smallest have just a few.

Most of the people interviewed for these profiles have moved on to new assignments, but the profiles offer a snapshot of the Foreign Service at work around the world. Meet Elizabeth Millard, the consul general in Casablanca, and see that consulates can be just as significant to the overall relationship with the country as the embassy in the capital. Meet Commercial Officer Richard Steffans and find out what it's like to manage trade relations in Kyiv, Ukraine, ranked one of the most difficult places to do business in the world. Head out with Environmental Officer Bruce Hudspeth, exploring Central Asia from the hub office in Astana, Kazakhstan. And meet Donald Moore, consul general in Port-au-Prince, to find out what a consular section does when disaster strikes without warning.

These are the men and women of the Foreign Service, and these are their jobs.

AMBASSADOR

Marie Yovanovitch ▪ Embassy Yerevan, Armenia

As U.S. ambassador to Armenia, Marie Yovanovitch is the chief of the diplomatic mission and the personal representative of the U.S. president there. The ambassador coordinates U.S. policy, including the operations of all the U.S. government agencies in Armenia, and represents the United States to the Armenian government, the business sector, and civil society. She is the chief executive officer of the mission and the interagency manager. She explains what is happening in Armenia to Washington policymakers. The ambassador is also the chief spokesperson for the United States in the country and the most visible U.S. government representative. "By telling America's story on a daily basis, I explain American values, beliefs, and culture in order to promote mutual understanding between the two countries," Ambassador Yovanovitch says.

The dissolution of the Soviet Union in December 1991 brought an end to the Cold War and created the opportunity for bilateral relations with the newly independent Republic of Armenia, a landlocked country in the Caucasus. The United States opened an embassy in Yerevan in February 1992 and has sought to help Armenia transition from communism and a command economy to democracy and open markets. Over the past 18 years, the United States has provided nearly $2 billion in assistance to Armenia, the highest per capita amount for a post-Soviet state.

Because more than a million Americans are of Armenian descent, Armenia tends to draw more interest in the United States than most other countries its size. Yovanovitch meets regularly with representatives of the Armenian diaspora on issues important to the Armenian-American community.

Located on the shore of Lake Yerevan, the U.S.

> *The ambassador coordinates U.S. policy and represents the United States to the Armenian government, the business sector, and civil society.*

mission occupies a 23-acre plot, one of the largest embassy compounds in the world. Ambassador Yovanovitch oversees a staff of almost 400 American and Armenian employees in an embassy that houses many U.S. government agencies, including the U.S. Agency for International Development, the Defense Department, the Peace Corps, and the Millennium Challenge Corporation. The U.S. mission supports efforts to build a stable, free-market economy in Armenia, and promotes reforms that strengthen civil society, the rule of law, and democracy.

Armenia fought a bitter war with Azerbaijan over the Nagorno-Karabakh region from 1988 to 1994, when a cease-fire was declared. As a result, Armenia's borders with Turkey and Azerbaijan have been closed since 1993. Although the borders with Georgia and Iran remain open, the 2008 conflict between Georgia and Russia temporarily restricted the flow of goods through Georgia to Armenia. This isolation creates serious challenges for Armenia. Yovanovitch and her team work to advance regional stability, the opening of borders, and the normalization of relations among Armenia and its neighbors. They actively support the historic steps Yerevan has taken to improve relations with Ankara. Protocols signed by those two countries in October 2009 aim to restore diplomatic relations and reopen the Turkey-Armenia land border.

Yovanovitch engages with government officials and civil society representatives to promote human rights and democratic development. In 2009, she received the Secretary of State's Diplomacy for Human Rights Award, which cited her advocacy of due process and transparent investigations for those arrested following the contentious February 2008 presidential elections, as well as her efforts to improve the electoral process in Armenia while maintaining a positive relationship with the Armenian government.

One area of particular interest to Yovanovitch is the advancement of women. She launched the country's first mentoring program for women, and she has conducted a sustained dialogue with the Armenian government on trafficking in persons. She explains that, while high-profile Washington priorities such as Turkey-Armenia normalization keep her busy, "one of the privileges of being ambassador is being able to focus on issues of special interest, such as creating greater opportunities for young women."

Daily activities for the ambassador include speaking with the media on current issues, meeting with Armenian officials and civil society leaders, and visiting U.S. government-funded projects. "There is no typical day. That's why I love the Foreign Service—and this job," Yovanovitch says. Her days often begin early and end late following a public event or a reception. She says Foreign Service work captures the spirit of John F. Kennedy's call to 'Ask not what your country can do for you. Ask what you can do for your country.'

"I immigrated to the United States when I was three years old," says Marie, "and have had all the benefits of American culture and education. In almost no other country would an immigrant be able to represent that country as an ambassador." Yovanovitch is a career Senior Foreign Service officer. Depending on the administration, between

Amb. Yovanovitch volunteering at a community center supported by USAID.

60 and 70 percent of ambassadors are appointed from the career Foreign Service, and 30 to 40 percent are political appointees from outside the Service.

Marie Yovanovitch, 51, was born in Montreal and grew up in Connecticut. She has a B.A. in history and Russian studies from Princeton University and an M.S. from the National War College, a degree she earned while in the Foreign Service. She joined the Service in 1986 after four years in the private sector. Prior to her appointment to Yerevan, she served as ambassador to the Kyrgyz Republic. Yovanovitch has also been a senior adviser to the under secretary of State for political affairs in Washington, D.C., and deputy chief of mission in Kyiv, Ukraine. Previous assignments also include Ottawa, Canada; Moscow, Russia; London, England; and Mogadishu, Somalia.

DEPUTY CHIEF OF MISSION

Dan Piccuta ▪ Embassy Beijing, China

The deputy chief of mission must be both Hindu and Buddhist at once, says Embassy Beijing DCM Dan Piccuta. Like the Hindu goddess Kali, the DCM must have many arms, with hands in dozens of pots across the full spectrum of U.S. government business inside the embassy, inside the Beltway, and inside the bilateral relationship. At the same time, he must project an unperturbed Buddha-like attitude that steadies the entire mission. The deputy must be the alter ego of the ambassador, ready to step into his or her shoes for an event, a day, or much longer. The DCM must be the ambassador's radar over the horizon, minimizing the number of surprises by working with the country team to assure the mission is ahead of whatever waves of activity are coming. The DCM must be the chief cheerleader for the embassy's employees, addressing quality-of-life and work-life balance issues. Finally, the DCM must be an honest broker on issues of both policy and management.

Embassy Beijing is one of the largest and busiest embassies in the world, with more than 950 employees, including the local Chinese staff. Adding the constituent posts—Shanghai, Guangzhou, Shenyang, Chengdu, and Wuhan—the

total is close to 2,000 employees, representing some 40 U.S. agencies. Mission China can average at least one visitor at the assistant secretary level or above every single workday. There are more than 67 formal, active dialogues between the United States and China, each with its own set of issues, visitors, and (sometimes) tangible results.

"Work in China is unlike anywhere else in the world," Piccuta says. The country today is a study in contrasts. The dramatic rise in urban living standards accompanying its increasing economic success comes against a backdrop of achingly poor rural life, while the explosion in Chinese Internet use has not been matched by political openness.

The deputy chief of mission plays a pivotal role in coordinating and facilitating major events, meetings, and visits. Piccuta engaged with U.S. leaders, academics and business representatives, as well as high-level Chinese officials, on issues of great sensitivity and importance to the United States.

Hosting nearly 300 temporary employees in Beijing for the 2008 Summer Olympic Games would have been challenging enough for any embassy. But combining that with a presidential visit was a first. "Never before had both the POTUS [President of the United States] and Olympic circuses been under one tent," Piccuta explains. Beijing welcomed an additional 600 temporary employees in support of the president's visit (dubbed "POTOlympicUS" by embassy staff).

During Piccuta's tenure, the embassy grew quickly, gaining 200 employees in two years. When quality of life was suffering, Piccuta made its improvement a priority. He succeeded in getting approval to provide more than 200 BlackBerries to embassy staff—not to keep them connected to the office 24/7, he says, but to free them from having to come to the office on a Saturday when checking in and checking e-mail was enough. In that spirit,

Meeting with Chinese Foreign Minister Yang in Beijing, 2009. From right: Secretary of State Hillary Rodham Clinton, Dan Piccuta, EAP Assistant Secretary Chris Hill, Climate Change Special Envoy Todd Stern, and Acting State Spokesperson Robert Wood.

Piccuta accompanies Secretary Clinton during her visit to Beijing, February 2009.

Piccuta tried to leave the office before dark to hit the gym most days, "to demonstrate that our work in China is a marathon, not a sprint, and that we can and must manage the pace."

Another major undertaking on Piccuta's watch was the move to a newly constructed embassy compound, the second-biggest and most expensive construction the U.S. government has ever undertaken. Piccuta had a hand in most aspects of the final phase of the construction project and the planning for moving almost 1,000 people spread around 17 locations in the city to the new offices. The stakes were high, especially given the known intelligence threat. It had to be done right the first time, and Piccuta says it was.

The DCM helps keep the embassy connected with its five constituent posts, each a significant consulate. Piccuta's attitude has always been to "share the wealth." He encouraged travel and exchanges of staff, especially local employees, to foster a shared sense of community among the posts. In the past few years, Mission China set up nearly two dozen Virtual Presence Posts. Under this program, embassy or consulate officers are assigned to cover—both virtually and through travel—cities and regions where the United States has no physical presence.

"A high-level Chinese contact once told me, 'You are like an amphibian, equally comfortable in the sea or on land, in China or in the U.S.'," he recalls. "I'd like to think that quality—of trying to see the world through the eyes of your interlocutors, to understand their point of view, to grasp their circumstances and motivations— allows me to communicate better, more clearly, and more effectively."

Daniel Piccuta, 55, joined the Foreign Service in 1986. He has been posted to China four times: he served in Guangzhou and twice before in Beijing. Dan has also

The deputy chief of mission must be an honest broker on issues of both policy and management.

served in Luxembourg (as DCM) and in Belgrade and Milan. Washington, D.C., assignments include tours in the State Department's Executive Secretariat in the 24-hour Operations Center, and on the Board of Examiners, which selects candidates for entry into the Foreign Service. He has a B.A. in history from St.

Vincent College. A member of the California Bar, he has a J.D. from the University of Southern California. He also studied in Shanghai and Taipei. He and his wife have one daughter. From Beijing, he moved to an assignment as foreign policy adviser to the commander of the U.S. Pacific Command in Honolulu.

CONSUL GENERAL

Elisabeth Millard ▪ Consulate General Casablanca, Morocco

There's no doubt about it: the job of consul general is one of the most rewarding and, dare we say, fun jobs in the Foreign Service. Elisabeth Millard says she's grateful every day to serve as consul general and principal officer for Consulate General Casablanca.

Consuls general, also known as principal officers, manage consulates, U.S. government offices located outside of capital cities in countries around the world. As consul general (CG) in Casablanca, Africa's third-largest

Elisabeth Millard (right) presenting awards after a race for people with disabilities in Casablanca.

city and Morocco's largest, Millard coordinates closely with the embassy in Rabat, but the job comes with lots of autonomy and responsibility. The CG oversees the work of each section: consular, economic, political, public diplomacy, management, and diplomatic security. She coordinates with the other agencies at her post, which include the Foreign Commercial Service and the Department of Homeland Security.

The consul general is deeply involved in all aspects of the U.S.-Morocco relationship. Located in Northwest Africa with Mediterranean and Atlantic coastlines, Morocco was the first country to seek diplomatic relations with the United States—in 1777—and remains one of the oldest and closest U.S. allies in the region. The Treaty of Peace and Friendship signed in 1787 is still in force, constituting the longest unbroken treaty relationship in U.S. history.

Casablanca is a city of contrasts: home to huge slums that have bred suicide bombers, it also gleams with opulence. On a walk along the Corniche, the wide promenade along the ocean, one is as likely to see a young woman in hip, revealing clothing as in a headscarf. The consulate is only 90 minutes by car from the embassy, so Millard is able to attend the weekly country team meeting. For a month in 2009, she commuted daily to Rabat to serve as acting deputy chief of

mission, and she served as chargé d'affaires there for several weeks in the absence of the ambassador. To make the long chauffeured commutes to Rabat more productive, Millard works on her BlackBerry. Wherever she is, she wants to be aware of any issue or problem that crops up, such as an American in trouble.

In most countries, a consulate covers a limited geographic area that defines the scope of its jurisdiction for consular services. For the U.S. mission in Morocco, the entire country is a single consular district and all consular services, including visa interviews, are conducted in Casablanca. At the office, Millard runs meetings, reads e-mails and cable traffic (reports coming in from Washington, the embassy, and other posts), and reviews and edits outgoing reporting cables. Most days, she has at least one event to attend outside the consulate, whether it's visiting a school, having lunch with a plugged-in activist, or accompanying a U.S. visitor to an official meeting. A great help in her official duties is strong language ability. "In a Francophone country like Morocco, speaking French makes the job so much easier—from reading the papers in the morning to interacting with Moroccans throughout the day."

Empowering her employees, both American and Moroccan, by ensuring they have the tools they need to excel, is key to Millard's work. She meets regularly with staff and tries to address any problems that may come up. She pays extra attention to those new to the Foreign Service, meeting with them to hear concerns and offer advice on assignments and career paths. "I wonder if being a mother helps me more acutely sense when someone is brooding or is unhappy," she says, "and reach out to that person to try to help."

One unique benefit for the CG in Casablanca is that the official residence is Villa Mirador, the historic house where

Millard coordinates closely with the embassy in Rabat, but the job comes with lots of autonomy and responsibility.

Winston Churchill lived and worked during the Casablanca Conference in January 1943. Millard and her husband seek every opportunity to share their lovely temporary home with visitors, hosting events several times a week. "We have hosted Moroccans from all walks of life and political persuasions," she says, "from orphans and disadvantaged youth to journalists, *imams*, political party leaders, government officials, and corporate tycoons." She hosts press roundtable discussions, movie nights, swimming parties for young Moroccans home from visitors' programs in the United States, and concerts featuring Moroccan and American performers.

While keeping a very busy representational schedule, Millard is always mindful of security. Located on a major thoroughfare in the heart of the city, Consulate General Casablanca was the target of a terrorist suicide bomber in 2007. The building has since undergone several security upgrades. The very real concerns help illustrate the dual and sometimes conflicting responsibilities of the consul general: to ensure the safety of employees and visitors but also to encourage a broad range of interactions between the consulate and Moroccans.

Elisabeth Millard joined the Foreign Service later in life than most officers. Before joining, she moved with her naval officer husband to postings in the United Kingdom, Bahrain, India, Finland, and Washington, D.C. At each post, she found meaningful work: as a banker in the Middle East, with USAID in India, and at the embassy in Helsinki, where she supported the new U.S. missions in the Baltics that were being established at the time. Joining the Foreign Service felt like a natural next step, so she took the exam in Finland and entered the Service in 1992. She has served twice at the National Security Council; as DCM at Embassy Kathmandu; and in India, Denmark, and the Czech Republic, as well as in the Operations Center in Washington, D.C.

Millard poses with the Harlem Globetrotters at an exhibition match in Casablanca.

USAID MISSION DIRECTOR

Hilda Arellano ▪ Embassy Cairo, Egypt

The U.S. Agency for International Development (USAID) is the lead federal government agency responsible for implementing America's foreign economic, development, and humanitarian assistance programs in support of the foreign policy goals of the United States. The agency is run by an administrator and receives policy direction from the Secretary of State. Primary priorities for USAID are to support and facilitate economic growth, agriculture and trade; global health; democracy and conflict prevention; as well as humanitarian assistance and disaster relief.

USAID Foreign Service officers work in partnership with private voluntary organizations, indigenous organizations, universities, American businesses, international

Hilda Arellano laying a corner stone for a dewatering project to protect Egyptian antiquities along the Nile in Luxor.

agencies, other governments and other U.S. government agencies. The main office of USAID in any country, known as the "mission," is part of the U.S. embassy and is run by a director, or, in the case of smaller programs, a representative.

Hilda "Bambi" Arellano led the USAID mission in Cairo from 2007 to 2010. The USAID mission in Egypt has been one of the world's largest for decades. Development assistance to that country has been more "political" than most other USAID programs. Tied to recognition of Egypt's contribution to peace in the Middle East since the 1978 Camp David Accords, the program was sustained at more than $800 million per year for two decades. During the last decade, the assistance has gradually been reduced to about $250 million a year. Although still in the top five, it is no longer the largest U.S. program. The mission director plays a key role in negotiating the future of the program, determining which activities to continue and which to cut. She aims to ensure that the program remains focused on sustaining the gains made.

USAID/Cairo has its own building in a different part of town from the embassy, so Arellano spent a lot of time traveling between offices to attend meetings. Her staff consisted of 41 Americans and 165 Foreign Service Nationals, so her job included a large management component. The Cairo office also has a large regional services role, providing support—contract services, financial management, administrative and legal services, and training—

Arellano frequently appears in media outlets, speaks at major conferences throughout Egypt, and plays an active leadership role in the donor community.

to USAID in Yemen, Lebanon, Morocco, Sudan, and Iraq. Cairo also provides financial management support to USAID programs in Afghanistan and Pakistan.

In most countries, USAID consults with local partners in the public and private sectors to develop an approach appropriate to each country's needs. But in Cairo, a large portion of earmarked funds is divided into different program areas in consultation with the government of Egypt. As a government-to-government program, it is centrally controlled and less flexible than most other USAID programs.

In spite of these restrictions, the USAID/Cairo program has been able to focus the majority of its activities at the decentralized level, explains Arellano, providing support for community groups, local governments, and organizations

to ensure the quality of service delivery where it matters most. She points to real progress in Egypt, with USAID assistance, in the diversity and strength of civil society organizations.

The 2004–2009 "Partnership for Prosperity" program sought to improve the quality of life for all Egyptians, through investments and technical assistance in the areas of education, economic growth, health, water management, agriculture, environment and natural resources, antiquities, and democracy and governance.

The USAID director's role in Egypt is highly visible, in large part owing to the exceptional importance the United States places on public diplomacy in the Middle East and the controversial issues surrounding democracy programming and declining funding levels over the past decade. Arellano frequently appeared in media outlets, spoke at major conferences throughout Egypt, and played an active leadership role in the donor community.

Arellano joined USAID in 1987 and has served in Ecuador (once as her first assignment and again as mission director in 1998), Guatemala City, Guatemala; La Paz, Bolivia (as mission director); Budapest, Hungary (as mission director for the Regional Services Center for Europe and Eurasia); Lima, Peru (as mission director); Baghdad, Iraq (as mission director); and in Washington, D.C., most recently as the counselor to USAID.

Arellano has a B.A. in political science from Cornell University, an M.A. in political science from the University of Texas at Austin, and an M.A. in teaching from Antioch College. She speaks Spanish, Portuguese, and French. Before joining USAID, Arellano lived and worked in Latin America and other developing countries

Arellano (second from right) visiting USAID-supported microfinance lending program participants in Minya, Egypt.

for 17 years. In 1971, she was posted to Peru and Bolivia for three years with the United Nations Volunteer Program, working on microcredit projects for rural women. After that, she worked with the World Bank and the United Nations Development Program, and then the Organization for American States. She and her husband, Jorge, have four children.

FCS COMMERCIAL OFFICER

Richard Steffens ▪ Embassy Kyiv, Ukraine

"The business of America is business," says Embassy Kyiv's commercial counselor, Richard Steffens, quoting Calvin Coolidge. Steffens runs the single-officer commercial office in Kyiv, which is responsible for trade promotion in Ukraine and neighboring Belarus. The main job of the commercial office in Ukraine, as in every other country, is to manage U.S. trade relations with the host country—helping U.S. companies enter the market, and operate and succeed there. His home agency is the Foreign Commercial Service, a branch of the Department of Commerce and one of the five foreign affairs agencies.

The World Bank rates Ukraine the 142nd-best place to do business in the world—making it one of the worst. Kyiv is considered an "emerging market" post, which means the commercial work there is labor-intensive, with a focus on the issue of corruption and on pushing government agencies to get out of the way of trade. In spite of serious challenges, commercial progress is being made in Ukraine. The Kyiv Commercial Office, which comprises the commercial counselor and 11 local staff, served more than 2,600 clients in 2009, 90 of whom were new to the Ukrainian market. Steffens' office reported 171 U.S. export successes during 2009, adding up to an export value of more than $425 million.

Commercial diplomacy can serve both U.S. and local interests. "We need to help U.S. companies export," Steffens says, "so that they can create jobs in America and pay the taxes that support everything else the U.S. government does." More broadly, he adds, "by getting U.S. companies to enter the market to invest in roads and airports, to sell pharmaceuticals and medical equipment, to partner with local colleges to provide better education, we help make the host country a better place to live and help create economic growth."

Steffens tells us he has never had a typical day as a commercial officer. If he ever does, he says, it will probably mean he's not

> *"I've always approached my job as a hybrid investment banker-diplomat."*

doing his job. Good commercial officers spend most of their time outside the office, on the road making contacts. "Last week, I was in Washington attending bilateral meetings on U.S.-Ukrainian trade relations," he says, "and then in New York briefing private equity funds on the business climate in Ukraine. Last month, I made a quick trip to Donetsk in eastern Ukraine to address a regional investment conference and to encourage the regional government to sign an agreement

with the U.S. Trade and Development Agency." Steffens also travels to the politically volatile Crimea, where he recently spent two days with the Crimean Tartar leadership, as well as a day at the mayor's office in the port of Sevastopol. He explains that greater U.S. business activity in Crimea could help to relieve the very high unemployment rate there.

Commercial counselors have enormous autonomy and independence, crafting their position at post to match the needs of the situation on the ground and their particular skill sets. They also have many stakeholders: the ambassador, the regional director at the Commerce Department in Washington, the half-dozen or so other Commerce Department agencies that may be operating in the country (in Kyiv, the Special American Business Internship Training Program and the Commercial Law Development Program), the local American business community, and companies in the United States trying to enter the market. "A successful commercial counselor manages to keep all these stakeholders reasonably happy."

Commercial counselors must have "a wide mental bandwidth," Steffens explains. One minute it is a call or meeting about an intellectual property issue, and the next it's a call related to financing a multimillion-dollar deal. "The commercial counselor must be able to comfortably switch between these roles in the same moment or same conversation," says Steffens. "This is the challenge, as well as the fascination, of the job."

Steffens is a member of the embassy's country team, and his office plays an important role in promoting economic development and political stability in Ukraine. When floods ravaged regions of western Ukraine and Moldova, the commercial office spearheaded a relief effort that provided more than $1 million in private-sector contributions.

Steffens attended business school at Wharton, and then went to Wall Street where he did turnaround work, followed by several years running a venture capital fund for

The Commercial Service Kyiv team and Boeing team at the signing ceremony for a major Boeing sale to Ukraine.

the State of New Jersey. Perhaps because of this background, he says, "I've always approached my job as a hybrid investment banker-diplomat. My job is to find the major deals in a country and get them done."

Steffens, 49, studied Russian in junior high and high school, and his career with the Foreign Commercial Service so far has been entirely Slavic-related. He joined the Foreign Service in 1991. Previous posts include Moscow and Vladivostok, Russia, and Prague, Czech Republic. He has an unpaid night job as a music producer for Ukrainian Records, seeking out the best of local pop stars and helping them produce new English-language versions of their songs. In December 2008, a newer version of a musical he had worked on as a writer/lyricist since the mid-1990s, "Mother Russia," played at Carnegie Hall in New York City. He speaks French, Russian, Ukrainian, and Czech. Steffens has been married for 22 years, and he and his wife have two children.

FAS AGRICULTURAL OFFICER

Holly Higgins ▪ Embassy New Delhi, India

Holly Higgins with a farmer in Gujarat, India.

The Foreign Agricultural Service (FAS) has primary responsibility for the U.S. Department of Agriculture's international activities. The USDA is represented overseas by more than 165 Foreign Service officers in 100 offices in 77 countries, managing agricultural policy and trade issues in their assigned regions. They play a key role in improving foreign markets for U.S. products and building new markets. In addition, the offices assist local importers who want to find U.S. suppliers for needed agricultural products. FAS also collects data and reports on local production, consumption, trade flows, and market opportunities for some 100 agricultural products.

"Every day, our office has to think about how 1.1 billion people are going to eat," says Holly Higgins, Embassy New Delhi's minister counselor for the Office of Agricultural Affairs, explaining the FAS interest in India in its most basic terms. Food security issues are central to the work of the agricultural officer (sometimes called "attaché"), and those issues cannot be separated from political and economic security and public health. Whether it is the trade relationship, food aid, or planning a long-term strategy for increasing understanding of U.S. scientific and regulatory approaches to food safety, it is all part of the day-to-day work of the agricultural officer.

Higgins, like almost all agricultural officers today, has regional responsibility, leading a team that covers India, Bangladesh, and Sri Lanka. The New Delhi office also helps support USDA efforts in the Maldives, Nepal, and Bhutan. Higgins travels often but is not on the road as much as she was in a previous assignment to Sofia, Bulgaria, where she was the only agricultural officer covering eight Eastern European countries. Running a bigger operation in New Delhi, she spends most of her time in the capital, while keeping in regular contact with staff throughout South Asia, including those in the new FAS office in Mumbai, which opened in 2010. Her team deals with "everything from food aid programs to press reports about food safety to reporting on the crop size and weather conditions," Higgins says. Her offices also help facilitate scientist exchanges under various programs to promote common understanding.

The U.S. trade portfolio with India is underperforming in comparison to other aspects of the bilateral relationship, so the FAS team is working to develop more markets and reduce barriers to the Indian market. They must be fluent in a wide range of scientific and technical areas, including transgenic crops, nutritional labeling, domestic farm policies, rural development, and international banking. They must understand local culture and politics, as well as regional and cross-border concerns. India has 26 states and 14 official languages, making communication a special challenge. While agricultural policy in India is formulated at the national level, implementation can be quite varied from state to state. "You really have to drill down to understand what is going on and what might be driving policy or market fundamentals," says Higgins.

Foreign Agricultural Service officers coordinate and leverage their work with many other U.S. government agencies. In collaboration with USAID, agricultural officers administer U.S. food aid programs. While a close relationship has long been in place between FAS and the Foreign Commercial Service, in recent years agricultural officers have expanded cooperative work with the U.S. Food and Drug Administration, USDA's Animal and Plant Health Inspection Service, and U.S. Customs and Border Protection. FAS also works closely with the State Department's Bureau of Oceans, Environment, and Science and the Department of Commerce's National Marine Fisheries Services on issues related to forestry (including climate change) and fisheries.

"Every day, our office has to think about how 1.1 billion people are going to eat."

Home to more than 1.1 billion people, India has a huge rural population. Well over 50 percent of the people are dependent on agriculture in some way, whether for employment or as a social safety net (growing their own food). U.S.

Higgins with a goatherder clan outside of Rajkot in Gujarat, India.

agricultural work in India varies widely, in part depending on the weather. During good years, India is not only self-sufficient in agriculture, but is also a regional breadbasket. But if the rainfall is poor and India's harvests fall behind, then New Delhi has to go to the world market and import food. Higgins' job, in part, is to make sure the United States is viewed as a safe and reliable supplier of food for India. So she and her colleagues support a growing two-way trade relationship in food and agricultural products. This involves negotiations with government regulatory bodies as well as working with the private sector to bring private-sector trade and investment groups together.

Higgins, 49, started working for FAS in 1983 as a Civil Service employee and entered the Foreign Service in 1990. Her previous postings include Sofia, Bulgaria; Milan, Italy; and Paris, France. Prior to joining USDA, she was a regulatory economist with the Commodity Futures Trading Commission in Chicago. Before that, she worked on Capitol Hill for a member of Congress from Iowa, writing agricultural trade legislation. Holly grew up on a farm in Iowa and graduated from the University of Iowa with a degree in economics. She is married with three children.

POLITICAL OFFICER

Dereck J. Hogan ▪ Embassy Moscow, Russia

The job of political officers is to analyze a host country's domestic and foreign policies, identify opportunities to advance U.S. interests, and actively promote those interests. Their value added is an understanding of the what and the why of the political situation on the ground, as well as where the United States wants the relationship to go and how to get there.

While reporting is critical and makes up the bread and butter of the political officer's job, it is not enough. "We can't afford that luxury," says Dereck Hogan, a political officer in Moscow from 2007 to

2009. It's not just about taking stock of the situation, he explains; you have to figure out how to work to align your host country's interests with U.S. interests. Good political officers are big-picture thinkers

and see how their issues connect to the larger U.S. strategy. They are also, critically, active listeners.

Hogan, 36, ran the "political external" division of Embassy Moscow's political section, which focuses on Russia's relationship with other countries, during a challenging time in U.S.-Russia relations. When Hogan arrived in 2007, a resurgent Russia was flush with petrodollars. President Vladimir Putin was popular and promoting the image of a strong Russia that wasn't going to be pushed around by the United States. At the same time, Washington was working hard to make sure Moscow saw Afghanistan as an area of mutual interest and was seeking greater collaboration.

Embassy Moscow is one of the five largest U.S. embassies. There are representatives from 29 different government agencies on the country team at post. The political section alone has 17 officers. At such a large post, you could meet someone new at work every single day. As one of two deputies in the political section, Hogan lived on the embassy compound so he could get to the embassy at a moment's notice. He was always in the office by 7 a.m. to check the Russian Foreign Ministry Web site to see what Moscow was focused on, who was visiting, and what was on the world stage for Russia.

"Good political officers are big-picture thinkers and see how their issues connect to the larger U.S. strategy."

Hogan met with his staff every morning to go over taskings. He took the management side of his role seriously, checking in regularly with each member of his staff, most of whom were junior officers, to discuss their professional goals. Hogan always encouraged officers to get out of the embassy regularly, and set a goal for himself and his staff to have at least two meetings with Russian contacts each day and produce at least two substantive cables a week, in addition to "spot reports" (quick briefs on breaking news).

An embassy is doing its job when it is staying ahead of Washington, Hogan explains, coming up with recommendations, and leading the way. But it is always a back-and-forth process. Washington has the more global perspective and sees Russia in the context of the president's overall national security policy and domestic interests. Colleagues in Washington also better understand how far Capitol Hill is willing to go on an issue.

Working on high-level visits takes up a lot of time for political officers in Moscow. At least every six weeks, Hogan was directly involved in a visit, either as a control officer (setting up the schedule and managing it), a site officer, or a notetaker, and sometimes all three. While visits eat up a lot of time, they also offer valuable and unusual opportunities. Hogan says he will never forget the time he spent stuck in traffic with Henry Kissinger, discussing how to engage China with the former Secretary of State.

Dereck Hogan at the Czar Cannon in Moscow.

One of the issues in which Hogan became deeply involved was the escalating tension between Russia and Georgia in 2007. Though the United States did not have a direct role in this conflict, U.S. diplomats did try to talk to both sides, perhaps helping delay what evolved into a brief 2008 war between Russia and Georgia. The lesson to take away, Hogan explains, is that "countries will do what they do—and sometimes the best we can do is try to mediate and minimize the conflict."

Hogan's evenings were often busy with receptions at other embassies and events at the ambassador's residence. He usually spent part of Saturday in the office, but kept Sunday free for family activities such as attending a local church, the theater or ballet, or going to the park or circus with his wife and young daughter.

"Russia has to be the most challenging and stimulating assignment you could have," says Hogan. In a culture that prides itself on intellect, embassy officers deal with a highly educated and sophisticated elite, and "knowledge builds your credibility." Having a 4/4 level in Russian certainly helped open doors. Hogan explains that while many officials speak English, it is always better to conduct meetings in Russian; it shows respect, and more information will be shared.

Hogan joined the Foreign Service in 1997. He has served on Provincial Reconstruction Teams in Uruzgan and Kunar Provinces, Afghanistan; and in Minsk, Belarus; Managua, Nicaragua; and Santo Domingo, Dominican Republic. In Washington, D.C., he was a special assistant to former Secretary of State Colin Powell, and a watch officer in the State Department's Operations Center. He has a B.A. from the University of Pittsburgh and an M.A. in public affairs from the Woodrow Wilson School of Public and International Affairs at Princeton University. He speaks fluent Russian and Spanish. Dereck is married to Anny Hogan, and they have a five-year-old daughter.

ECONOMIC OFFICER

Susannah Cooper ▪ Embassy Abu Dhabi, United Arab Emirates

"Like all economic officers, I am responsible for reporting on economic issues, following economic developments and policies, and delivering economic démarches," says Embassy Abu Dhabi Economic Section Chief Susannah Cooper. Economic officers advance U.S. economic and commercial interests through diplomacy.

Cooper works in the United Arab Emirates (UAE), a loose federation of seven emirates that shares a southern border with Saudi Arabia and an eastern border with Oman. The UAE constitutes the largest Middle Eastern export market for the United States. Embassy Abu Dhabi is a large mission that works with the UAE on a wide variety of issues, most notably regional economic issues related to Iran, Iraq, Afghanistan, Pakistan, and other countries. "While the bilateral relationship is historically based on political and security ties," Cooper explains, "in recent years cultural, educational, and commercial ties have grown significantly." The economic relationship between the United States and the UAE has blossomed: more than 750 American companies are now based there, and more than 40,000 U.S. citizens live there.

In Abu Dhabi, Cooper's job is to keep U.S. government agencies apprised of economic developments and policies that affect U.S. interests in the UAE. The execution of that goal is complicated by the fact that the UAE imports huge amounts of American goods and has the third-largest economy in the Middle East.

Cooper spends much of her time on issues related to nuclear power and renewable energy. Although, historically, the UAE economy was based on hydrocarbons, a sector in which many U.S. firms participate, the UAE is now investing in clean energy technologies to meet a growing demand for electricity and to diversify the economy. The embassy tries to play a constructive role in this process.

> *Cooper's job is to keep U.S. government agencies apprised of economic developments and policies that affect U.S. interests in the UAE.*

Cooper's economic team helped finalize a bilateral energy cooperation agreement "supporting greater cooperation on the development and application of renewable energy technologies." In 2009, the United States and UAE negotiated and signed a nuclear power cooperation agreement, which has led to technical cooperation on nuclear safety, security, and safeguards, as well as the creation of a Gulf Nuclear Energy Infrastructure Institute to train regional nuclear power officials.

As the economic section chief, Cooper supervises six employees (five Americans and one Locally Employed Staff member). She is the primary adviser to the ambassador on all economic issues and works closely with the Commerce Department representatives, who directly promote U.S. exports. She also works closely with the representatives of other federal agencies covering aviation (Federal Aviation Administration), financial affairs (Treasury Department), and customs cooperation (Department of Homeland Security/Immigration and Customs Enforcement).

A typical day for Cooper involves meetings with government officials "to discuss bilateral cooperation, review key economic developments, encourage economic liberalization and discuss upcoming bilateral visits." She gets involved in the planning for the many high-level official visitors to the UAE, and often attends meetings during these visits.

Though she speaks Arabic, having spent most of her career in the Middle East, Cooper conducts most of her meetings in English, and the business culture, hours, and attire are similar to what they would be in the United States. She notes that "the UAE is a modern country, so the work environment is very much like that in any developed country."

Her role as economic officer has also allowed Cooper to assist with the coordination of foreign assistance to countries such as Afghanistan, Pakistan, Yemen, and Haiti. She has worked with the UAE government to provide these countries with billions of dollars for development projects involving education, health care, and other important issues.

"The economic officer covers the majority of policy issues that

Cooper on a trip to Abu Dhabi's offshore Zirku Island oil export facility.   PHOTO CREDIT: ZADCO

are not political in nature," Cooper says, "which makes the work very diverse and rewarding." The opportunity to help coordinate humanitarian aid, along with many other aspects of the job, makes for a unique and fascinating career.

Cooper, 37, grew up in Scarborough, Maine. She joined the Foreign Service in 1997 after completing a B.A. in international affairs from Sweet Briar College and an M.A. in Arab studies from Georgetown University. Besides Abu Dhabi, she has served in Riyadh, Saudi Arabia; Kingston, Jamaica; Doha, Qatar; and Tunis, Tunisia. She and her husband, a Foreign Service consular officer, have a four-year-old son and a two-year-old daughter.

CONSULAR OFFICER

Donald Moore ▪ Embassy Port-au-Prince, Haiti

Haiti is the Western Hemisphere's poorest country, so consular work at Embassy Port-au-Prince is especially challenging. Proximity to the United States, combined with extremely difficult economic, social, and political conditions, creates strong emigration pressures that lead people to risk their lives attempting to travel to the United States using illegal means, often aboard dangerous vessels.

Donald Moore holding a Haitian adoptee granted humanitarian parole.

It was on Donald Moore's watch as consul general, head of the Embassy Port-au-Prince consular section, that Haiti was struck by a massive earthquake on January 12, 2010, which brought tragedy and destruction on a massive scale, killing more than 230,000 people. Consular officers immediately began working to provide emergency services to Americans in the consular district. Foreign Service colleagues from posts near and far joined in the assistance effort. American and local staff slept in the office or in tents on the embassy grounds, dealt with minimal sanitation and hygiene facilities, ate military ready-to-eat meals, and worked 12 to 18 hours a day.

The consular staff helped American citizens and adoptees evacuate Haiti in a round-the-clock effort.

The evacuation of American citizens on U.S. military flights began two days after the quake and continued for more than a month until the resumption of commercial flights on February 19. The consular staff helped American citizens and Haitian adoptees evacuate Haiti in a round-the-clock undertaking. Moore's staff not only helped organize the effort and coordinated with the U.S. military and Haitian national police, but also provided an empathetic ear to the many traumatized American citizens while firmly enforcing strict guidelines to determine eligibility for evacuation. They set up makeshift offices by the tarmac at the airport and ran a frenetically paced control room there. More than 16,400 Americans were able to leave

Haiti in one of the largest evacuations ever managed by the U.S. Department of State.

Moore says the consular staff demonstrated a clear understanding of what the regulations allow, the ability to make solid, often difficult decisions, and excellent customer service skills even in the most trying of circumstances. "We are from the U.S. government and we are here to help" was right on target in this case, he adds.

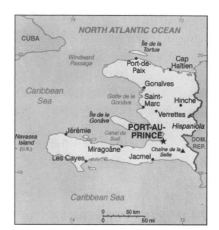

The two main responsibilities for all consular officers are to assist American citizens and facilitate legal travel. The top priority for all consular officers worldwide is to protect American citizens. Consular officers provide a wide range of emergency services to Americans, including visiting them in jails and hospitals. They process passport applications, serve as notaries, and register births of Americans overseas. "We are in the business of public service to American citizens, no matter where they may be and regardless of the hour or the emergency," explains Moore.

Foreign Service personnel assigned to Haiti receive both hardship and danger pay. Beset as the country is by violence, instability, and crumbling infrastructure, travel to

Moore with Assistant Secretary for Consular Affairs Janice Jacobs at the opening of the new embassy compound in Port-au-Prince.

and from the embassy in Port-au-Prince and within many areas of town is restricted. American staff often travel in armored vehicles. Physical infrastructure—roads, water supply, electricity, and communications—has long been in bad shape, but was made significantly worse by the 2010 earthquake. Political unrest during recent years repeatedly triggered the evacuation of much of the U.S. staff, causing a tremendous backlog in visa applications that has made the work of the consular section even tougher.

The U.S. mission in Port-au-Prince is a large embassy comprising about 1,000 employees from 15 U.S. government agencies. The consul general manages the consular section and oversees the efficient delivery of services in Haiti. Moore is a member of the country team and reports directly to the deputy chief of mission. He supervises 15 Foreign Service officers, three family member employees, and 33 Locally Employed Staff.

Moore makes customer service a top priority, noting that all visitors, both Haitian and American, will remember their experience with the consular section. "Often the most direct contact a foreigner has with an American is for a visa interview," Moore explains. "The impression we give will have a lasting effect on how we are viewed as a people."

Most mornings, Moore walks through each section of the consular office, checking in with staff and addressing personnel issues. He inquires about any American citizen emergency cases. He meets with his section heads each day and often participates in policy discussions at the country-team level.

Moore joined the Foreign Service in 1992. He has served at six posts in consular positions, including Milan, Italy; Paris, France; Tirana, Albania; and Washington, D.C. Moore was born in Fort Pierce, Fla. He has a B.S. in broadcast production and a J.D. from the University of Florida, Gainesville. He also has a master's degree in international private law from the University of Paris. Before joining the Foreign Service, he served in the Judge Advocate General Corps with the U.S. Navy and as an assistant state's attorney in Florida. Don speaks French, Italian, and Albanian. He has one son from a former marriage. While in Haiti, Moore was promoted to the Senior Foreign Service and received the 2009 Barbara M. Watson Award for Consular Excellence. After Haiti, he moves on to a second assignment to Italy, this time as consul general in Naples.

PUBLIC AFFAIRS OFFICER

Christopher Teal ▪ Consulate General Guadalajara, Mexico

This is a historic time in the relationship between Mexico and the United States, and public affairs officers for the U.S. mission in Mexico have a direct role in moving the relationship in a positive direction. Public Affairs Officer Christopher Teal serves as the spokesman for Consulate General Guadalajara, explaining U.S. policies to residents of the large seven-state area of western Mexico. Teal has the dual role of

Chris Teal looks on as Secretary of State Condoleezza Rice and Mexican Foreign Minister Patricia Espinosa sign an agreement on emergency management cooperation in Puerto Vallarta, October 2008.

being the "eyes and ears" of the consulate, reporting on the local situation, but also the "face" of America to the public and the local government. He promotes educational and cultural initiatives that bring American experts and artists to Mexico and send Mexicans to the United States on exchanges through Fulbright Scholarships and other programs.

The U.S. embassy in Mexico City is one of the largest, and the U.S. mission in Mexico includes nine consulates, making it the largest overall U.S. diplomatic presence in the world. Consulate General Guadalajara is larger than many embassies, with about 100 Locally Employed Staff and 50 Americans from the State Department and other federal agencies, including the Federal Bureau of Investigation and the Drug Enforcement Agency. Due to the complexities and extent of the ties between the United States and Mexico, coordination between the embassy and the consulates, as well as among the many government agencies working in Mexico, is paramount. The nonstop stream of VIP visitors to Mexico requires constant engagement; in his first year at post in 2008, Teal served as lead control officer for then-Secretary of State Condoleezza Rice's visit and later as press lead for President Barack Obama's visit.

The most significant bilateral issues that Teal must follow and explain on behalf of the United States are counternarcotics and security, immigration and visas, and economic development and trade. Immigration is always a major area of interest and concern throughout Mexico, so Teal spends a lot of his time explaining the visa process and immigration policy. The wave of violence associated with the Mexican government's fight against drug cartels makes security a top concern: Teal fields many questions about bilateral assistance programs such as the Merida Initiative, which aims to combat the threats of drug trafficking, transnational crime, and money laundering. On top of that, the unfortunate position of Mexico as epicenter for the H1N1 virus meant that the public affairs and consular teams had to help keep the large American community across Mexico informed and facilitate U.S. assistance to local health authorities as they tried to cope with the crisis.

"Insatiable curiosity makes for a good FSO, but this is especially true in public affairs."

Much of Teal's time is spent meeting with contacts in the government, the academic world, and the media. He often participates in public events, traveling frequently to engage Mexican audiences throughout the consular district directly. "Insatiable curiosity makes for a good FSO, but this is especially true in public affairs," Teal says. "There is always more to learn, and by learning we can also share more about ourselves and our country."

Teal also plays a management role in the consulate, overseeing a staff of four Locally Employed Staff, a Mexican intern, and one entry-level FSO. He regularly advises the consul general on major issues of the day and how best to position the consulate in response. Consulate General Guadalajara has no political or economic section, so Teal often finds himself filling those roles as well, reporting on local issues.

Teal's work with local media is rewarding and difficult. The security dangers tied to the cartel

Teal with a group of student folk dancers at an elementary school in Guadalajara.

violence in Mexico put press freedom at risk, as the cartels frequently threaten media outlets. Several international nongovernmental organizations have listed Mexico as the most dangerous place to practice journalism in the Western Hemisphere. Teal and his team work actively with local journalists to help increase their capacity to cover high-risk stories while staying safe. The right to information and freedom of expression is critical to democracy in Mexico, so helping Mexican journalists maintain their ability to keep their compatriots informed about what is happening in their country is a top priority.

The public affairs officer is one of the most visible U.S. government figures in Guadalajara. This offers unique challenges, as well as opportunities to meet and interact with individuals from across the spectrum of society, from business and government leaders to artists and intellectuals. "The variety of work and the challenges of leading a public affairs section make this one of the most interesting jobs in all of government," Teal explains. "The fact that we can have a real and immediate impact on people's lives is tremendously rewarding. There is nothing I would rather be doing."

Teal, 40, was born in Pontiac, Illinois, but grew up in Arkansas, Texas, and Washington, D.C. He studied political science, and has a B.A. from the University of Arkansas and an M.A. from George Washington University. Before joining the Foreign Service, Chris worked with journalist Juan Williams on his biography of Thurgood Marshall. He joined the U.S. Information Agency in 1999, just as it was being merged into the State Department. His first tour was as a consular officer and press officer in Santo Domingo, Dominican Republic. He then went on to Lima, Peru, and spent two tours in Washington, D.C., most recently at the Foreign Press Center covering African affairs. Teal is married with one son. In his limited spare time, he enjoys writing; *Hero of Hispaniola*, his book about the first African-American diplomat, Ebenezer D. Bassett, was published in 2008 (Praeger).

MANAGEMENT OFFICER

Rachna Korhonen ▪ Embassy Kuwait City, Kuwait

President Obama with Korhonen, logistics officer for the presidential visit to Kuwait, June 2008.

A management officer is the chief operating officer and the business manager of the embassy, overseeing all day-to-day operations: logistics, administrative support, finance, budget, hiring, motor pool, facilities, community liaison activities, and anything else required to keep the embassy running. Management officer positions include human resources officer, finance officer, general services officer, and facility manager. At smaller embassies, there may be just one supervising management officer and one general services officer to cover all the management activities, while larger embassies have a management counselor who oversees a number of other management officers in finance, personnel, and general services positions.

Embassy Kuwait, where Rachna Korhonen spent one year as general services officer (GSO) and one year as human resources officer, is a busy place. This mid-sized embassy in the Middle East supports numerous government agencies, with more than 100 American employees, more than 150 U.S. military personnel, and some 360 Locally Employed Staff, only two of whom are Kuwaiti. The rest are Palestinian, Jordanian, Indian, Bangladeshi, Syrian, etc. One of the interesting challenges for Korhonen was managing staff members of so many different nationalities, each with varying expectations but all needing to comply with the same regulations and standards. As GSO, Korhonen supervised a staff of 45 local employees who run the embassy warehouse, motor pool, travel section, and shipping department, as well as manage the customs, procurement, contracting, and housing operations.

"Everything starts and also finishes in human resources."

The embassy oversees a broad bilateral relationship with Kuwait, and also serves as a support base for operations in Iraq and Afghanistan. Many Foreign Service personnel heading to assignments in either country will first pass through Embassy Kuwait's Iraq Support Unit (ISU). The unit supports U.S. government travelers heading to Iraq and Afghanistan, including obtaining flights and access to military bases for them. Daily United Airways flights from Washington, D.C., to Kuwait mean that the ISU processes more than 300 delegations per year.

Embassy Kuwait also hosts a high-level visitor almost every single day, many heading to Iraq or Afghanistan, and every visit is supported by the management staff. During the year she served in a general services officer position, Korhonen was often in charge of arrangements for the motorcades and sometimes served as overall control officer for visits, facilitating all logistics required.

Most GSOs do not sit at a desk all day, but are always on the move, solving problems in the embassy and in the residences, problems that can be quite urgent. A good GSO is a skilled diplomat, managing expectations and competing demands coming in from all around the mission. "Compromise was the word of the day," recalls Korhonen.

As a human resources officer during the second year of her tour, with just four other employees in an office much calmer than that of the GSO, Korhonen was responsible for hiring (and sometimes firing) local staff, counseling and training them, and evaluating their performance. "For a management officer, a human resources tour often is an eye-opener," Rachna explains. "Everything starts and also finishes in HR." On a typical day, Korhonen held at least six meetings related to hiring. She designed a training plan for each section in the mission, encompassing classes in the United States at the Foreign Service Institute, local training, and independent study options. She also designed customer service training for all of the management staff.

Korhonen, 45, joined the Foreign Service in 2004 following a successful career in the private sector, during which time she lived with her family in a small town in New Jersey. She has a degree in computer science and math. Her first Foreign Service tour was Mumbai, India; Kuwait City was next. From

Rachna Korhonen with the local guard force for a National Day event in Kuwait, May 2008.

there, she went on to Kirkuk, Iraq, and will move next to Riyadh, Saudi Arabia, to serve as the embassy's supervisory general services officer. Korhonen says the Iraq job is the best job she's ever had. She enjoyed letting the world see that the United States placed an Indian-American woman in a diplomatic post in Kirkuk. "I love seeing people's reaction when they are waiting for an 'American diplomat' and out I come."

Korhonen speaks Hindi, Punjabi, and Urdu, and she learned to speak Gujurati and Marathi while serving in Mumbai. She is married with three children, ages 10, 19, and 22. Her husband was employed on the local economy in Kuwait, which was a challenge but worked well for him.

REGIONAL SECURITY OFFICER

Nicholas Collura ▪ Embassy Sana'a, Yemen

Yemen is not a safe place for Americans. For Embassy Sana'a, the regional security office is the hub in this critical terrorism-threat environment. Regional Security Officer Nicholas Collura is involved in the simplest everyday decisions, such as whether a certain store or restaurant is off limits to the embassy community or what type of vehicle is needed for a certain event.

The commute to and from the embassy, procedures for access to the embassy facilities, and the safety of personnel, property, and classified information—these are all daily concerns for the regional security officer (RSO). While the security threat level is higher in Sana'a than many other places, RSOs posted in 265 U.S. diplomatic missions worldwide must be engaged in all aspects of security for the embassy and the embassy community.

Embassy Sana'a is a mid-sized critical-threat post in Yemen, which borders Saudi Arabia and Oman. Yemen is the poorest country in the Middle East. The terrorist group known as al-Qaida in the Arabian Peninsula (AQAP) is based there. On September 17, 2008, Embassy Sana'a was struck by one of the worst terrorist attacks in Yemen in more than a decade. This attack, claimed by AQAP, took place at the embassy gates but did not breach the walled compound. It paralyzed the embassy and resulted in the death of 17 people, including six Yemeni security officers, one embassy guard, and the attackers. Collura and the rest of the security team mobilized quickly and secured the post. Although the physical and procedural security of the embassy had held, the RSO office identified additional security measures to implement. In early January 2010, Embassy Sana'a closed for two days in response to credible threats by AQAP of an imminent attack on American interests in Yemen.

Without a strong security team in Sana'a, the embassy would not be able to provide the services or conduct the diplomacy required to implement U.S. foreign policy. One of the key issues Collura manages on a daily basis is "staying one step ahead of individuals who wish to do the embassy and its staff harm." This requires constant monitoring of the security environment and ensuring that the security staff is ready to handle any issue that might arise.

Maintaining a constant state of readiness is extremely challenging, requiring strong managerial skills on the part of the RSO to keep the staff motivated, equipped, and focused. Diplomatic security officers like Collura must also balance these tight security requirements with the need to ensure that U.S. embassies are inviting and approachable places for those with legitimate business with the U.S. government. For most people, the embassy is the closest they will ever come to setting foot in the United States. Regional security officers know that the experience should be as positive as possible.

The embassy security office is extremely busy, constantly monitoring the quickly changing security environment in the capital and in the rest of the country. The RSO makes sure all employees know what their responsibilities are in the event of an emergency and are prepared—through training and drills—to carry them out. The RSO is also the principal adviser to the ambassador on security-related issues and is responsible for all security programs at post. In Yemen, as in most countries, this job is demanding, the stakes are high, and the hours long. The RSO is never completely off duty. Although each embassy has a duty officer on call 24 hours a day, the security officer has to be reachable at all times as well, in case of emergency.

Collura investigates hostile intelligence attempts to subvert U.S. personnel and policies overseas. Above all, every day he monitors the security environment, which

This job is demanding, the stakes are high, and the hours long.

requires continued close coordination and liaison with Yemeni security forces. The RSO's ability to make and maintain working relations outside the embassy—with local security forces and governments, businesses, and other embassies—can make a critical difference in emergency situations. The more contacts and allies the RSO has, the better the flow of information and cooperation will be.

Another key role of regional security officers like Collura is liaison with local American businesses and nongovernmental organizations on security matters. RSOs exchange information on the local security environment and advise these entities on

Nicholas Collura (back left) on a trip to
Mulkulah, in southern Yemen, with U.S.
Ambassador to Yemen Stephen Seche.

security issues. They also manage local chapters of the Overseas Security Advisory Council, a public/private partnership between the State Department and some 3,500 U.S. companies, educational institutions, religious groups, and nongovernmental organizations. Managing training and assistance programs can also be in the RSO's portfolio. Certain governments receive significant U.S. funds to enable them to become better security partners for the United States. RSOs identify recipients and help administer such security assistance training programs.

When posted in the United States, diplomatic security officers like Collura protect the Secretary of State and certain visiting dignitaries, investigate passport and visa fraud, and handle other criminal investigations. They also conduct individual security investigations. They work at the State Department headquarters in Washington, D.C., or in field offices throughout the United States.

Collura, 38, joined the Foreign Service as part of the Diplomatic Security Service in December 2001. Prior to joining DS, he served as a law enforcement officer for the state of Florida for 10 years. His first assignment for DS was in the Miami field office. From there, he went to Tel Aviv, Israel, and then Dhahran, Saudi Arabia. Sana'a is his third Foreign Service tour. In 2009, he was assigned to the Naval War College, where he earned a master's degree. His next assignment is deputy RSO for Consulate General Peshawar, Pakistan, an unaccompanied post (he cannot bring his family). Nick is married with two children.

PROVINCIAL RECONSTRUCTION TEAM DIRECTOR

Jim DeHart ▪ PRT Panjshir, Afghanistan

Nowhere do Foreign Service officers work more closely with the military than on Provincial Reconstruction Teams, like the one in Panjshir, the only civilian-led U.S. PRT in Afghanistan. Jim DeHart, a political officer, is on a one-year tour at Forward Operating Base Lion as PRT Panjshir Director. As he put it, the position is embedded in a foreign culture (the U.S. military) within a foreign culture (Afghanistan).

Panjshir lies northeast of Kabul, about two hours away by car, but PRT personnel almost always take the quicker and safer helicopter route. The province is a cul-de-sac fortress, surrounded by the mountains of the Hindu Kush—bare, exposed granite rising as high as 20,000 feet. The only feasible way in is through the canyon known as the Lion's Gate. In the valley, subsistence farmers scratch out a living growing wheat and corn in a manner unchanged for generations. A proud and insular people, Panjshiris are predominantly Tajik except for a community of Hazara and a handful of Kuchi nomads traversing the highlands each year.

DeHart, far left, with PRT Military Commander LTC Eric Hommel (center), Panjshir Governor Hajji Bahlol (front right in suit), the Provincial Director of Information and Culture (front far right in suit), and other officials.

Panjshir has never been conquered, and hundreds of rusting Russian tanks strewn among the rocks serve as a reminder of the Soviet Union's 10-year-long failed military campaign. And even when they controlled 90 percent of Afghanistan, the Taliban still failed to take that valley. Ahmad Shah Massoud, the charismatic "Lion of Panjshir" who led the fight against the Soviets, was assassinated two days before 9/11, but is still a powerful presence among the local population. U.S. forces dropped into the valley soon after 9/11 to help Massoud's forces run the Taliban out of Kabul. Panjshiri enmity for al-Qaida and the Taliban make the valley a much safer place for coalition forces than the rest of the country. PRT Panjshir is the only team protected by local Afghan guards rather than by a U.S. security force.

The PRT structure emphasizes civilian-military integration and teamwork at all levels. DeHart reports to the senior civilian officials at Bagram Air Base and also to the U.S. embassy in Kabul.

> *The PRT structure emphasizes civilian-military integration and teamwork at all levels.*

As PRT director, DeHart is responsible for building a strong integrated civilian-military team with a shared focus on U.S. counterinsurgency objectives. His work is not that different from that of his counterparts in other provinces, except that the permissive security environment enables the PRT to run continuous missions to every corner of the province. His responsibilities include engaging with the governor, other officials, and district and community leaders to advance governance and development; coordinating efforts with other international actors and nongovernmental organizations; and supporting visits from the embassy and military commands. He sees the biggest challenge as ensuring the right balance between U.S. assistance and building Afghan capacity and ownership. "Better, more capable Afghan institutions are the goal, and we're beginning to see those," he says.

The core military component of the Panjshir PRT is commanded by a U.S. Air Force lieutenant colonel and comprises just under 40 soldiers, sailors, and airmen,

as well as a squad of military police who conduct training for the Afghan National Police. The civilian component is growing, and as of late 2009 included State, USAID, USDA, and the Army Corps of Engineers.

Regular workdays for DeHart include meeting with the Panjshir governor, the public works director, or the education director, to discuss ways the PRT could support their efforts to deliver services to the people. Or he hikes to a village to assess development needs there. He joins the military on a horseback journey into the Hindu Kush to assess progress on a school being built by the PRT. He takes a four-wheel-drive vehicle up a goat trail to deliver humanitarian supplies to a remote village before winter sets in. He guides various American TV crews around the valley, explaining the history and politics of Panjshir. Everywhere he goes, Jim tries to meet with the elders and other villagers to put a friendly face on the PRT, explain what the team is doing and find out what is going on in the neighborhood.

DeHart, 45, began his career with the State Department in 1992 as a Presidential Management Intern in what was then the Bureau of Refugee Programs. He joined the Foreign Service in 1993, and has also served in Istanbul, Turkey; in Melbourne, Australia; and at NATO headquarters in Brussels. In Washington, D.C., he has served as a watch officer for the State Department's Operations Center, director for Central Asia on the National Security Council Staff at the White House, and deputy director for Caucasus and Central Asian Affairs at State. He also worked for two under secretaries for political affairs as a special assistant for Europe and Eurasia. Following a year as a Rusk Fellow at Georgetown University, Jim spent 40 weeks in Dari language training before heading to Afghanistan.

DeHart's father was a career consular officer, so as a child Jim lived in Australia, Hong Kong, the Dominican Republic, and Mexico. The family moved to Oregon when he was 10. He has a B.A. from Gonzaga University and an M.A. in international affairs from George Washington University's Elliott School. He and his wife, a high school teacher, have two children, ages 10 and 14. Following his tour in Afghanistan (an unaccompanied posting), he heads back to Washington to serve as office director for Afghanistan in the State Department.

DeHart with a Deh-Kalan village elder.

USAID DEMOCRACY OFFICER

Bruce Abrams ▪ Embassy Lima, Peru

Bruce Abrams at a USAID-sponsored human rights seminar in Bogotá, Colombia, in January 2004.

The work of a USAID mission in any country depends on the particular development challenges facing that country. Most missions have some combination of technical program offices addressing the following issues: democracy and governance, agriculture and the environment, education and training, global health, economic growth and trade, global partnerships, and humanitarian assistance. Typically, the USAID mission has a director and a deputy director; an executive officer responsible for administration and operation of all support systems in the mission; a contracts officer; and program officers, who coordinate with the host government, oversee programs, and manage relationships with program-implementing organizations in the country. USAID missions rely on a professional staff of local employees for technical and political analysis. They are the backbone of any USAID mission.

As chief of USAID/Peru's Office of Democratic Initiatives, Democracy Officer Bruce Abrams oversees a team of four Americans and five Peruvians at Embassy Lima. The team designs and manages individual contracts and grants, the vehicles through which USAID delivers goods, services, and technical assistance and training to Peruvian institutions or individuals.

The U.S. government's foreign assistance priorities in Peru are to help the country firmly anchor its democratic institutions, convert the advantages of economic openness into broad social benefits, and assert state control over its territory. USAID projects help the government of Peru identify and combat public-sector corruption; mitigate and manage social (and sometimes violent) conflict; help local government deliver better services and govern more democratically; and strengthen the role of civil society in all aspects of Peruvian life.

> *"As a democracy officer, I have the opportunity to be engaged in some of the most interesting and challenging questions in society."*

"As a democracy officer, I have the opportunity to be engaged in some of the most interesting and challenging questions that a society deals with," says Abrams, "which involves channeling conflict and competition through processes and institutions so that the result is, in Lincoln's words, government 'of the people, by the people, for the people.'" He is quick to point out that the aim of his office is not to export U.S. democracy to Peru, but to "modestly assist others in freely seeking their own social, economic, and political aspirations."

The USAID democracy office in Peru has a particularly close relationship with the embassy's political section, sharing contacts and perspectives on political, governance, and human rights issues there. USAID officers in Peru, as in other countries, have the benefit of working with local partners who are doing the work of building democracy, so they often have a valuable inside view of the local situation and the society's needs. Democracy officers—technically called Crisis, Stabilization, and Governance Officers—also work closely with the embassy's public affairs section to coordinate relations with the media and cultural figures. Their home office back in Washington is the Bureau for Democracy, Conflict, and Humanitarian Assistance.

In 2010, Peru held local elections, with national elections scheduled for 2011. In preparation, the USAID mission designed a support program to strengthen democratic values and increase participation in the political process.

Most days, Abrams attends internal meetings to track progress on project activities; works on analysis of political, social, and economic trends that might affect democracy in Peru; meets with contacts and counterparts to develop relationships; and, if he's lucky, has an opportunity to "enjoy the wonderful food, culture, music, and people of Peru." Abrams relishes having a wide array of international friends in Lima, and exploring its parks and beaches, as well as areas outside the city, with his family.

Abrams accepts a gift on behalf of the U.S. mission at a local government project in Ayacucho, Peru, November 2009.

Bruce Abrams, 46, was born in Syracuse, N.Y., but grew up in New Haven, Connecticut, where his father worked as a professional artist and his mother as an archivist at Yale University. He has a B.A. in American history from Boston University and a master's degree in urban planning from UCLA. He cites a post-college, 10-month backpacking journey through Latin America as greatly influencing his future path. He worked on political campaigns and then for the Los Angeles city government for three years before joining the

Peace Corps and serving in Hungary in the early 1990s. From there, he got a job as a locally hired contractor with the USAID office in Budapest, and then worked in another contract position for USAID Washington, advising USAID missions in Central and Eastern Europe on local governance projects. He was in Belgrade in March 1999 when NATO bombed the city.

After joining USAID in 1999, Abrams' first assignment was to the mission in Bogotá, Colombia. In 2004, he volunteered for a nine-month stint with USAID in Baghdad, where he helped design and manage the first generation of democracy programs there. From 2004 to 2009, he served as deputy, then chief of the Office of Democracy for USAID in Egypt. Bruce is married and has two young children.

REFUGEE COORDINATOR
Nancy Cohen ▪ Embassy Belgrade, Serbia

The job of a refugee coordinator, a regional position, offers an extraordinary mix of policy and humanitarian assistance program re-sponsibilities. Refugee coordinators track, analyze, and report on refugee movements and the situations that produce them, as well as assess needs and evaluate ac-tivities and interventions funded by the U.S. govern-ment. In 2010, there were 26 "refcoord" positions overseas, including in embassies in Kabul, Baghdad, and Bangkok. The positions belong to the Bureau of Population, Refugees, and Migration (PRM). Refugee officers play a key role in alerting Washington to emerging crises in the region and suggesting ways the  U.S. government might intervene to protect refugees or improve their conditions.

As the regional refugee coordinator in the Balkans, political officer Nancy Cohen is based in Belgrade, Serbia. Embassy Belgrade is a medium-sized post, with about 100 Americans and about 300 locally engaged staff. The current facility is a hodgepodge of adjacent buildings along city streets. A new embassy is planned that will move the mission to a beautiful park-like setting.

The United Nations labels the Balkans one of the five most pressing, protracted refugee situations in the world. The others are the plights of Afghan refugees in Pakistan and Iran; the Rohingya in Bangladesh; Eritreans in Sudan; and Burundian refugees in Tanzania. Although the last Balkan wars ended in 1995, re-gional conflicts continued through 2004, and the legacy of displacement, poverty, and statelessness remains. Nearly 500,000 people continue to live outside their home regions throughout the Balkans in 2010 as a result of regional conflicts.

Displaced populations differ around the world, and the solutions for them vary; however, the structure of the refugee coordinator job is similar from post to

post. Refugee coordinators report to PRM and to the deputy chief of mission at their home embassy, as well as to the DCMs of all the other posts they cover. Despite numerous bosses, Cohen explains, a refugee coordinator enjoys tremendous autonomy, overseeing tens or hundreds of millions of dollars in humanitarian assistance.

The refugee coordinator monitors and evaluates implementation of PRM-funded projects throughout the Balkans. In 2009, the bureau provided more than $12 million to international organizations and nongovernmental organizations to assist refugees and internally displaced persons throughout the Balkans. For the most part, the projects focus on returning refugees and displaced persons to Kosovo; integrating internally displaced persons in Serbia and Montenegro; and providing legal assistance to help the displaced from Kosovo exercise rights or obtain social services. In addition to monitoring implementation of multimillion-dollar programs, the Balkans refcoord develops and manages an administrative budget of about $200,000—something that reporting officers rarely get to do before becoming a deputy chief of mission.

The job requires a significant amount of local travel and some conference travel to Geneva or Washington, D.C. Cohen spends an average of 20 percent of her time on the road. On a typical day in Belgrade, she might meet with the representative of the United Nations High Commissioner for Refugees to review the organization's operating plans or discuss a project or problem. She might conduct a site visit to monitor an NGO partner's project or meet with a government official. Her contacts are varied, from foreign ministers to Roma refugees, taking her from presidential palaces to garbage-dump residences. Her reporting ranges from political cables and weekly activity reports to monitoring reports.

Her contacts are varied, from foreign ministers to Roma refugees, taking her from presidential palaces to garbage-dump residences.

Refugee coordinators often find themselves in areas of political instability. While the Balkans is one of the more developed locations for a refcoord, Cohen still encountered political volatility in Serbia leading to the firebombing of the embassy and political uncertainty in Kosovo that earned her danger pay. Prior to Kosovo's declaration of independence in 2008, the political uncertainties surrounding the province's status required Cohen to get involved in regional contingency planning for possible population flows within or across borders and boundaries. Although tensions ran high, the declaration of independence did not spark major movements. In fact, since independence, increasing numbers of displaced persons have returned to Kosovo.

"It is common to hear FSOs who have served in areas as different as Serbia, the Horn of Africa, Bangkok, and Kabul describe their refcoord tours as the best of their career," Cohen says. "Wherever you find yourself, it's a great job."

Nancy Cohen calls New York City, San Francisco, and New Orleans home. Before joining the Foreign Service in 1993, she had worked as a photographer, labor organizer, paralegal, systems analyst (for the Treasury

Nancy Cohen at the opening of a milking station in Kosovo, awarding certificates for completion of a business planning course.

Department and the Smithsonian), English as a Second Language teacher on a refugee resettlement project, and as a volunteer for Volunteers in Service to America.

Cohen joined the Foreign Service as an unconed generalist (according to the policy of the period), single, and nearing 40. She was an economic officer for 10 years and then switched to the political cone. She has spent nearly all of her career overseas, covering human rights in Tunisia and environment and science in Brazil, and heading the political/economic section in Lithuania. Many of her assignments were guided by tandem and school considerations related to an 11-year marriage to another FSO and the needs of her daughter, now 13. Following her Serbia posting, she moves to a job in PRM's Office of Europe, Central Asia, and the Americas, and then to an assignment as a Pearson Fellow working on Capitol Hill.

REGIONAL ENVIRONMENTAL OFFICER

Bruce Hudspeth ▪ Embassy Astana, Kazakhstan

Environmental issues transcend national borders and have political, economic, security, and humanitarian implications. As the regional environmental officer (REO) for Central Asia, running the environmental "hub" office in Astana, Bruce Hudspeth is on the road half the time, traveling to and from the six countries he covers: Kazakhstan, Kyrgyzstan, Tajikistan, Uzbekistan, Turkmenistan, and Afghanistan.

Based on the idea that environmental problems can be most effectively addressed regionally, the 12 regional hub offices around the world complement the work of the bilateral environment, science, technology, and health officers. The regional environmental officer engages with all the countries of a region to promote environmental cooperation, sharing of environmental data, and adoption of environmentally sound policies of benefit to all countries in the area.

Bruce Hudspeth on a trip to the once-vibrant "port" city of Muynak on the Western Aral Sea.

Boats in the desert where the Aral Sea once was.

Hudspeth reopened the Central Asia Regional Environmental Hub Office in 2008 after it had been closed for almost two years. (Following uprisings in Andijon, Uzbekistan, the Uzbek government insisted that the U.S. embassy close several regional offices.) The hub office is located in Embassy Astana, a medium-sized post in the remote northern steppes of Kazakhstan in the heart of the Eurasian continent. When the Kazakh government moved from Almaty to the new capital of Astana, the U.S. embassy followed suit and moved to this brand new city, which today is thriving, offering fascinating architecture and a modern lifestyle—despite being the second-coldest capital in the world!

Kazakhstan, like the rest of Central Asia, inherited a Soviet legacy of pollution and neglect of the environment for the sake of industrial development. Along with Uzbekistan, it is home to the Aral Sea, considered by many to be the premier ecological catastrophe of our time. Water is scarce, and its transboundary management has become a geopolitical issue. Kazakhstan was also home to the Soviet nuclear program, where above-ground testing at Semipalatinsk was conducted until the 1963 Test Ban Treaty, resulting in serious public health problems that persist to this day.

The ESTH acronym—environment, science, technology, and health—offers a guide to the issues that Hudspeth covers: climate change, endangered species, environmental awareness, the geopolitics of water resource management, negotiations for bilateral science and technology agreements, renewable energy, space technology (including the Baikonur launch complex), HIV/AIDS, and tuberculosis, as well as the long-term health consequences of 40 years of nuclear weapons testing.

Hudspeth is integrated into the political-economic section, where he not only covers regional issues but also serves as the de facto environment officer for Embassy Astana. He coordinates closely

with the other Central Asian posts' environment officers and serves as a bridge between them and Washington, as well as the "eyes and ears" of the Bureau of Oceans and International Environmental and Scientific Affairs in Central Asia. In that role, he makes policy recommendations and works closely with other U.S. government agencies. Hudspeth attends regional conferences and maintains contact with local government officials throughout Central Asia, as well as with nongovernmental organizations. Environment officers have no budget for projects, so Bruce is constantly trying to match up worthy initiatives with funding sources.

Environmental officers in all but the largest embassies are almost always economic officers who cover these issues as part of their portfolios. However, in Central Asia, ESTH officers are so busy with the economic matters that drive most of their work that they have little time for other issues. As the REO, Hudspeth has no other competing priorities, so he is able to assist and complement the work of ESTH officers.

On any given day, Hudspeth might be anywhere in the region, meeting with local groups and government officials. He may fly to Almaty for a meeting and back to Astana that evening to be at the Ministry of Agriculture's climate change conference. When in his office, he's drafting reporting cables from his last trip and preparing for the next trip, arranging meetings as well as logistics. He might prepare a briefing paper on the desiccation of the Aral Sea or write the new edition of a bimonthly environmental newsletter. He delivers a démarche on swine flu or food security, and attends the newly established U.S.-Kazakhstan Energy Working Group to explore ways to cooperate on renewable energy. He accompanies a visiting U.S. Forest Service delegation to meetings in Astana and then flies to Dushanbe for the Carnegie Institute's annual renewable energy conference.

Science diplomacy is one of the best ways to promote a positive image of the United States abroad.

Hudspeth seizes every opportunity for public diplomacy, speaking at conferences and meetings on the advantages of scientific cooperation. He sees science diplomacy as one of the best ways to promote a positive image of the U.S. abroad. The REO position is a great fit for someone who enjoys taking initiative, creative problem-solving, travel, and giving speeches. "Environmental diplomacy is the 21st-century diplomacy," says Bruce, so this is the job of a lifetime for him.

Hudspeth, who is from Corvallis, Oregon, has a degree in mathematics and, prior to joining the Foreign Service, ran his own business. He is married and has five adult children. He was almost 45 when he joined the State Department in 1992; his first assignment was to the newly opened embassy in Almaty, Kazakhstan. Other postings include Montevideo, Uruguay; Kyiv, Ukraine; Shenyang and then Beijing, China (following one year of language training in

Hudspeth against a classic Astana background, including President Narsultan Nazarbayev's palace.

Washington, D.C., and one year in Taiwan). Astana will be Bruce's last Foreign Service posting: he faces mandatory retirement at age 65.

ENTRY-LEVEL OFFICER

Carolyn Dubrovsky ▪ Embassy Kathmandu, Nepal

Carolyn Dubrovsky at work in the Kathmandu consular section.

Before heading to their first assignments, all entry-level officers go through orientation training, called the A-100 course. There they are introduced to the vast array of issues they will face as representatives of their government abroad. Entry-level officers (ELO) serve in assignments that are no longer than two years, and are eligible for tenure after 36 months of service, which usually occurs during the second tour.

Entry-level officers, who previously were called junior officers, are most often assigned to consular positions for their first, and sometimes second, tour. They are required to serve in a consular position for at least one year before tenure. However, these early years also enable officers to pursue a wide variety of opportunities in the embassy. They act as control officers during high-level visits, set up and speak at outreach events, and support and attend representational events at the ambassador's residence and elsewhere. ELOs often have a chance to do an exchange with colleagues in other sections of the embassy or even at other U.S. posts in the region.

Carolyn Dubrovsky manages the Refugee and Asylum Follow-to-Join Unit in Embassy Kathmandu's consular section that handles what Dubrovsky calls "a regular but not over-whelming" nonimmi-

grant visa caseload. Each of four units is run by an ELO, supervised by the deputy consul and the consular chief, and supported by 14 local staff and three American consular assistants.

Embassy Kathmandu is a medium-sized embassy in South Asia with about 50 direct-hire Americans and 450 Locally Employed Staff. Prior to her arrival in Nepal, Dubrovsky was given eight months of Tibetan language training (most ELOs do not get more than six months of language training before their first post-ing). She already spoke Nepali, having spent two years in Nepal as a student. Because so many Tibetans reside in Nepal, the addition of Tibetan language made Dubrovsky an even more valuable resource for the embassy.

Dubrovsky and her colleagues regularly handle issues affecting U.S. citizens in Nepal, and they have to be ready to help any U.S. citizen in need at any time, day or night. "This is our primary function," says Dubrovsky. "It may be something as simple as putting extra pages in a passport or, in the most serious cases, help-ing a family cope with the death of a loved one overseas."

Dubrovsky manages visa cases for the family members of people who have claimed asylum or been resettled in the United States as refugees, many of whom are Bhutanese or Tibetan. She is responsible for making sure that qualified applicants are reunited with their families in the United States as quickly as possible. These cases can involve complicated is-sues of relationship, identity, or nationality fraud, but must be handled with extreme sensitivity, given the precarious circumstances in which many of these individu-als reside in Nepal. She and her

> *"Sometimes the most unexpected assignments and responsibilities turn out to be the best."*

colleagues work closely with the Department of Homeland Security, international nongovernmental organizations, and the regional refugee coordinator at post.

"Consular officers have varied and interesting work," Dubrovsky says, "and need to employ a broad range of skills to be effective." She cites customer service skills, knowledge of visa law and local law, and a deep understanding of cultural, economic, and political contexts of the country as important keys to success. Each ELO in the consular section manages a unit, and they all face a range of issues every day. Consular officers in Kathmandu start their mornings with nonimmigrant

Dubrovsky conducts an interview with a visa applicant.

(visitor) visa interviews. In the afternoon, they work on immigrant visa cases and provide American Citizen Services, as well as work on special projects. They visit local jails, hospitals, and orphanages, and engage in regular outreach programs that may involve giving a presentation on student visas or doing an interview with a local radio station.

When working on visa cases in Kathmandu, the most common issues are document fraud and misrepresentation. Consular officers are the first line of defense in recognizing such misrepresentation and making efforts to stop it, thus protecting U.S. interests.

Dubrovsky's arrival in Nepal coincided with a doubling of the workload for her unit. With the help of local staff, the unit was able to revise and streamline the processing of cases, decreasing processing times and resolving a backlog of older complicated cases. The effort was aimed at reuniting families, but also served as a valuable experience in managing cross-cultural barriers and using resources efficiently.

Dubrovsky, 28, joined the Foreign Service in 2007 as a political officer. She has a B.A. in biology from Smith College and master's degrees in international relations and public administration from the Maxwell School of Citizenship and Public Affairs at Syracuse University. She worked as a contractor for the Defense Department for a year before joining the State Department. She is married to another entry-level officer, Konstantin Dubrovsky. "Be prepared to go wherever the Foreign Service needs you," Carolyn advises those considering a Foreign Service career. "Be realistic and keep an open mind. Sometimes the most unexpected assignments and responsibilities turn out to be the best."

OFFICE MANAGEMENT SPECIALIST

Elizabeth Babroski ▪ U.S. Mission to the OSCE, Vienna, Austria

The Organization for Security and Cooperation in Europe (OSCE) is a major forum for the 56 participating member-states to work together on issues of peace, security, and human rights in Europe and Central Asia. A legacy of the historic 1975 Helsinki Accords, it is the only fully inclusive trans-Atlantic, European, and Eurasian political organization. Over more than 30 years, commitments to democracy, rule of law, human rights, tolerance, pluralism, and media freedoms have been hammered out at the OSCE and its predecessor, the Conference for Security and Cooperation in Europe.

The U.S. Mission to the Organization for Security and Cooperation in Europe represents the interests of the U.S. government to the OSCE. USOSCE, as it is called, is part of Tri-Missions Vienna, which also includes U.S. Embassy Vienna and the U.S. Mission to International Organizations in Vienna. For Office Management Specialist (OMS) Elizabeth Babroski, this complexity makes her job that much more enjoyable, providing it with a multilateral dynamic. Although each part of the Tri-Mission is focused on separate policy issues and located in separate buildings with separate ambassadors, Babroski explains, the members of the community "feel like we are all part of the same team." In fact, they are on the same management team: one management office supports all three U.S. missions in Vienna, managing security, human resources, finance, and general services.

Babroski serves as office manager and executive assistant to the U.S. ambassador to the OSCE, working at what she calls "command central." Running this busy front office involves managing the ambassador's schedule, arranging his travel, and coordinating all of his activities. She must always ensure that the rest of the mission is aware of front office priorities, and that the ambassador is fully briefed on what is going on inside and outside the mission. She coordinates the activities of the front office with the rest of the U.S. mission, as well as with other countries' OSCE missions, and with the OSCE chairmanship and secretariat. Babroski also supervises the ambassador's driver and the protocol assistant and works closely with the staff of the ambassador's residence, often supervising activities related to representational events held at the residence.

Elizabeth Babroski at OSCE headquarters.

The ambassador is often away from the office at committee meetings at OSCE headquarters, at other events in Vienna, or out of town. In order to maintain lines

Babroski at OSCE headquarters, housed in the historic Hofburg Palace in Vienna.

of communication, Babroski and other staff rely on smart phones to keep in touch. She regularly interacts with officials of many foreign governments, as well as staff at the other American missions in Vienna and in U.S. embassies in other OSCE member countries. USOSCE has about 35 American employees and 20 local staff. Its offices are located in Vienna's 19th district—a 25-minute drive from OSCE headquarters in the first district.

An office management specialist has many duties at an embassy, but each of them falls under the umbrella of the primary responsibility: coordinating moving parts. This includes everything from necessary, if occasionally mundane, office work (such as filing, shredding, and filling out paperwork) to crucial logistical tasks (such as fielding high-level phone calls, coordinating the ambassador's meetings and travel, and communicating with other staff members to keep operations moving smoothly). "An OMS must be proactive, able to prioritize and manage time effectively," says Babroski. "Good judgment and a sense of humor help, too." The job of an OMS requires dedicated, flexible, and professional individuals who help orchestrate the complex components of a U.S. mission. An ambassador's OMS tends to be someone who has "honed the tools of the trade" and is thus well-prepared to fully support a chief of mission.

In Vienna, Babroski works closely with the ambassador's driver, protocol assistant, and other staff members to ensure that the ambassador's schedule is accurate and hassle-free. In a typical day, Babroski attends meetings, schedules events, interacts with her foreign counterparts, distributes correspondence, checks cables, organizes phone calls for the ambassador, and receives visitors.

"I enjoy the responsibility and diversity of skills required to support a senior official, along with

Running this busy front office involves managing the ambassador's schedule, arranging his travel, and coordinating all of his activities.

the challenge of moving to a new post every few years," says Babroski. She also enjoys learning languages and experiencing other cultures. Elizabeth strives to maintain a balance between work and family, noting that "home is where you are, so make the most of it!" She is enthusiastic about the job, and says she is most proud of "representing the U.S. in a positive way that helps others around the world understand American values and interests."

Babroski, 46, joined the Foreign Service in 1992. She holds a B.A. in French and has a 16-year-old son. Previous posts were Port-au-Prince, Haiti; London, England; Suva, Fiji; Oslo, Norway; Paris, France; Bridgetown, Barbados; and Singapore.

INFORMATION MANAGEMENT OFFICER

Mark Butchart ▪ Embassy Pretoria, South Africa

The information management officer (IMO) is analogous to the chief information officer employed by many businesses and government organizations. As the senior information management professional at post, the IMO provides oversight and operational control of classified and unclassified information technology for the mission. This usually includes responsibility for international satellite and leased-line operations, all data processing, telephone and radio systems, videoconferencing systems, regular mail and diplomatic pouch operations, local area network administration, and technology training.

As the IMO for Embassy Pretoria, Mark Butchart is responsible for all information resource management activities throughout the embassy and the three consulates—Cape Town, Johannesburg, and Durban. More than 1,000 employees (locally hired South Africans and Americans) staff the U.S. mission to South Africa, the largest on the continent, which supports more than 30 U.S. government agencies working in the country. South Africa has the strongest economy and most advanced technology in Africa, but still lags far behind the United States when it comes to telecommunications capabilities and infrastructure.

Information management officers run the information resource management (IRM) section of the embassy, which in a medium or large mission is usually split into three main offices. These are the Information Systems Center (which is the primary computer support section); the Information Programs Center (which supports the diplomatic pouch and mail operations, as well as the telephone and radio systems, and manages the post's classified computer network); and the Information Technical Center (which maintains all telecommunications connectivity between the posts and Washington, D.C.). This career track usually begins with assignments as information management specialists or information

management technical specialists (radio, telephone, and digital technicians), graduating to positions as information programs officers or information systems officers, before being assigned as an IMO.

One of Butchart's key responsibilities is to "translate" highly technical issues and information into laymen's terms for post management. He spends a lot of time communicating with Washington, D.C., offices, as well—especially in relation to the problem of inadequate bandwidth in South Africa. He manages a staff of about 30, and part of that job involves protecting his staff's time and explaining the limits of their services—for example, why they cannot repair embassy staff members' personal computers on U.S. government time.

The IMO must be flexible, versatile, and ready to be called on to occupy other positions in the embassy if the need arises. Butchart has served as acting management counselor and management officer when those officers were away from post. He also was selected to serve as an election observer during the 2009 elections in South Africa.

Most days, Butchart arrives early to work, in part to avoid Pretoria's traffic congestion. He always faces his e-mail queue first and last each day, making sure it is clear before he heads home. He attends embassy country team and management section meetings, and usually has four or five unanticipated meetings each week.

In the IRM offices, preparations for the 2010 Soccer World Cup, held in South Africa, began in 2009. The staff prepared for an influx of approximately 130 temporary employees, all of whom needed IT and telecommunications support from the mission. Butchart served as liaison with the relevant offices in South Africa and Washington, D.C., to determine the requirements and then work to develop a way to

> *"As long as our customers are fully supported and can work with a minimal amount of aggravation, then IRM has done its job."*

address these needs. In addition, his team had to ensure that the embassy continued to run smoothly during the World Cup, so Butchart had to balance the demands of the visitors with day-to-day embassy operational requirements.

"The tools we provide to our customers—telephones, radios, computers—should work seamlessly and effectively," says Butchart, "facilitating their ability to perform in the most efficient and effective manner possible. That is why we are here." Maintaining a humble posture, he says that for the most part, resource management staff toil silently in the background, facilitating the work of diplomacy. "As long as our customers are fully supported and can do their important work with a minimal amount of technically related aggravation, then IRM has done its job," he says.

Butchart (center) playing with the Pretoria Blues Band.

Mark Butchart, 48, is an Air Force veteran from Atlanta, Georgia, who began working for the State Department in 1986 as a communications electronics officer. In 1989, he worked as a contractor for the State Department in Albany, Georgia; then joined the Foreign Service as an information management specialist in 1992. In addition to Pretoria, he has been posted to Bonn, Germany; Guangzhou, China; Mbabane, Swaziland; Tel Aviv, Israel; Lagos, Nigeria; and Washington, D.C. He is part of a tandem couple, married to Jenny, a financial management officer. He cautions that State relies on tandem employees themselves to find positions in the same mission in order to be assigned together. Butchart and his wife were posted to different continents during his South Africa assignment: she was in Bogotá, Colombia. In 2010, they were reunited with assignments in Washington, D.C., where Mark was selected for a Pearson Fellowship to work in a congressional office on Capitol Hill.

FACILITY MANAGER

Gary Hein ▪ Embassy Cairo, Egypt

Gary Hein in front of the chief of mission residence and Cairo II office building.

The primary role of a facility manager is to ensure the availability of services—electricity, heating, ventilation, air conditioning, water, etc.—necessary for the U.S. mission to function effectively. The American taxpayer has invested in thousands of U.S. government buildings overseas, and it is the job of the embassy's facility manager to coordinate maintaining, preserving, improving, and protecting the physical infrastructure of the mission. The building services must be provided in a facility that is safe and clean. The facility manager is also responsible for ensuring that employee housing is functional and safe.

Embassy Cairo is huge, with a physical infrastructure to match. As the senior facility manager, Gary Hein is responsible for a vast assortment of real estate in the city. The U.S. mission comprises three large compounds and more than 300 employee residences scattered throughout Cairo, a crowded urban landscape of more than 15 million people, which serves as the crossroad between Africa and the Arab world, Europe and Asia.

Hein also has regional responsibility for the American Presence Post in Alexandria, which requires extra care as one of the Secretary of State's Culturally Significant Properties. Hein is responsible for supporting more than 1,500 people who are part of the U.S. mission, representing 38 different government agencies. His team includes some 225 local staff, most of whom are Egyptian. While smaller embassies have only one facility manager (or none—in the smallest posts the general services officer does the job), Hein works with two deputy facility managers and an engineering team.

Hein explains that his job has many moving pieces. His office is part of the management section, which processes about 12,000 work orders annually, handles more than 100 make-readies (preparing housing for the arrival of a new employee to post), and manages millions of dollars worth of projects. "Between language barriers, cultural differences and harsh weather conditions, there is plenty of potential for things to go wrong. From time to time they do. Having trust in my team allows me to leverage our collective resources," Hein says. He points to follow-up and communication as the two key elements of the job that determine success or failure.

The facility manager position encompasses budget planning and workplan devel-

> *Gary Hein is responsible for a vast assortment of real estate in the city.*

opment. Hein manages approximately $8 million worth of projects, as well as a $1.2 million budget for routine maintenance and repairs. Coordination is one of the most important aspects of the job, according to Hein: "My mantra is communicate, coordinate, and notify." He leads a group called the Cairo Construction Coordination Committee, which meets throughout the year and provides an opportunity to discuss upcoming projects and the impact those projects will have on the mission. Communication is key to managing overlapping projects, which often draw from the same finite support resources.

Safety is another critical piece of the facility manager job. Hein serves as the post occupational safety and health officer (POSHO). Many safety deficiencies are due to a lack of training or knowledge, so Hein tries to ensure that his staff is up to date on all of the regulations and safety standards they need to know. He manages local staff development, encouraging employees to take advantage of training opportunities available at the mission and to gain familiarity with building codes and State Department regulations. As part of staff development, Hein manages a training and mentoring program, with an emphasis on professionalism and morale improvement.

Hein spends about half of each day in various scheduled and unscheduled meetings, from management team meetings and the community welfare gathering to discussions of specific projects. He also researches codes and regulations

Gary Hein with the embassy engineering team in Cairo.

as he prepares justifications for projects, responds to taskers, and drafts position papers and project recommendations. Personnel issues and responding to customers take up part of each day, as well.

The facility manager is part of the management team, and works with all sections and offices in a U.S. mission.

"The work of a facility manager helps form the first, and often most lasting, impression on new officers and their families, local staff, and official visitors, as well as the public." The role of the facility manager is not limited to keeping the lights on, Gary explains. He is also able to help promote the embassy's mission, identifying outreach opportunities that promote a positive image for the embassy. Outreach activities he initiated during previous tours include a ceremonial tree planting, safety promotion with the host government and, in Dar es Salaam, projects to establish safe water wells for local communities.

Hein, 43, was born and raised in Colorado and earned a liberal arts degree in 1989. Before joining the State Department in 1991, he worked as a project foreman in the construction industry. His first Foreign Service post was Belgrade, Yugoslavia. Other postings have been Prague, Czech Republic; Oslo, Norway (with responsibility for Copenhagen, Denmark); Dar es Salaam, Tanzania; Antananarivo, Madagascar; and Ottawa, Canada (with responsibility for six consulates and one American Presence Post). He met his wife, Ana, in Belgrade, and they have two children.

MEDICAL OFFICER

Mark Cohen ▪ Embassy Nairobi, Kenya

Dr. Mark Cohen runs a large health clinic in Nairobi that serves more than 1,000 people. He is the regional medical officer (RMO) for Embassy Nairobi, providing primary health care to the embassy community there, as well as to the U.S. mission communities in the Republic of the Congo, the Democratic Republic of the Congo, Burundi, Rwanda, Uganda, and Tanzania.

"Each post within the region has its own unique challenges," Dr. Cohen explains. "We have to follow disease trends across a number of areas—Ebola in Uganda, Rift Valley Fever in Tanzania, malaria in Burundi, and gastrointestinal illness just about everywhere." But tracking and treating diseases are only part of the job. "We must be prepared to manage everything from sprained ankles to injuries from car accidents, unusual insect stings, snake bites, jet lag, and everything in between."

In the RMO job, "the challenges are the rewards," explains Cohen. "I get to serve a remarkable community in ways that I never expected. I have the luxury of time with my patients that isn't rushed. I can explain things, ask more questions, and listen to my patients. In the embassy community, my patients are my colleagues and my friends. I know their families. I am given a great trust; earning it is my reward."

Foreign Service medical providers are the RMOs, nurse practitioners and physician assistants (called FS health practitioners), psychiatrists, and medical technologists serving at U.S. missions around the world. There are nearly 60 regional medical officers and 112 additional Foreign Service health practitioners overseas, as well as 21 regional psychiatrists and 12 regional medical technologists. At some small posts, health practictioners are local or family member hires. These medical providers offer routine health care, including physical exams, vaccinations, and health screenings.

> *"I have the luxury of time with my patients that isn't rushed."*

Embassy medical providers also provide urgent and emergency care; work closely with local providers, clinics, and hospitals; assess the suitability of local care; and arrange medical evacuations when necessary. They are on call 24 hours a day, seven days a week. They often become acquainted with unusual illnesses not found in the United States, and they need to keep current with local conditions. Because mission employees travel to the far reaches of Kenya, Dr. Cohen must be familiar with hospitals and local healthcare providers throughout the country, including places the official community frequents for vacation and training.

"The travel is great," says Cohen of his job, "and I get to see and appreciate how medicine is practiced in many places. I've met so many dedicated medical professionals all over the world, and even—maybe especially—when resources are limited, they provide exceptional care in great earnest." Cohen spends about a third of his time on the road visiting the other posts he covers in the region. On these trips, he usually meets with the ambassador or the deputy chief of mission to review medical issues particular to that mission, as well as the management officer with direct responsibility for the health unit at each embassy.

While visiting other posts, Cohen always spends time meeting with health unit staff. "The local-hire health practitioners at post are the most important contacts I have," he says. "They know the community, the local medical resources, and conditions better than anyone." He spends time with the post health practitioner, seeing patients in consultation, reviewing medical records, visiting local hospitals and clinics, and reviewing health unit operations. "Lunch or dinner out with the health unit staff is nearly always part of a regional visit. We build relationships that will last for many years, relationships that depend as much on good medical care as on trust and communication and respect ... and a good meal together."

Embassy and consulate health units vary depending on the size of the mission, the local medical capacity, and the needs of the community. Some posts have just one medical provider. Because Nairobi is one of the largest missions in sub-Saharan Africa, it has both a regional medical officer and a Foreign Service health practitioner, as well as two nurses, two administrative assistants, a regional medical officer/psychiatrist, and a regional psychologist.

Individual patient care is the primary responsibility for all Foreign Service medical practitioners, says Cohen, but much of his time is spent on missionwide or regional issues, such as planning for a response to pandemic influenza and managing country- and region-specific issues, such as malaria. Medical practitioners serve as experts for general medical issues at post and advise the ambassador and embassy community. They are active members of the management section, offering their expertise on issues such as local sanitation and hygiene, travel cautions, and emergency planning.

Dr. Cohen visiting with children in Jinja, Uganda.

Cohen calls himself a chief cook and bottle washer for the embassy community. He says "the job requires a flexibility to work with patients by e-mail and phone, strong knowledge of local medical conditions that may be unique to the region, solid emergency skills, and the ability to research and identify all sorts of medical conditions."

Mark Cohen, 56, joined the Foreign Service in 2004. Before Kenya, he served in Moscow, Russia, where he met his wife. He grew up in southern New Jersey and has a B.S. from American University, an M.S. from George Washington University, and an M.D. from New Jersey Medical School. He practiced medicine in Auburn, N.Y., from 1985 until joining the State Department in 2004.

DIPLOMATIC COURIER

Edward Bent ▪ Embassy Bangkok, Thailand

Ed Bent (right) managing pouches in Frankfurt, July 2009.

"I enjoy travel," says Diplomatic Courier Ed Bent. "You have to in this position!" Based at the diplomatic courier regional hub in Bangkok, Thailand, Bent is charged with ensuring the safe conveyance of classified and sensitive diplomatic material. He manages the movement of diplomatic pouches across international borders in observance of the Vienna Convention on Diplomatic Intercourse and Immunities. Even in today's digital world, certain information, supplies, and equipment must still be delivered by hand. Diplomatic couriers (part of the Diplomatic Security Service) have a vital role in U.S. foreign policy endeavors, yet are an unheralded group that quietly carries out its sensitive security mission.

Couriers do much more than simply transport pouches from point A to point B. They interact with foreign officials, as well as U.S. embassy staff, in all the countries they visit, ensuring that regulations and policies relating to the movement and protection of diplomatic pouches are followed. They manage schedules that can be shifted due to inclement weather (snow in the mountains of Kyrgyzstan, monsoons in Bangladesh) and other unforeseen obstacles.

Bent's first assignment was to Frankfurt, where he served for 28 months following specialist orientation training and a three-week course in diplomatic courier operations. The Frankfurt division is affiliated with the U.S. consulate there, a large post with about 900 employees. In February 2010, Bent participated in a special

mission to deliver 5,000 kilos of material to the Sarajevo construction site for the new U.S. embassy building. Following several delays, he boarded a charter aircraft, an old Antonov AN-12. Although the Ukrainian crew on the plane spoke no English, they communicated friendship by providing their passenger with all the coffee and cookies he could eat. He enjoyed a stunning view of the snowcapped eastern Alps from the low-flying aircraft, which reached an altitude of only 10,000 feet above the mountain peaks.

When on the road, the courier's hours are long and irregular. In September 2010, Bent spent three weeks as a crewmember of a large cargo container ship. He had control of the diplomatic cargo for 384 consecutive hours on that trip, traveling from California to China, and was the only American among the crew of Eastern Europeans and Asians. He was on board for 120 hours without the cargo, called "deadheading." One night during the journey, they experienced sustained winds of 45 knots ripping through the Pacific while trying to avoid a severe hurricane off the coast of Asia.

There are approximately 100 diplomatic couriers worldwide. The Diplomatic Courier Service has four regional offices: Washington, Miami, Bangkok, and Frankfurt. In addition, there are six smaller hubs: Dakar, Manama, Pretoria, Sao Paulo, Seoul, and Sydney. The home office is located in Rosslyn, Virginia.

Although he is on the road most of the time, Bent has a somewhat regular routine. He wakes up early and prepares for a departure or a return flight—the destinations vary widely. Advance notice is not always available, so every day can be an adventure. From Frankfurt, Bent regularly traveled to locations in Europe, Central Asia, the Middle East, and Africa, as well as to Washington, D.C. In his first year on the job, Bent performed more than 50 courier missions covering 400,000 miles, from a short trip to Luxembourg to the longest journey, to Seoul; the cargo ranged from a single pouch to thousands of kilos of goods. His travels are conducted using trucks, ships, trains, commercial airlines, and cargo planes. Upon return from a mission, there is always a significant amount of paperwork to complete, including trip and expense reports.

In his first year on the job, Bent performed more than 50 courier missions covering 400,000 miles.

During his first assignment with the Foreign Service, Bent was recognized several times for outstanding service. After noting excessive cargo costs during one particular trip, he was able to reduce the charges, earning his first of two "Extra

Ed Bent on the tarmac in Sarajevo.

Mile" awards. Bent was appointed as the first Innovation Program Monitor for the Frankfurt Courier Region and, later, for the Global Diplomatic Courier Service. He prepared standard operating procedures for courier activity at the Frankfurt airport.

Diplomatic couriers come from all walks of life. Some are retired military, some come from other government agencies, and others are former police officers or even attorneys. Ed notes that the life of a courier can be glamorous, but it can also be arduous. Couriers must cope with long workdays and travel in all political and meteorological conditions. They must ensure that the stipulations of the Vienna Convention are met, contend with customs, and understand that they are accountable for what they transport. Some countries can be difficult to deal with in this regard. This is where tact, diplomacy, and the ability to think on one's feet comes into play. Bent says: "I am proud that our trips ensure that our colleagues working in embassies and consulates around the world are safe, because they have operational communication channels."

Bent, 56, holds a B.S. degree in engineering and has studied economics and business administration at the graduate level. A native of Berkeley, California, he joined the Foreign Service in January 2008. Before becoming a diplomatic courier, Bent worked as a financial planning specialist and corporate manager. His background also includes command and staff positions in the field artillery branch of the U.S. Army. Bangkok is his second post.

LOCALLY EMPLOYED STAFF

Mimy Santika ▪ USAID Mission, Jakarta, Indonesia

Locally Employed Staff working in USAID missions around the world are partners in development with their American colleagues as well as local organizations. An integral part of the team for any USAID program, Locally Employed Staff (who previously were called Foreign Service Nationals) have—in addition to technical skills—a level of cultural sensitivity and understanding of the local context that American USAID staff, who rotate to a new country every few years, cannot match.

Mimy Santika began working for USAID Indonesia in 1991, spending three years in the agriculture and environment office before moving over to the democracy program, where she would spend the next 12 years. She was especially focused on work with nongovernmental organizations in Aceh (on the northern tip of Sumatra) and Papua (the western half of the island of New Guinea), two politically sensitive areas at opposite ends of the country. She often made long trips to both regions to meet with contacts there.

USAID Mission Indonesia has had a strong democracy program for many years, and Santika has enjoyed working on projects that aimed to promote political awareness in the population, fair elections, political party development, and the strengthening of civil society. Santika was part of the USAID team that provided assistance to Indonesia in conducting its first free and fair elections in 1999, through support to local NGOs as well as international organizations experienced with democratic election processes.

The full U.S. mission in Indonesia (which includes the USAID mission plus the embassy and consulates) is considered large, with 1,400 Locally Employed Staff based at offices in Jakarta, Aceh, Medan, Surabaya, and Bali. In a large country of 240 million like Indonesia, spread out over more than 14,000 islands, local staff play a critical role, providing insights about priorities and the needs of people in Indonesia. As Santika notes, "LES are a source of information and the institutional memory for the embassy."

> *Santika was part of the USAID team that provided assistance to Indonesia in conducting its first free and fair elections in 1999.*

Santika is a technical specialist for the education sector program—a complex and politically sensitive effort to improve the quality of basic education in public and private schools in Indonesia's decentralized environment. The education initiative is a high-profile presidential initiative, so the White House is interested in how it proceeds. Santika joined the Education Office at USAID in 2006 and manages activities implemented at the district and school level, assisting in the improvement of education management and governance in seven provinces (Aceh, North Sumatra, West Java, Banten, Central Java, East Java, and South Sulawesi). She provides leadership and technical direction for the design, implementation, management/administration, monitoring, and evaluation of the education program.

Mimy Santika with elementary students in Pare-Pare, South Sulawesi.

Santika engages and negotiates with senior-level officials and representatives from the Indonesian government, as well as donor agencies, nongovernmental organizations, and the private sector. Santika and her LES colleagues collaborate to promote the sustainability of projects and to gather lessons learned (best practices) from existing activities and other donor programs.

The $150 million education program, encompassing preschool through higher education, is run by a group of 13 in the USAID mission—eight LES and five Americans. Typical days involve responding to implementing partners, reviewing and preparing reports, maintaining collaboration with Indonesian officials and donor partners, and monitoring project activities. The goal is to help the local government strengthen the education system to become more accountable and effective in providing services to schools, students, teachers, and principals. Most of the education projects are in the final stages of implementation, so the main focus is now on institutionalizing best practices with the local government and facilitating requests to replicate the program in other areas in Indonesia.

With almost 20 years of experience with USAID, Santika says the role of local employees has changed dramatically: "We are empowered and have more responsibilities than we had in the 1990s." There are much broader training and other skill-development opportunities for LES today. As a senior LES, Santika acts as a mentor for colleagues and encourages them to participate actively, providing opinions, "because we know more about our own country." She feels that the views of local staff are usually appreciated and welcomed.

In another leadership role, Santika has served as an FSN (now LES) Committee member since 2004; and in 2009, she was elected to be chair of the Indonesian Employee Association, which acts as a liaison between the LES and embassy management. She has also served as an Equal Employment Opportunity liaison.

Mimy Santika, 51, and her husband come from different ethnic groups. She is Minang, from West Sumatra, while her husband is Sundanese, from West Java. They have two children, a 25-year-old son and an 19-year-old daughter. Santika was raised in Jakarta and has an agricultural degree from Bogor Agricultural University. She spent six years in the United States while her husband was on a scholarship to Michigan State University from 1984 to 1990.

LOCALLY EMPLOYED STAFF

Edgar Zamudio ▪ Consulate General Tijuana, Mexico

Locally Employed Staff—previously known as Foreign Service Nationals—are the local employees serving in every U.S. post in the world. They provide the institutional memory for the missions, remaining at post as their American colleagues transfer to new assignments every few years. Most are citizens of the country where they work. With their intimate understanding of the politics, culture, and society of their country, they provide valuable insight into effectively addressing complex situations and overcoming challenges in a cross-cultural environment. LES work in U.S. missions as, among other things, political and economic assistants, warehouse managers, drivers, electricians, interpreters, security guards, and budget specialists.

Special Consular Services Assistant Edgar Zamudio works in arguably the most challenging American Citizen Services post in the world, Consulate General Tijuana. Less than 20 miles from San Diego, Tijuana is another world. No garden vacation spot, the district is a hotbed for illegal activity, offering temptations that get Americans into no end of trouble. Zamudio has seen it all.

Twenty-five percent of all U.S. citizens arrested outside the U.S. are arrested in Tijuana. Every morning starts with e-mails and calls from concerned family members in the United States. "On a normal day, we have from one to six Americans arrested," says Zamudio—but they're not the average tourists.

"We frequently deal with runaways, drug addicts, and the homeless or mentally ill," he explains. Easy access to illegal drugs attracts a significant number of Americans, who inevitably visit parts of Tijuana where drugs

> *Twenty-five percent of all U.S. citizens arrested outside the U.S. are arrested in the Tijuana district.*

are dealt, increasing their odds of becoming victims of crime. Accidental drug overdoses are common. The availability of veterinary medicines used in "suicide cocktails" brings some Americans to Tijuana to take their own lives, explains Zamudio. The red-light district also attracts Americans, exposing them to criminal activities in and around bars and brothels.

Part of Zamudio's job is to visit Americans when they are first arrested by the Mexican authorities. He helps ensure that family members are contacted, explains their rights, and provides other consular services. He checks in on them regularly. If a prisoner is ill or has another problem, he works with the authorities to find solutions.

Once an American is sentenced, Zamudio works to facilitate a transfer to a U.S. prison to serve the remaining time. He personally has helped more than 50 families work their way through the complex prisoner transfer process. As an LES based in Tijuana, he ensures continuity in the section, knows the history of arrest cases, maintains local contacts, and understands how to apply local laws and procedures to optimize American prisoners' welfare.

During the prison riots at La Mesa Prison in late 2008, Zamudio was part of the team responsible for accounting for the more than 250 American prisoners in a prison with more than 8,000 residents and almost no records. His team was the only link between family members and inmates for the first several weeks. Unfortunately, three Americans were killed in the riots. As part of his job, Zamudio also handles U.S. citizen death cases, assisting next of kin with identifying and transporting remains and preparing documentation.

Consulate General Tijuana is a medium-sized post in northwest Mexico with a staff of about 50 American direct-hire employees and 100 Locally Employed Staff working for the various agencies at post. It covers all of Baja California and Baja California Sur. American Citizen Services work in Tijuana is unique, in part because of the proximity to the U.S. border and San Diego. "Daily border crossings are routine, as many people live in one country and work or attend school in the other," says Zamudio. The work is divided between American tourists and American expats living in Mexico. It is, as Zamudio explains, "quite brisk and

fairly predictable—drownings, car accidents, lost and stolen passports, etc."

In January 2010, immediately following the devastating earthquake in Haiti, Zamudio was chosen to join a relief team sent to help evacuate U.S. citizens from Port-au-Prince. "The minor inconveniences of working 18-hour days and sleeping on the embassy floor were nothing in comparison with the suffering of the people I was

Edgar Zamudio visiting the state penitentiary in Mexicali, Baja California, to complete documents for a prisoner transfer to the United States.

helping—people who had lost everything," Zamudio says of the experience. "It was an amazing privilege to work beside my State Department colleagues from all over the world, as well as those from other U.S. government agencies. Just knowing we helped make a difference in someone's life was a huge personal reward. The experience helped me to see the world differently and appreciate the little things in life."

Zamudio, 29, was born and raised in Tijuana. He has a bachelor's degree in international business and language studies from the State University of Baja California, and a master's degree in international negotiations from Claude Bernard University Lyon 1 in France. Edgar has worked for Consulate General Tijuana for five years, starting in the Foreign Commercial Office with a focus on "match-making" for American companies looking for partners in northern Mexico. There he became familiar with the fundamental economic needs of people on both sides of the border. He then spent two years as a consular assistant at Consular Agency Cabo San Lucas. In 2008, he took up his current position as special consular services assistant.

PART II

Foreign Service Work and Life: Embassy, Employee, Family

By Shawn Dorman

THE EMBASSY AND THE COUNTRY TEAM

Embassies are located in the capital city of each country with which the United States has official relations, and serve as headquarters for U.S. government representation overseas. U.S. consulates are ancillary government offices in cities other than the capital. American and local employees serving in U.S. embassies and consulates work under the leadership of an ambassador to conduct diplomatic relations with the host country.

The Department of State is the lead agency for conducting U.S. diplomacy and the ambassador, appointed by the U.S. president, reports to the Secretary of State. Diplomatic relations among nations, including diplomatic immunity and the inviolability of embassies, follow procedures framed by the 1961 Vienna Convention on the Conduct of Diplomatic Relations and Optional Protocols, ratified by the U.S. in 1969.

The foreign affairs agencies that make up the Foreign Service—the Department of State, the U.S. Agency for International Development, the Foreign Commercial Service, the Foreign Agricultural Service, and the International Broadcasting Bureau—are part of the overall U.S. mission in a country and usually have their offices inside the embassy. Each embassy can also be home to the offices of other U.S. government agencies and departments, in some countries as many as 40 different entities. Agencies with a significant overseas presence include the Department of Defense, the Central Intelligence Agency, the Drug Enforcement Agency, the Treasury Department, the Federal Bureau of Investigation, and the Department of Homeland Security.

Most U.S. ambassadors have two titles. The first—ambassador extraordinary and plenipotentiary—is the international diplomatic title conveying the responsibility for relations with the host government. The second—chief of mission—has a more internal focus, representing the responsibility for management of the embassy.

The chief of mission leads the country team, an interagency group made up of the head of each State Department section in the embassy and the heads of the other U.S.

69

government agencies represented at post. Depending on the size of the U.S. mission and the breadth of America's relations with the country, the team can be quite large.

The country team meeting represents a regular occasion for the sharing of information among sections and agencies, and an opportunity to coordinate activities. It is where the ambassador can give instructions, share new priorities, request input or feedback, and be briefed on what is going on in the country and throughout the mission.

There's a saying some in the military like to use: "If you've seen one country team, you've seen one country team." The effectiveness, utility, and dynamics of country team meetings depend heavily on post leadership and vary widely from post to post and from year to year. Personalities and styles do matter, and the ambassador sets the tone.

The country team usually meets once a week. Ambassadors run their country team meetings differently, but, typically, each section and agency head (or a designated representative) will give a brief report on what the office is focused on that week and will raise any issues that might be of interest to the wider embassy community. Regular interagency consultation offers an opportunity to ensure that the various departments and agencies in the mission know what the others are doing and are not working at cross purposes. Embassy division chiefs attending the country team meeting return to their offices and brief their staff on relevant information from the meetings.

The first country team was established by the Truman administration in Germany in 1951. Following World War II, with economic assistance programs and Defense Department activity overseas growing, there was a need for more coordination of the overall U.S. mission. The "Clay Paper," named for General Lucius Clay, one of the architects of the Marshall Plan, was a memorandum of understanding among the Defense Department, State Department, and Economic Cooperation Administration that established the original concept of the country team: "To insure the full coordination of the U.S. effort, U.S. representatives at the country level shall constitute a team under the leadership of the ambassador."

A decade later, President John F. Kennedy initiated the practice of providing each chief of mission with a letter outlining his or her authority and expectations for the country team. The authority covers all executive branch employees, except those under a military commander.

"You are in charge of the entire United States diplomatic mission," the Kennedy letter states, "and I shall expect you to supervise all of its operations. The mission includes not only the personnel of the Department of State and the Foreign Service, but also the representatives of all other United States agencies which have programs and activities in (country name). I shall give you full support and backing in carrying out your assignments."

Depending on who is in the White House, between 30 and 40 percent of ambassadorships are filled by political appointees, the rest coming from the career Foreign Service. Many political appointee ambassadors have strong business

MINDS WIDE OPEN:
THE FSN-FSO RELATIONSHIP
By Galina Sabeva

When I left my job as a correspondent for Reuters in 2003 to join the American embassy in Sofia as a political assistant, I had only a vague idea what to expect. A glossy job description in the newspaper, coupled with my misperception about embassy work, led me to believe that I had landed an important, if not glamorous, job. I knew very little then about the ups and downs of working as a Foreign Service National, a term used for the local employees working for U.S. missions abroad. *Note: The term has been officially changed to Locally Engaged Staff, but most people still use the more familiar FSN.*

I was given a tiny desk in the embassy basement, with no access to the classified diplomatic area. A set of complex security instructions and a long list of acronyms added to my confusion. An FSN colleague, who had worked at the embassy for more than 10 years, offered soothing advice: "Once you get over the strange rules, it can be quite interesting." But it was the deputy chief of mission, an energetic former journalist for *USA Today*, who gave me a clear perspective on what to expect. I'd probably have a hard time getting used to the embassy's protocol-conscious environment, he said, and I would have neither the visibility nor the access of my previous job. But, he added, "These limitations aside, the job is rather exciting." This conversation was an important reality check for me, and got to the essence of the FSN job. There are certain limitations, but also opportunities—it's up to the individual to accept the former and explore the latter.

Why the U.S. Embassy?

I joined the embassy when working for America wasn't the most prestigious job. The U.S. was involved in an unpopular war in Iraq, while anti-Americanism was peaking in Europe. Trust among Americans in their own administration hovered near record lows.

Strange as it may sound, FSNs don't generally join the embassy for competitive pay, work benefits, and job security. Consecutive post–World War II

American administrations have pursued policies aimed at spreading democracy, and the U.S. diplomatic service has played a key role in advancing these policies. Locally hired employees in an American embassy have the unique chance to observe the inner workings of a global superpower's diplomatic machine and see how it conducts diplomacy on a day-to-day basis.

Despite their vivid awareness of their country's power, I have seen very little arrogance, if any, in the men and women who actually conduct U.S. diplomacy. At the same time, I have often been surprised at how my otherwise amiable American colleagues have difficulty taking "no" for an answer when pursuing U.S. foreign policy goals with forceful determination. I have had the opportunity to observe American idealism and pragmatism, two interwoven, but also often contradictory, strands in U.S. diplomacy. And during the war in Iraq, I saw diplomats upholding policies with which they did not necessarily agree, and doing so with professionalism and loyalty to their government.

As someone born and raised in Europe, where diplomacy is primarily a behind-the-scenes occupation, I have been fascinated, at times disconcerted, to watch how the embassy has used bold public diplomacy as a policy tool.

An (Extra)Ordinary Job

I am often asked how it feels to be a foreigner at a U.S. embassy. The honest answer is that although exciting, it is not always easy. All the challenges related to an ordinary job, such as communication, career development, motivation, and workplace safety, are amplified by intercultural differences, political sensitivities, and security issues related to the specifics of diplomatic work.

When they pass through the embassy gate, local employees in effect give their loyalty to a foreign government. In some regions, local employees pay a high price for working for America, and at some high-threat posts they have paid with their lives. So it is important that loyalty works both ways and that the local staff know that their advice and effort are valued by their American colleagues.

Interpersonal communication between the local staff and American employees of the embassy can be a challenge. This is a delicate area that requires tact and patience on both sides. For the FSN, there is no full information cycle. Because of the classified nature of diplomatic work, FSNs often work on projects with no corresponding access to the final product or feedback on their input. In most political sections, FSNs and FSOs are physically separated due to information security requirements.

Yet in some cases, being an FSN is an advantage. Sometimes FSOs stick to the safest approach to sensitive issues, telling mission leaders what they want to hear. I have often seen ambassadors look to FSNs for an unvarnished view.

Trust and Loyalty

The formula for a successful relationship between FSN and FSO is the same as in any relationship—trust and understanding. Although the work standards and the nature of the FSN-FSO relationship vary from post to post depending on political and cultural issues, there should be a clear understanding of each other's functions. Some (in my experience most) diplomats see the local staff as an inseparable part of embassy operations, while others regard FSNs as second-class employees. It is vital, however, for diplomats arriving at a new post to approach their local colleagues with open minds. It is also up to the FSNs to prove they are full-fledged members of the embassy team, performing up to the highest American standards of work excellence and professional ethics.

The FSNs are at the embassy for the long term, preserving institutional memory, providing valuable knowledge about the domestic scene, acting as liaison between the mission and host-country representatives. Every three to four years, they have to prove themselves anew and get accustomed to a different leadership style. FSNs don't know what to expect, and vice versa. The relationship between FSNs and junior officers is tricky. The need to educate your supervisor is a delicate matter; yet this is what many FSNs must do. "Managing up" requires tact on the part of the FSN and the right attitude on the part of the officer, some of whom come to post with little idea about the local employee's role.

Career advancement—a vital motivating factor for FSOs—is another challenge for FSNs. There is an "iron ceiling" beyond which they cannot advance, so there must be a strong effort on both sides to keep the local staff challenged. I have had bosses who have gone out of their way to assist the local staff's professional development. In one case, political section FSNs were invited to accompany high-level political delegations to the U.S. on U.S. government-funded Volunteer Visitor Programs, thus raising the local employees' profile while achieving mission goals.

The Human Factor

Working alongside my American colleagues and watching them in action has been one of the greatest benefits of the job. It is amazing how many of them have joined the Foreign Service to work for their country, believing in an ideal. I have worked with interesting people, including a former financier for Armani who left the fashion house to serve at the State Department, and a brilliant economic officer who used to act in movies and probably could have been a star if he hadn't chosen to pursue a diplomatic career. I have had the chance to work for both career and political ambassadors with radically different styles who actively sought local employees' opinions. "There is hardly a better adviser on what is happening on local soil than the local staff," one ambassador used to say.

The local employees take pride in their U.S. colleagues' professional achievements and share their occasional frustrations. The American and local staff are united by common values, but also human bonds, which sometimes last long after the FSO departs post. There are numerous cases of collegial solidarity. One excellent example is the worldwide FSN Emergency Relief Fund, established and sustained by American colleagues to help FSNs in need.

A Special Relationship

There are some 43,500 local employees working in more than 270 overseas U.S. posts. In many ways, their work is similar to any other job, with ups and downs, joys and disappointments. What makes embassy work unique, from the local staff perspective, is the special relationship between the FSN and the FSO.

Over the past several years, we have seen growing appreciation of FSN work. Former Secretary of State Colin Powell deserves special recognition for acknowledging our contributions to American overseas missions. While the institutional framework is important, it is ultimately up to individual FSNs and FSOs to take up the challenge and make their relationship work. In my own case, it has worked much more often than not.

A lot has changed since my first day at the embassy. Over the past seven years, Embassy Sofia's local staff has doubled and the Bulgarian employees like myself have taken on increasingly greater responsibilities. I have come to truly enjoy my job, its diversity, and its dynamics. Being a foreigner working at an American embassy has not become easier, and the same limitations are still in place. But so are the growing opportunities.

I haven't regretted for a minute taking up the challenge.

Galina Sabeva, a former Reuters correspondent, is a political specialist at the U.S. embassy in Sofia, Bulgaria.

backgrounds, but come to the job without international affairs experience or an understanding of how an embassy functions or the best way to manage the interagency process. Some political ambassadors bring with them the power that comes with a personal relationship with the president. The American Foreign Service

Association has long urged an end to the practice of giving out ambassadorships as campaign spoils, arguing for qualified ambassadors in all cases.

The country team—when it works well—is where everything the U.S. government is doing in a country comes together. However, because the number of programs and agencies operating out of U.S. embassies continues to expand, a unified purpose is not always evident in all areas of activity. That said, the country team usually serves as the focal point of embassy coordination, and does the job of keeping members informed of what's going on in the country.

While the exact text of the letter varies from president to president, the overall message is the same: the ambassador is in charge. The challenge for chiefs of mission to remain in charge continues to grow, however, as the scope of U.S. government activities widens, along with the growing presence of non-Foreign Service personnel and agencies overseas, especially since 9/11. The global terrorist threat and the wars in Iraq and Afghanistan have resulted in a major upsurge in the number of military personnel overseas, as well as personnel from other security-related agencies such as the FBI and Department of Homeland Security.

Most embassies have a Defense Attaché Office (DAO) headed by a defense attaché—the DATT. The DAO, which may have representatives from more than one military branch, represents the U.S. Department of Defense and advises the ambassador on military matters. The DAO also implements bilateral military engagement programs and reports on political-military developments in the host country. U.S. Marines serve a critical protection role, guarding embassies and consulates around the world, working closely with the State Department Bureau of Diplomatic Security.

The military role in public affairs and foreign assistance work that best fits the mandates of the State Department and USAID—has grown since 9/11. Resources play a key role here: the military is simply much better funded and staffed than the foreign affairs agencies, and has filled in where there are insufficient civilian resources. In 2010, the Obama administration—including Secretary of Defense Robert Gates—focused on strengthening the civilian diplomatic function. However, by early 2011, stark budget realities along with new congressional leadership were pointing to a possible swing back toward the familiar fallback mode for the foreign affairs agencies, "do more with less."

Each member of the country team regularly reports back to his or her own home agency in Washington, receiving instructions and coordinating activities with officials, as well as among embassies in the region or elsewhere, depending on the issue. The country desks at the State Department manage the day-to-day relationships between the U.S. and other countries. They are the primary points of contact in Washington for ambassadors and the State Department's embassy offices. Desk officers tend to everything from coordination of policy inputs and high-level visits to managing the flow of information from Washington to the embassy.

These desks (offices) are organized into the six geographic bureaus of the State Department, which are in the domain of the Under Secretary of State for Political

Affairs, known as P. These are African Affairs, European and Eurasian Affairs, East Asian and Pacific Affairs, Near Eastern Affairs, South and Central Asian Affairs, and Western Hemisphere Affairs. The functional bureaus of International Narcotics and Law Enforcement, and International Organization Affairs, are also under the political affairs umbrella.

So-called functional bureaus are involved and informed based on global issues rather than geographic regions. The Under Secretary of State for Democracy and Global Affairs (called G) covers the bureaus of Democracy, Human Rights and Labor; Oceans and International Environmental and Scientific Affairs; Population, Refugees, and Migration; and the Office to Monitor and Combat Trafficking in Persons.

The other under secretaries are responsible for Economic, Energy and Agricultural Affairs (E); Arms Control and International Security Affairs (T); Public Diplomacy and Public Affairs (R); and Management (M). The Under Secretary for Management covers a wide array of functions, including the offices and bureaus of Administration; Consular Affairs; Diplomatic Security and Foreign Missions; Human Resources; Information Resource Management; Medical Services; Overseas Buildings Operations; Resource Management; and the Foreign Service Institute.

The nerve center of the State Department is the Operations Center. Almost always the first place called when something critical or newsworthy happens overseas, the Ops Center (as it is familiarly known) manages the flow of information during a crisis, finding and briefing the Secretary of State and other officials who need to know. Watch officers are on duty 24 hours a day, seven days a week, monitoring the world and trying to stay abreast of world affairs and any events that may have an impact on the United States.

The Operations Center is a smart place to spend a year if you don't mind working a rotating shift schedule. The best place to gain a true sense of the rhythm of "the building" and the flow of high-level communication, the Ops Center is also a networking hub that can facilitate access to choice assignments.

Embassy reporting is sent to the State Department, but it is also shared with multiple federal agencies that may have an interest in the subject. When an embassy sends a report—still known as a "cable"—the author and the post decide on the level of classification and on how widely to share the message. It may be distributed further after receipt in Washington.

State Department communications have been more widely distributed in recent years as part of a post-9/11 emphasis on increasing information-sharing among government agencies. In 2010, hundreds of thousands of classified State Department documents were allegedly downloaded by an American military private and shared with the founder of the Web site WikiLeaks, who then proceeded to post and share them widely, with the media and on the Internet. This devastating breach of the protection of classified documents has led to a re-evaluation of information-sharing policies. Access has been tightened as a result.

THE VISIT:
THE FOREIGN SERVICE ON CALL
Secretary of State Hillary Clinton Goes to Indonesia
FEBRUARY 2009

Secretary Clinton's arrival in Jakarta.

When a Secretary of State visits a particular country, the entire Foreign Service staff at the embassy there goes into overdrive for days, weeks, or even months of preparation, depending on the goals of the trip and how much advance warning is given. Embassy personnel work with the Secretary's staff and any number of Washington offices to make numerous decisions along the way: What does the Secretary need to know? Who will she meet and what will she say? What policy objectives will be pursued? Where will she go and how will she get there? Thousands of substantive, logistical, protocol, and security questions must be answered. Often, despite thousands of hours of coordination and planning, when the day of the visit finally arrives, the only thing staving off chaos is the quick thinking and tireless ingenuity of the embassy's Foreign Service officers, specialists, and local employees on the ground.

In February 2009, Secretary of State Hillary Rodham Clinton made her first overseas trip after taking office. The following are descriptions of a "day in the life" of several Foreign Service officers who worked on the Secretary's visit to Jakarta, Indonesia, the second stop on a four-city Asia tour. We hear from a political officer, a management officer, an economic officer, and a public diplomacy officer.

SETTING THE AGENDA:
THE PAPER TRAIL
By Matthew A. Cenzer, Political Officer

Thursday, February 5

8:30 P.M. It is the end of Jakarta's day, but the start of Washington's. Working with Political Counselor Joe Novak and the rest of the political section team, assigned by the ambassador to handle the substantive elements of the Secretary's visit, I begin to coordinate the many papers necessary for the visit. I call our country desk at the State Department in Washington to discuss which papers the Secretary's staff wants and which papers we, at post, think she should have. She will need briefing checklists (the memos read by the Secretary before every major meeting) for meetings with Indonesian officials. We have decided that a number of background papers would also be useful. Secretary Clinton has not visited Indonesia since 1994, and we need to bring her up to speed. While we sleep in Jakarta, our colleagues in Washington work on the papers.

Friday, February 6

8:00 A.M. Thanks to our colleagues in Washington, the papers are already waiting in my inbox this morning. I circulate them to embassy colleagues for additional input and ask for responses by 11 a.m., the first of many deadlines. The deputy chief of mission and the ambassador need time to review and approve every paper. Next, I speak with political and economic section colleagues, who will draft other necessary papers on an enormous range of topics, from Indonesia's upcoming elections to an overview of U.S. assistance programs. I ask for papers by 2:30 p.m.

9:00 A.M. I meet with Ambassador Cameron Hume to discuss writing the cable that will set the scene of the visit (called, not surprisingly, the "scene setter"). His guidance is clear, if intimidating: "The Secretary must be able to have a good visit even if she reads nothing but this cable." The message needs to spark the Secretary's enthusiasm about Indonesia and convince her to press forward on the priorities we identify. I start writing.

11:00 A.M. I receive briefing checklists from colleagues; the papers are on time and they are good. I check them for format and consistency and pass them on to the political counselor for review.

12:00 P.M. I complete a draft of the scene setter and give it to other sections for clearance. I send the papers reviewed by the political counselor to the front office, where office managers have devised a matrix to keep track of every paper.

2:30 P.M. Background papers begin arriving. More reviewing, formatting and editing—then on to Joe and the front office.

3:00 P.M. Deputy Chief of Mission John Heffern arrives to discuss the scene setter; he likes it, but it is too long. The Secretary is extremely busy, so our message has to be brief and focused; every word has to count. We cut anything already included in other papers and review the cable again.

4:00 P.M. Papers start to come back to me from the ambassador's office with his changes and questions: How many troops has Indonesia sent on peacekeeping missions? How fast has our trade grown in the past five years? I call expert colleagues to get the answers.

5:00 P.M. We check the matrix and see that over half of the papers are complete. I have a rare moment of downtime while waiting for the other half to come from the ambassador's office.

6:00 P.M. The ambassador has reviewed the scene-setting cable and made a few suggestions. I incorporate them into the text and proof it again.

7:00 P.M. The last few papers come out of the ambassador's office. We review them one last time to make certain everything is perfect.

8:00 P.M. We send the papers to the desk (the State Department's Indonesia office in Washington, D.C.), and follow up with a phone call, during which we discuss additional papers that might be needed. Our Washington colleagues promise to review these and let us know tomorrow morning what we have left to write.

8:30 P.M. I push the "send" button for the scene-setting cable. This workday is over, but there will be more papers tomorrow!

ADVANCE TEAM WORK
By Scott Kofmehl, Economic Officer

Saturday, February 14

9:00 A.M. Economic Counselor Peter Haas and I pick up Eugene Bae, Secretary Clinton's lead advance official, and head straight for the airport, where the Secretary will ultimately arrive. The ambassador has designated Peter as the visit's overall control officer, and I am his liaison with the Secretary's advance team. We visit every event site four to six times before "game day" to negotiate details with Indonesian officials, develop minute-by-minute event scenarios, and coordinate all event logistics. For every event, Peter has assigned an embassy site officer who is responsible for all the details. At the airport, the site officer negotiates how many vehicles will be allowed on the tarmac, discusses rain contingencies, and decides where the press will be positioned.

10:30 A.M. Secretary Clinton told her staff that she wants a "sense of place" wherever she visits. She wants to see more of Indonesia than the insides of government ministries and hotel conference rooms; she wants to interact not just with officials, but with average Indonesians. To ensure that this happens, we drive to another event site—a poor neighborhood that participates in several USAID-supported programs—and meet with the community leader. The biggest variable for this site is security. We need a meaningful but safe event site with effective photo ops.

12:00 P.M. We are off to our next meeting: preparation for a live taping of a popular Indonesian teen television show, *Dahsyat!* ("Awesome!"), best described as an Indonesian mix of MTV's *TRL* and *The Tyra Banks Show*. Appearing on a teen variety show is not a typical Secretary of State activity, but it will make for an excellent outreach opportunity. Along with our public diplomacy colleagues from the embassy, we meet with the show's producers and hosts to go over plans and try to ensure the taping will go smoothly.

2:00 P.M.   Off to the National Archives Museum, the event site for a dinner with civil society leaders. Planning this dinner, which includes 70 guests, is more complicated than wedding planning: Whom should we invite? Who would cater? Are there Internet and printer connections for the Secretary's speechwriter?

4:30 P.M.   Earlier today, Eugene asked us to coordinate a meeting with the event site officers to review all nine events. Sitting around a hotel suite, the embassy staff discusses every detail of the Secretary's schedule. Peter and I joke that we function as neurotransmitters: we receive taskings, identify people with answers, and relay those answers to Eugene.

7:00 P.M.   Peter and I meet with Eugene to review the day's notes as he prepares for a call with the "plane team," the staff that travels with the Secretary and is coordinating this four-city trip. The plane team has the final say in any visit decision. There is natural uncertainty with a new Secretary and staff, as standard operating procedures are still developing.

9:00 P.M.   Peter and I go back to the embassy to catch up on e-mail. I distribute the next day's schedule to embassy colleagues. We just keep asking: What's next? What information do we need? Who else needs the information that we have received from Washington?

11:30 P.M.   We drop off event scenarios at the ambassador's residence. Tomorrow, we will visit the USAID-supported neighborhood projects and the Archives Museum again, as well as the presidential palace, the foreign ministry, and the Association of Southeast Asian Nations Secretariat.

GAME DAY
By Tristram Perry, Public Affairs Officer

Wednesday, February 18

1:00 P.M.   The embassy is calm after three frenzied weeks preparing for Secretary Clinton's first overseas trip. Indonesia is her second stop, between Japan and South Korea—but, as Ambassador Hume says, "the only one with the chance to change U.S. foreign policy." We've scheduled a lot of press events, and despite countless walkthroughs and meetings, what happens, happens.

2:00 P.M. I flip TV channels until I see the plane landing. The Secretary emerges in a red suit, walks down the stairs, and greets our ambassador and other dignitaries. My embassy colleagues are there in the background, discreetly managing the baggage, traveling press, and members of the delegation. The Secretary moves toward a singing choir waving U.S. and Indonesian flags. Unprompted, she wades into their midst, creating a lasting public image of her trip.

2:45 P.M. Time to go. My Indonesian colleague Dian and I head to the Indonesian Foreign Ministry for the first official press event of the visit. When we arrive, the local reporters are jostling for position, but the mood is upbeat and festive. Even the hardened foreign correspondents seem excited.

4:00 P.M. The diplomatic security agent gives us the signal—five minutes to go. We position ourselves on the edge of the crowd and make sure the photographer is in place. Secretary Clinton and her group emerge from their vehicles and are whisked inside. We rush into the hall, where a wall of television cameras point at two empty podiums.

5:15 P.M. The Secretary and Indonesian Foreign Minister emerge from their meeting, all smiles, and make statements. As they depart, we spot a traveling reporter who'd missed

Secretary Clinton with Indonesian President Susilo Bambang Yudhoyono.

the van. We will be late to our next event at the National Archives, but our colleagues Rob and Kira from the consular section are already there, so we have time to take a detour and get the reporter to her hotel.

8:30 P.M. Fifty of Indonesia's leading civil society figures are dining with the Secretary as we wait to enter, crammed alongside 30 reporters at the base of a narrow flight of stairs. The building's design—historic Dutch colonial—leaves room for just six television cameras. The signal is given, and we rush to get the equipment upstairs. There is some confusion because the National Archives' staff have taken Al-Jazeera's spot. They move just in time for the Secretary's first words. Her speech is broadcast across Indonesia and internationally.

10:30 P.M. My colleagues and I drop off our equipment and return to the office to prep for the next day. I send a flurry of reminders to our team and head home after midnight. We still have the "Awesome" show early in the morning, and then several other press events to manage. For now, bedtime.

WHEELS UP!
By Michael Mullins, Management Officer

Thursday, February 19

    6:30 A.M.   We reserved the hotel ballroom for the Secretary's meet-and-greet with the embassy community, but a wedding party lasted well into the night and left us little prep time. As the ballroom filled with bomb-sniffing dogs, security personnel, hotel staff, and 600 guests, the information management team works feverishly to bring Consulates Surabaya and Medan into the event via video. We establish the connections with 30 minutes to spare.

    9:30 A.M.   Nearly 400 people from the embassy community, including local staff and family members, arrive by bus for the meet-and-greet. Everyone is in place an hour ahead of time, and Secretary Clinton enters to great applause.

    10:30 A.M.   Afterward, diplomatic security personnel hold everyone in the ballroom without warning—including motorcade drivers! We persuade them to let out the drivers, and once the Secretary's motorcade departs, dozens of people rush for their buses home. Many Americans mistake the press bus for their own, while others call their personal drivers, creating a traffic jam.

    12:00 P.M.   Lights flash and sirens blare as the motorcade zips through the bustling Jakarta traffic. Suddenly, the motorcade stalls. We see a minibus, broken down and blocking the road—a regular feature on Jakarta roads. Finally arriving, we count on a 45-minute site visit before the next movement. But only 10 minutes later journalists run for their vehicles: the Secretary is leaving early! We scramble and contact the airport to inform them that we are ahead of schedule for the first time during the visit.

    1:00 P.M.   We line up the baggage and equipment planeside 90 minutes before departure. Security begins its careful inspection and bags slowly travel up the conveyor belt. We expect plenty of time—and perhaps even lunch. Radio squawks and mobile ringtones shatter that first peaceful moment of the day. "How could she be early?" shouts a disbelieving staffer. Two dozen camera crews focus their cameras on the loading gear blocking the Secretary's aircraft. Scant minutes later, sirens announce the motorcade. Mercifully, we slam the cargo hold shut just as the Secretary's car turns onto the tarmac.

    4:00 P.M.   As the Secretary's plane crosses the threshold of no return—halfway to the next destination—it's time to celebrate a job well done. We'd arranged a "Wheels Up" happy hour at the hotel, and the lobby begins to fill with staff. David, the motor pool dispatcher, calls to ask if the drivers are invited. Of course they are! They arrive in their Indonesian batiks worn in honor of the Secretary, and the Americans break into applause and line up to shake their hands. With pride (and relief) we all toast a job well done.

NOT JUST A JOB: THE FOREIGN SERVICE LIFE

The World Is Home

The Foreign Service is not like other careers. As a Foreign Service officer or specialist, you live the profession, and so does your family. Serving overseas with one of the foreign affairs agencies, there is no punching out at the end of the day. Foreign Service employees represent the U.S. government 24/7, a fact of life that presents both challenges and opportunities. Challenges, because anything you say or do can be taken as said or done on behalf of the U.S. government. Opportunities, because your connection to the U.S. government provides you with all-star access in many parts of the world—to people, to information, to understanding and, occasionally, to influence.

Foreign Service employees can expect to spend at least two-thirds of their careers overseas, and to transfer from one assignment to the next every one to four years throughout their careers. So if stability and a comfortable routine are what you value, the Foreign Service may not be for you. But if what you seek is a way to serve your country, challenging and meaningful work, lifelong learning, and the opportunity to live internationally and speak foreign languages, then the Foreign Service might be the right fit.

Coming on Board

After accepting an offer to join an entering class of State Department generalists or specialists, you will be given a date to report for orientation and the start of your new career. You will move to the Washington, D.C., area and attend orientation and training at the National Foreign Affairs Training Center in Arlington, Virginia—still generally known by its original name, the Foreign Service Institute, or FSI.

FSI has a college campus feel to it. While new Foreign Service employees must wear business attire for the initial training, many of the language and other classes are more casual. Periodically throughout a Foreign Service career, employees will cycle back to Washington and through FSI. Time spent in training at FSI, usually lasting from a few weeks to about a year, offers the opportunity to learn a language or advance a professional skill—and be paid for doing so.

For State FSO generalists, the first course is always A-100 orientation: basic training for diplomats. Each A-100 class is composed of between 30 and 100 new FSOs, depending on hiring needs and the budget climate. During the hiring boom of 2009 and 2010, part of the Diplomacy 3.0 initiative to increase the State Department Foreign Service by 25 percent, classes averaged more than 90 people each.

A-100 is an intensive program, a crash course in diplomatic work and life. More information is being squeezed into less time, as the length of the course has been trimmed several times to accommodate the increased flow of new hires. In the early 1990s, A-100 lasted nine weeks and included two overnight offsite exercises. By 2010, the course was down to five weeks, with one offsite exercise.

The course is designed to describe the role, structure, and function of the State Department and to clarify the terms of Foreign Service employment. A-100 covers everything from handling a press briefing or a hostile audience (sometimes the same thing!) to how to fill out a travel voucher or pick a domicile. It is an introduction to the job and to the bureaucracy. And there is a lot of bureaucracy to navigate in the Foreign Service.

The A-100 experience has long been seen as a rite of passage, bringing new hires together to create a community of colleagues and friends that lasts well beyond the training period. Many A-100 classes have e-mail groups and social networking sites that continue for years, keeping people in touch while they travel the world. Friendships made during orientation can last a lifetime, although the larger the classes become and the shorter their duration, the harder it may be to create strong communities.

State specialists begin their careers with a three-week course at FSI called "Orientation for Foreign Service Specialists" that is roughly comparable to the A-100 class for generalists. Then they go on to training in their specialty.

New USAID officers have a five-week orientation in Washington, and then move on to specialized training and the fulfillment of language requirements needed for tenure. The initial training phase in Washington before the first assignment can last from four to 12 months or more, depending on the job and whether language study is required. New USAID officers spend their first overseas tour rotating through various USAID offices at a mission and completing training requirements.

Bidding

During orientation, each new State Department generalist class is given an official "open assignments" list of upcoming vacant jobs around the world to be filled by the members of that particular class. If there are 100 people in the class, the bid list will have about 100 positions on it, occasionally a few more than the total number in the class. These positions are all over the world, on all continents except Antarctica. This is an exciting time for new employees and their families, as they begin to picture themselves in various countries and start to realize that the overseas life they had dreamed about will actually become a reality very soon.

New entrants are encouraged to think first about their own and their family's preferences and priorities for their careers. Do they want to learn a new language? Work in their chosen career track for each assignment or try something else? Be posted to a particular region of the world? Seek a posting where a spouse or partner will have good job or educational opportunities? The possibilities are endless, but new generalists are asked to turn in a list of three top personal priorities (a preference list).

TWENTY-EIGHT MORE WEEKS:
LIFE IN LANGUAGE TRAINING
By Brendan M. Wheeler

The recording ended and I leaned back in my chair.

"Tell me what you got," the instructor said, her face full of hope that this time I would understand.

A shy smile of apology crawled across my face. My three classmates sat patiently. One gazed outside at flocks of leaves colored gold and maroon riding gusts of November wind across the green of the Foreign Service Institute campus. Unlike me, my classmates understood the 60-second recording the first or second time they heard it.

"Once more," our instructor said. "Just listen for nouns you know."

Our instructor pressed 'Play' and, for the fourth time that afternoon, an Arab man's rumbling baritone voice filled the classroom. I sat stiffly, listening hard, trying to understand the clearly spoken sentences.

"Anything?" my instructor asked when the recording stopped.

A moment passed. I looked up, my brow furrowed.

I'm never going to learn Arabic, I thought.

■ ■ ■

Five months earlier, with 40 other new Foreign Service officers, I had stood before the administrator of the United States Agency for International Development and took the oath of office. The administrator said that our class marked the beginning of an effort to recapitalize the corps of Foreign Service officers who serve as development professionals in USAID missions around the world.

The swearing-in ceremony marked the beginning of my career as a crisis, stabilization, and governance officer, responsible for designing and managing humanitarian assistance and democracy and governance development programs for USAID. But before I could head out to my first overseas post, before my adventure could begin, I had to learn a foreign language—a challenge I had avoided since high school.

USAID requires all new FSOs, before their first postings, to display functional proficiency in a foreign language—a skill every FSO must have in order to achieve tenure in the Service. Those sworn into the Service with me spoke Spanish, French, Russian, Mandarin, Arabic, Portuguese, Italian, German, Polish, Hebrew, Guarani, Vietnamese, Bulgarian, Japanese, Moore, Nepalese, and Serbo-Croatian. I had a little experience with Arabic, but not nearly enough to achieve the required level of proficiency.

USAID enrolled me in a 44-week basic Arabic course at the Foreign Service Institute. Classes met for seven hours a day, five days a week. Starting with the alphabet, I began the difficult work of learning to speak, read, and write Arabic. Our instructors introduced dozens of new vocabulary words and multiple new grammar points each day. Any week I integrated seven or eight new words and one new grammar point into my speech I considered successful. I struggled to meet that goal.

■ ■ ■

I paced the hallway outside the testing room.

"You'll do great," my instructor said.

"We'll know in an hour," I said.

My instructor smiled warmly—the same smile of encouragement she had used six weeks earlier when I struggled to understand that recording.

The two examiners sitting inside the room waved me inside.

"*Ahlan*, Mr. Wheeler," they greeted me. "*Sabah ilkheer.*"

"*Sabah ilnoor,*" I responded, closing the door behind me. I breathed deeply and took my seat.

An hour later, I paced the hallway again, wide-eyed, waiting for the results.

"How'd it go?" a friend asked. She awaited the results of her test, too.

"Hard. Not sure."

I thought about how my struggle with German in high school had led me to avoid studying languages in college and graduate school.

Now I have to learn Arabic to keep my job! I thought. *I must be crazy.*

"Mr. Wheeler," the lead examiner said. "We're ready. Please come back in."

I sat stiffly, my hands clasped in front of me. I smiled wanly, anticipating bad news.

"You did well."

"I did?"

"Right where you should be after 16 weeks."

"I am?" A broad smile spread across my face. The examiners laughed at my surprise. I laughed, too.

"But you need to work very hard. Focus on noun-adjective agreement and pronunciation," the lead examiner said. Together, they began a long critique of my performance.

■ ■ ■

After class that day, I stopped by a window. A low canopy of chunky, gray clouds hung overhead. A raw December wind tormented two students crossing the lawn. I thought about how warm and green the campus would look in July when I would complete my course.

Seven hours a day, five days a week … for 28 more weeks. I exhaled. *I can do it.*

Brendan M. Wheeler joined the Foreign Service in 2008, and serves with the U.S. Agency for International Development. His first posting is Addis Ababa, Ethiopia.

Then, when the open assignments list is handed out, each member of the A-100 class will review it, research posts of interest, weigh them against their stated personal priorities, and put together a bid list including all the jobs on the list ranked high, medium, or low. The State Department will remind you, however, that the needs of the Service come first. If you are the only Cantonese speaker in the class and an officer is needed in Guangzhou, that's probably where you're headed. But it may not be; as you will hear constantly in A-100 and throughout your career, "It depends!"

Foreign Service generalists who enter the Foreign Service without a language must gain proficiency in one before they can be tenured. They will therefore be directed to a language-designated position with training for one of their first two assignments.

For generalists, the first two postings (also called tours) are directed assignments, which means that while each FSO submits a "bid list" (also known as a "wish list"), it is the Bureau of Human Resources that will decide, based primarily on the needs of the Service. Each FSO is assigned to a career development officer from HR who will act as a counselor to help the employee navigate priorities and options.

Bidding on first assignments will make the full import of "worldwide availability" evident. While efforts are made to ensure that everyone gets a post that meets at least one of their preferences, there is no guarantee. If your skills and abilities qualify you as the best fit for a certain position, you may find yourself assigned to it whether you ranked it high or low. After the first two tours, FSOs do have more say in the process; but networking with the bureaus and posts overseas will be required.

Every new State FSO will spend at least one year in a consular position, and most will spend more time than that doing consular work. A small percentage of non-consular officers may do two consular tours before working in their designated cone, but that is usually a choice. Officers have five years and three chances to get tenure, and are considered conditional employees until they are tenured. That said, close to 97 percent of all FSOs receive tenure within the allotted time. As with certain universities, the Foreign Service is extremely difficult to get into, but once in, it's fairly easy to stay in.

Until 2009, new officers could assume that their first assignment would be overseas: almost never was an officer assigned to Washington out of A-100. With the hiring surge starting in 2009, however, some incoming officers were assigned to one-year Washington jobs, either as country desk officers at the State Department or to jobs dealing with "functional issues" such as food security, refugee assistance, or environmental affairs. These officers were going on to consular positions overseas for their second tours.

The assignment process for A-100 classes generally works well, in part because one person's dream assignment is someone else's idea of the worst. While certain posts get more high bids than others (think Europe), most new employees are reasonably satisfied with their first assignments. Every post is interesting in some way.

One year before an assignment ends, officers will review a new open-assignments list and submit a new "preferences" list, which might be different than the one submitted before the first tour. They will also submit a bid list for their follow-on assignments, consisting of a rank-order list of 20 jobs.

Specialists are given open-assignments lists during orientation that are specific to each career track. They bid only on jobs in their own tracks.

For both generalists and specialists, "Flag Day" is the culmination of the orientation period: the day when assignments are handed out, along with a small flag for the country of assignment. Flag Day is one of those life events that is never forgotten. Then, flag in hand, it's time to rush to the Internet, FSI Transition Center, library, or even to the map, to start to get a real picture of where on earth is going to be home for the next couple of years.

Training

After their orientation course, new FS employees go off to whatever specialized training they need before heading out to their first assignments. Those going to consular tours complete the Basic Consular Course, popularly known as "ConGen." The 31-day course aims to teach those going to consular positions overseas about immigration law and visa regulations, how to conduct interviews, and how to assist Americans overseas. Role-playing sessions in the training center's mock jail cell are notorious and do offer a sense of what a consular visit to a jailed American citizen overseas can involve.

New State Department generalists should expect to spend three months to a year in training, with strong efforts made by HR to keep training to under a year. For State specialists, the time varies depending on the position, and can last anywhere from one month to about nine.

Each time an officer or specialist bids on an onward assignment there are training considerations. Many assignments will require a return to FSI for language training, tradecraft training for a particular career track, or area studies. Positions that require language study are included on the appropriate open-assignments list far enough in advance for bidders to factor in the needed training time.

FSO Career Path

FS employees develop and manage their own career paths, and no two careers are exactly the same. In general, State FSOs will find at least one or two regional and/or functional "home bureaus" to which they will return for more than one posting. For example, Arabic speakers will most likely be assigned to Arabic-speaking posts a number of times, and become known to, and at home in, the Bureau of Near Eastern Affairs. Consular officers will have the Bureau of Consular Affairs as a home bureau. Regional bureaus are based on geographic areas, while functional bureaus are tied to issues such as human rights and the environment.

While there are boxes to check and requirements to meet along the way, there is a reasonable amount of freedom to tailor a Foreign Service career to individual interests and needs. Some people prefer to spend their careers outside Washington and return rarely to headquarters. Others will spend more time in Washington. Many FSOs try to plan for more time in the United States at certain times of life, such as when a child is in high school.

FSOs also have interesting opportunities for excursion assignments outside the State Department. These include the war colleges of the Armed Forces, offices on Capitol Hill, and certain nongovernmental organizations. Some FSOs go to Princeton University for a one-year master's degree program, while others head to Georgetown University to help out at the Institute for the Study of Diplomacy.

OUTSIDE OPPORTUNITIES:
SABBATICALS, FELLOWSHIPS, AND DETAILS
By Kelly and Steve Adams-Smith

A career in the Foreign Service offers unparalleled opportunities to live in exciting locales while working on issues others may only read about in the headlines. There simply aren't many professions that offer the opportunity to change jobs—and countries—every few years. That dynamism is more than enough to keep most people hooked on this career, but the Foreign Service offers even more challenge and variety through numerous exchange programs and continuing education opportunities.

Among the offerings for mid- and senior-level State Department officers and specialists are one-year details to other agencies and branches of government, as well as opportunities to work in think tanks, universities, and private companies. Those participating in such programs are able to reinvent themselves for a year, pursuing interests that are related to their FS jobs but also enhance their skills, allowing them to bring new insights and best practices back to the State Department.

DETAILS TO OTHER AGENCIES. Eligible officers from a variety of functional areas of expertise find time spent in another executive branch agency eye-opening and rewarding. Perhaps the most prestigious of these interagency details is to the staff of the National Security Council, where officers and specialists fill a range of jobs from policy director to office manager. The other foreign affairs agencies also regularly take State Department detailees, as do the CIA and the Department of Homeland Security. Every year the Office of the U.S. Trade Representative (USTR) takes as many as eight FSOs, usually economic-coned officers.

The State Department also sends numerous FSOs every year on details to the Department of Defense. Some senior FSOs serve as faculty or advisers at the various War Colleges. State is also assigning an increasing number of officers as political advisers, known as POLADS, to U.S. military service chiefs in the Pentagon, to regional combatant commanders, key functional commands, and various other locations in the United States and abroad.

CONGRESSIONAL FELLOWSHIPS. Good relations with Capitol Hill are vital for the State Department. Through the Pearson Fellowship, State provides up to 16 employees each year to Congress to work with House and Senate members or on congressional committees as foreign policy advisers. Similarly, State chooses two employees each year for the American Political Science Association's Congressional Fellowship, which combines work on a congressional committee or member's staff with coursework on legislative/executive branch relations at the Johns Hopkins School of Advanced International Studies (SAIS) in Washington, D.C.

INTERNATIONAL ORGANIZATIONS AND FOREIGN GOVERNMENTS. If working for an international organization is more your style, State details officers to the United Nations, World Bank, NATO and NATO's multinational force observer missions, and other international organizations. Or, if you'd like to experience what it is like to work in the foreign ministry of another country, State allows FSOs to participate in numerous diplomatic exchange programs with European countries, the European Union, Australia, New Zealand, and Japan. These one-year exchange programs are normally followed by a tour of duty in the American embassy in that country.

PRIVATE SECTOR, ACADEMIA, AND THINK-TANKS. If you'd like to experience life in the private sector, there are opportunities available to work in a major corporation for a year through the Executive Council on Diplomacy's Corporate Placement Program. If academia appeals to you, State officers and some specialists can take advantage of one-year programs at Princeton, George Washington University, Columbia, or other universities. Think-tank placements are also an option, with FSOs spending time at the Council on Foreign Relations and other institutions.

The Dean and Virginia Rusk Fellowship is one of the most highly sought Foreign Service fellowships. This program, established in 1985 at Georgetown University's Institute for the Study of Diplomacy, is open to mid-level officers who wish to expand their professional and international horizons by teaching and taking classes. While not limited to tandem couples, the fellowship encourages married officers and professionals to apply and work together.

For those reaching the Senior Foreign Service, there are numerous opportunities to be a Diplomat in Residence. These officers serve as State's regional recruiters based in universities all over the United States. They travel often, answering the questions of students interested in the Foreign Service, conducting Foreign Service exam prep sessions, and mentoring the next generation of Foreign Service personnel.

Steve and Kelly Adams-Smith, with their children Benjamin and Sophia, at Semester at Sea headquarters in Charlottesville, Virginia.

One of the most unusual outside-of-State opportunities is the Una Chapman Cox Sabbatical Leave Fellowship. This one-year sabbatical, offered to two FSOs a year, was established by the Una Chapman Cox Foundation, an entity dedicated to strengthening the Foreign Service. Sabbatical winners pursue a combination of work, travel, lecturing, teaching, study, research, writing or other activities that is both rewarding for the officer and beneficial to the Foreign Service.

As a tandem couple with a little more than a decade of Foreign Service experience, we found these continuing education opportunities extremely attractive. Steve, a management officer with a degree in political science, jumped at the chance to spend a year as an American Political Science Association Congressional Fellow. That program provides the opportunity to learn about the legislative branch and its role in American foreign policy.

Following a 10-week course on "Congress and Foreign Policy" at SAIS, APSA fellows representing government, journalism, and academia join doctors and scientists sponsored by the Robert Wood Johnson Foundation for an additional six-week orientation program that prepares the group for work as congressional staffers. For Steve, the fellowship was not only stimulating intellectually, it was also fun, offering the chance to do something that, while related to his Foreign Service career, was not what he anticipated doing when he joined the Foreign Service as a management officer. The fellowship also gave Steve a chance to rekindle his interest in politics and other branches of government while helping the State Department maintain good relations and understanding with Congress.

At the same time, Kelly, an economics officer, spent a year as an Una Chapman Cox Sabbatical Leave Fellow. She was detailed to the Institute for Shipboard Education's Semester at Sea program, a study-abroad program based at the University of Virginia. Each semester, Semester at Sea's ship, the

Kelly on the Semester at Sea ship with Archbishop Desmond Tutu.

MV Explorer, circumnavigates the globe carrying 700 students from 250 American universities. The students visit a dozen ports while taking a full course load, earning academic credit from the University of Virginia. Kelly, a Semester at Sea alumna whose interest in the Foreign Service was sparked by her SAS voyage, helped Semester at Sea strengthen its ties with the State Department and the U.S. embassies in countries the *MV Explorer* visits. She also helped the State Department take advantage of the public diplomacy and recruitment opportunities offered by the program.

Each of these programs opened our eyes to new ideas and ways of doing the government's business. We returned to the State Department recharged and refreshed, with renewed commitment to public service. After spending the previous two tours overseas, the flexibility of our sabbatical work schedules also helped ease the transition to life in the United States for our two children, who have spent nearly all of their young lives abroad. These benefits of our fellowship year will pay off personally and professionally for years to come.

Kelly and Steve Adams-Smith are a Foreign Service tandem couple. They joined the Foreign Service in 1997 and have served together in Moscow, Tallinn, Sofia, and Washington. In 2011 they both completed Foreign Service fellowships. They live in Arlington, Virginia, with their two children.

State specialists do not have as much flexibility as generalists to do many different types of jobs. They join the Foreign Service with more particular skills and are expected to pursue their chosen career track for most of their assignments.

USAID hires its FSOs for a number of specialized career tracks, known as backstops. They range from technical areas such as agriculture, private sector, and health to support functions such as contracting, legal, and financial control. The number of tracks ebbs and flows depending on funding for various program areas, but generally there are over a dozen. A master's degree or equivalent is needed for almost all USAID's backstops, and the agency hires a good number of Ph.D.-holders. Two years of overseas development experience is also required for most USAID career tracks.

FSOs at USAID are encouraged to move between regions, and can move between backstops as well. But the fairly extensive technical knowledge required for certain specializations prevents a lot of switching, and extra training is not provided. Promotions are based on a variety of assignments with ever-increasing responsibility. In a small agency like USAID, promotions tend to come fastest for those who pursue managerial positions, because managing resources and programs is the core of the agency's day-to-day work.

Given the difficult posts that comprise the majority of the USAID world, and the pressing needs of staffing ever-larger missions in post-conflict and active-conflict zones such as Afghanistan and Iraq, the USAID assignments process is ever-evolving. An FSO's first assignment is directed, ideally to a post that has a range of USAID programming and expertise, as well as adequate mentoring. Subsequent assignments are made through a competitive bidding process very similar to that of the State Department. As of 2011, USAID FSOs coming into the Service can expect to serve in one-year unaccompanied posts more than once during a career.

Up or Out

The personnel system is designed to keep Foreign Service employees moving up the career ladder; the higher up the ladder one goes, the fewer positions there are. The position of ambassador is the top rung on the Foreign Service career ladder, and relatively few make it to that position. Historically, 60 to 70 percent of all ambassadorial positions go to career Foreign Service employees (usually but not always State generalists). The political, non-career appointees, however, tend to get the ambassadorships in the countries that many consider the most desirable places to live, such as Paris and London.

State Department generalists and specialists, as well as USAID, Foreign Agricultural Service, and Foreign Commercial Service officers, compete for promotion with their colleagues through annual sessions of selection boards, also called promotion boards. The boards consider annual performance evaluation reports and rank members of each career path, or cone, by grade level. Only the top-ranked officers and specialists are promoted.

State FSOs are hired into a specific career track, formerly called a "cone"— Consular, Economic, Management, Political, or Public Diplomacy. However, officers can and do take assignments outside their track. As mentioned earlier, all officers will do consular work for at least one year during their first two tours.

Each April, Employee Evaluation Reviews (EER) are due for all State and USAID FSOs and for State specialists. EERs are the main documents reviewed by promotion panels as they determine who gets promoted each year. Employees must be engaged in their own EER process, ensuring required counseling sessions with a supervisor are held, and documenting performance to highlight. For State FSOs, each performance review includes input from a "rating officer" (usually the employee's direct supervisor)

WHAT IF I DISAGREE?
DISSENT IN THE FOREIGN SERVICE
By Ambassador Thomas Boyatt

Sporadically, the media becomes enthused by a "whistleblower" or an act of "telling truth to power." Usually such interest is *ex post facto*. For example, a career employee of the Securities and Exchange Commission warned of the Bernard Madoff Ponzi scheme years before it collapsed in 2009—in time to save investors billions of dollars. He was ignored until the damage became public. The lesson is that to be effective within bureaucracies, dissent must be institutionalized.

In the U.S. federal government (and probably in the world) such institutionalization exists in only one place—the U.S. Department of State. For more than 40 years, whistleblowers and those prepared to tell truth to power have been protected and respected there. Such support exists equally within the formal bureaucratic system and within the informal—some would say more powerful—system in which professional reputation is paramount.

In the State Department itself, the combination of the turmoil over the Vietnam War and the advent of white-collar unions in the early 1970s led to the establishment of an official mechanism for disagreement called the "Dissent Channel." Procedures were promulgated in the *Foreign Affairs Manual (FAM)*, State's regulatory compendium, enabling any Foreign Service employee to write a dissent message addressed to the Secretary of State and sent through the Secretary's Policy Planning Staff. Such messages cannot be stopped or altered by supervisors at any level, ambassadorial or otherwise. The director of Policy Planning is required to provide a substantive response within 30 to 60 days.

The Dissent Channel has been used to ventilate differing views on sensitive policy challenges from Vietnam, the Middle East, and Cyprus in earlier times to Bosnia, Iraq, and Afghanistan more recently. Hundreds of dissent messages have been sent over the decades. Some have led, immediately or eventually, to policy changes. Perhaps most important, the dissent process has influenced the quotidian policy debate. Senior officers are more tolerant of differing views, more willing to discuss and debate rather than issue dicta. The permanent policy discussion is more open and vibrant because of the existence of the Dissent Channel.

Outside the official State/Foreign Service structure, the informal system has strongly supported those with dissenting views even longer. In 1969 the American Foreign Service Association (the professional association and union for the Foreign Service) joined with the family of the recently deceased Ambassador William Rivkin to create the annual Rivkin Award. This award recognizes officers working constructively within the system to change policy and performance for the better. An independent panel of judges makes the award that includes public recognition at a reception in the State Department's elegant Benjamin Franklin Rooms and a cash stipend. Since 1969, the Rivkin Award (now for mid-grade officers) has been joined by the Harriman (for junior officers), Herter (for senior officers), and Tex Harris (for specialists) awards. In a culture where peer regard is very highly prized, the AFSA awards for constructive dissent bestow extraordinary distinction. Moreover, most awardees have gone on to enter the Senior Foreign Service and to account for a much higher percentage of ambassadors than the Service as a whole.

Ambassador Boyatt testifying on Capitol Hill in 2007.

In addition to the informal and official dissent structures, the unique aspects of the foreign policy process are also significant. First, foreign policy is in a constant state of becoming; the policy struggle continues 24/7. It is never settled. From a micro perspective, U.S. ambassadors make representations to the 190 countries and institutions with which we have diplomatic relations virtually every day. The reactions to these démarches, duly reported, change the status quo and provide opportunities to discuss, consider, and perhaps change American policy. From the macro perspective, every presidential or congressional election; every senior leadership change; major international events; and a host of other factors constantly bombard the policy process. The foreign policy debate is unending.

Second, upon entering the Foreign Service and after each promotion, FSOs swear to "uphold and defend the Constitution of the United States against all enemies, foreign and domestic." We do not swear allegiance to a president or an administration. At least implicit in this oath is the requirement to "tell it like it is" and to give our best policy advice.

Finally, it is important to understand that dissent is part of a continuum that begins with advocacy. The most effective way to influence the permanent policy process is to convince superiors of the validity and utility of your views. Being right with some consistency helps. Being wrong is also an option. A certain humility on the part of policy advocates (and thus potential dissenters) is useful. There is always the possibility, however remote, that superior officers—like parents—may be right from time to time.

Official and informal dissent structures and the unique aspects of the foreign policy process provide background and context. Important questions of when and how to dissent remain. Certainly, formal dissent is not to be undertaken lightly. The key element is that you must believe the national interest is threatened. This assertion leads to the prime directive.

Dissent is about the national interest, not individual world views. You may object to the "War in ____" (fill in the blank). But if you are not an expert in the country or region and/or you do not have some level of responsibility for policies there, leave the dissenting to others. On the other hand, if you have the *bona fides* and your advocacy has not been successful, then you should consider formal dissent. If you choose that option, keep the following in mind:

Articulate the case for change succinctly. Be precise. Record your years (hopefully) of experience in the country or area and your current responsibilities in the matter. Your immediate supervisors will know of your experience and authority; others may not.

Have a plan for success (your dissent becomes policy) and for failure (your dissent is dismissed). If the former, have the next steps outlined in detail and ready to table. If the latter, know how you will proceed—simply go back to work and live to fight another day; seek a transfer; or submit your resignation and go public.

Many, if not most, Foreign Service officers will not face the hard choices of formal dissent. The vast majority will have an impact on policy through advocacy. Those who do choose formal dissent are too valuable to lose, in my view. Accordingly, I am not a strong supporter of resignation even though I understand that occasionally it will be the only way. From the perspective of 50 years of involvement, I would argue that particular foreign policies are not as critical with the passage of time as they seem to be in the heat of the moment.

Still, dissent has become institutionalized in the culture of the State Department and the Foreign Service, and the nation has greatly benefited thereby.

Thomas D. Boyatt, an FSO from 1959 until 1985, served as ambassador to Colombia and Upper Volta (now Burkina Faso) and chargé d'affaires in Chile, among many other postings. A past president of the American Foreign Service Association, he is currently president of the Foreign Affairs Council; chairs the Academy of American Diplomacy's "Foreign Affairs Budget for the Future" project; and lectures, teaches, and consults. Ambassador Boyatt received AFSA awards for dissent two times: the William R. Rivkin Award in 1970 while serving in Nicosia, and the Christian A. Herter Award in 1977 while serving as country director for Cyprus. In 2008, he received the Lifetime Contributions to American Diplomacy Award from AFSA.

and a "reviewing officer" (often the deputy chief of mission or someone else a step above the supervisor in the embassy hierarchy). Employees being evaluated have space to comment, an area known as "the suicide box" because they can hurt themselves with ill-advised comments. Filling this out is something of an art learned over time.

A typical Foreign Service career lasts about 20 years, though many FS employees serve 30 or more years. Average age for entry into the State Foreign Service is early thirties, though some do join right out of college and others join much later. The Foreign Service Act of 1980 mandates that each foreign affairs agency establish rules to govern "time-in-class" and "time-in-service." FSOs must be promoted into the Senior Foreign Service within 27 years. In addition, members can spend only a limited amount of time at any one grade (10 to 15 years, depending on the grade) without promotion. Those who do not advance in time are "selected out" of the Service.

Those who do cross the threshold into the Senior Foreign Service may serve for a total of 30 or more years. Foreign Service employees are eligible for retirement with a full pension at age 50 after 20 years of service. Many Foreign Service members go on to new careers after retirement. Unlike the Civil Service, Foreign Service employees are required by law to retire at age 65, or sooner if they come up against time-in-class restrictions.

Not everyone who joins the Foreign Service joins for an entire career, although the attrition rate remains fairly low. Reasons for resigning are most often connected to family issues such as spouse employment or other personal or professional reasons.

Foreign Service employees represent and implement the policies of the U.S. government. Embassy reporting informs Washington and, at times, influences policy or policy direction. Foreign Service employees may not agree with all U.S. policies, but can usually still find a way to do the job. They can put forth alternative views, sometimes informally through meetings and discussions at post. If an employee wants to make a formal dissent, there is a mechanism for this called the Dissent Channel. The message goes to the Secretary of State and does not have to be cleared by the employee's supervisors (see sidebar, p. 94). When an employee feels that he or she cannot do the job because of disagreement over policy, resignation is the option of last resort.

THE FOREIGN SERVICE FAMILY

Foreign Service life for accompanying family members can be a roller coaster ride. There is the excitement of poring over a new bid list and imagining life in exotic cities you have to look at a map to find. FS life comes with airline tickets, a usually-nice place to live with no mortgage or rent, subsidized schooling for the kids at often-outstanding international schools, and an extensive built-in support system from the embassy.

The Foreign Service is not the Peace Corps (although some do like to call work-ing for USAID "the Peace Corps for grown-ups"), and FS families don't usually find themselves hiking to their new homes laden with heavy backpacks. For bet-ter or worse, Foreign Service life overseas is structured in a way that helps create and support a lifestyle that maintains many of the comforts of home in America.

U.S. embassy and consulate communities overseas can be tight-knit, though the feel of the community varies greatly depending on the location, the size of the U.S. mission, the level of hardship, security issues, post management, and other factors. While it varies greatly from post to post, common wisdom has it that the smaller the post and the more difficult the conditions in the country, the better the morale and the closer the community. Community and morale are also highly influenced by post management and the involvement of the ambassador and deputy chief of mission in community life.

Foreign Service family life is also largely dependent on the situation on the ground in whatever country is home at the time. Because the Foreign Service is on the front lines of world events, families will directly feel the impact of whatever is happening in the host country. Political unrest, terrorism, natural disasters— these are things that can alter reality at post in an instant. When the situation be-comes unstable or dangerous, an evacuation may be ordered or authorized from the State Department. The post may "draw down" to only "essential personnel" (sometimes called "emergency personnel"); and all others, including all family members, will be evacuated from the country. Evacuation status is then re-evaluated every 30 days until the situation is stable enough to warrant a return of employees and families.

When a family is evacuated, they have some choice about where to set up camp while waiting to return to post. Many go to Washington, D.C., where sup-port is strongest. Temporary housing is paid for by the government, and a per diem living allowance is also given. The State Department Family Liaison Office has staff responsible for assisting Foreign Service families on evacuation status as well as families of employees serving in unaccompanied positions.

In general, Foreign Service employees transfer with their families every one to three years if overseas, or after one to five years in Washington. Officers may be granted a waiver to allow more time in Washington when needed for medical or family reasons.

The number of unaccompanied positions has risen to more than 900 since 9/11 as the U.S. has engaged in two wars and the threat of terrorism has grown around the world. In 2010, most of the 23 unaccompanied posts (including Provincial Reconstruction Teams) were in Afghanistan, Iraq, and Pakistan, with "limited ac-companied" posts in Algeria, Chad, Lebanon, Yemen, and elsewhere (limited ac-companied refers to posts that have some restrictions on families; spouses may be allowed but no children). Foreign Service families coping with unaccompanied tours receive a "separate maintenance allowance" to help defray the costs of having spouses living in different places. All family members of employees serving under the chief of mission are supported by the State Department Family Liaison Office (FLO). Information about unaccompanied tours and available support and programs for families can be found in the FLO section of the State Department Web site.

TAI TAI:
A DIPLOMAT'S WIFE IN THE MIDDLE KINGDOM
BEIJING, CHINA
By Donna Scaramastra Gorman

I lead a double life here in China. In one life, I'm a stay-at-home mom, wife of a government worker, payer of bills, packer of lunches, master of all things domestic. But in my other life, I'm a *tai tai*. The literal translation is "wife," but the word implies so much more, indicating privilege, position, and wealth. It marks me as an important person, well to do, even sophisticated.

Imagine that. I own a couple of pairs of jeans and a pile of T-shirts, most of which are marked with baby spit-up. I've been known to take the garbage out in my pajamas. And sometimes (ssshhh, don't tell) I eat my kids' leftover mac-n-cheese over the kitchen sink. None of that matters in China. Here, I'm a *tai tai*.

I wasn't prepared for this aspect of Foreign Service life back when we signed on the dotted line all those years ago and shipped off to our first overseas post. I pictured adventures aplenty. I imagined laughing at dinner parties with exotic friends, haggling in foreign languages at vegetable markets, maybe even riding a camel, or hiking on the Great Wall of China. I've done those things, and more.

What I didn't anticipate was the isolation I would sometimes face as the wife of a diplomat in foreign, not-always-friendly cities. I thought I would learn to blend in on any continent. I never stopped to think that I might spend my life sticking out, marked as different in ways both good and bad. But that's how it is. With each new assignment, I've found new ways that I simply don't fit in. Try as I might, I will never blend in here in Beijing.

I live in a gated, guarded community on the outskirts of the city, in a house that was assigned to me by the U.S. government. There are guards stationed round the clock, young Chinese men from the countryside. The houses, occupied mostly by foreigners, have garages with automatic door openers, balconies, guest bathrooms, and American appliances. Our own house is spacious, if somewhat shoddily constructed. You wouldn't give it a second glance if I plunked it down in the middle of suburban Virginia. Here, though, when compared with housing for the local Chinese, it's a veritable palace.

The guards live in a nearby barracks. Stroll past, peek through their gate, and you'll see clotheslines strung between squat brick buildings, hung with T-shirts and blankets. Bicycles are propped near dormitory doors, where the guards sleep several to a room. You might see one of the guards in his shirt-sleeves, rocking back on his heels and smoking, waiting for his shift to start. Every four hours or so, the guards all line up, one behind the next in their crisp olive uniforms, and march across the street from their barracks to our villas.

On our side of the wall, the streets are tidy, swept as they are by an army of workers, hedges clipped neatly, trash cans emptied. I can't tell you where these workers live, exactly. Probably in the nearby *hutong*, a collection of ram-shackle houses clustered together in cramped, dirty alleyways just down the road from our compound. Many of the *ayis* live there—the women who cycle onto the grounds daily to help us clean our houses, iron our clothes, and mind our children. And I wonder: What do they think of us? Their houses seldom have running water, so they have to pay to use a communal shower. I've seen many of them cooking outdoors, stirring noodles in pots over Bunsen burner contraptions just outside their front doors. How did I ever imagine I was going to fit in here, with my microwave oven and my hot water heater?

Back in the States, I'm a solidly middle-class wife and mother of four. Back home, we struggle to make the payments on our tiny townhouse, to fill the car with gas, to buy an occasional meal out. But here, because I have a house and a car, people assume I'm rich. I'm a foreigner, a *laowai*, driving my car past their columns of bicycles, spending obnoxious sums of money on imported cereal, butchering their language every time I open my mouth. Even my four children serve to set me apart: they're the ultimate status sym-bol in a country with a one-child policy.

Though I struggle to speak the language and to pick up on cultural cues, I live in an English-language bubble. There's no such thing as a casual conversa-tion: every word out of my mouth has to be planned in advance, finished in my head before I can toss it off my tongue. Even now, after almost three years here, many of the guards stare at the ground when I greet them in Chinese. Am I somehow insulting them by addressing them? Am I being overly friendly? Still I keep at it, greeting them daily, and some have finally begun to respond.

Xie xie, I say, when someone holds a door for me, and I instruct my chil-dren to say thank you, too. Chinese people really don't say thank you as often as Americans, explains my Chinese teacher, but still I keep at it. Better to err on the side of courtesy than to make a bad impression, after all.

I'm polite. I'm friendly. I want people to like me, despite the linguistic, economic, and cultural barriers between us. What they see is a *tai tai*, but I want to be a regular person. I want to blend in. I've gotten to know the manager at the little shop down the road, and we struggle to chat in Chinese. Talking with him, I feel as though I'm carving out a place for myself within this community, as an ordinary shopper, there to buy milk and bread like everyone else. That's the image I try to project—ordinariness.

The Foreign Service attracts adaptable people, but it can't create chameleons. I've learned to adapt in so many different ways, to laugh at the strange events unfolding around me, to swallow my fear and leap feet first into new situations. But I haven't learned how to blend in. Instead, I'm struggling to stand out with grace: to smile for the picture-taking locals; to con-

Donna Gorman and her family at the Great Wall of China.

verse with strangers about my family size; to admit, during nearly every conversation I start on any given day, that I simply don't understand what I'm hearing.

It's taken years in the Foreign Service to finally understand that I'm never going to fit in, that maybe I'm not supposed to fit in. I thought, when we started down this path, that I would grow to be the kind of person who could navigate through any city with ease, the kind of person who could read the faces of passersby in countries across the globe. I was wrong. Instead, my life as a diplomatic spouse has turned me into the kind of person who is comfortable being uncomfortable, who never quite fits in anywhere.

Finishing up a three-year tour in China, I'm still an outsider, and many of my everyday interactions are fraught with confusion. How to tell the taxi driver he's made a wrong turn? How to ask the tailor to shorten a hem? How to understand what the *ayi* is telling me about how my daughters spent their morning while I was away at work? But I've learned to laugh at myself, and accept and cherish the fragments of comprehension, glimpses of understanding, that come my way.

Inside of my house, here in Beijing, I'm just your average American mom, helping my kids with their homework as I prepare dinner, and that's how it should be. But out in the wide world, I'm a *tai tai*, floating above the crowd, somehow assumed to be worthy of respect, and I suppose that's okay, too. I struggle every day to stay afloat in this strange world, while at the same time striving to keep my feet firmly planted on this foreign soil.

Donna Scaramastra Gorman is a freelance writer whose work has appeared in Newsweek, *the* Washington Post *and the* Christian Science Monitor. *She moved to Amman, Jordan, in 2010 with her husband and four kids. Previous posts have included Moscow, Yerevan, and Almaty.*

Singles and Tandems in the Foreign Service

Single Foreign Service employees tend to have greater flexibility and freedom to pursue the career and opportunities they desire, but they lack the immediate support system of family members traveling with them. The lifestyle overseas can be exciting but at times lonely, at least until networks and friendships are established.

Foreign Service singles tend to be seen by the bureaucracy and often by colleagues as more available and less encumbered than their married colleagues, and they face unwritten expectations that they should be the first to step up to volunteer for unaccompanied and danger posts and to work holidays. These pressures are not official, but they are real. On the other hand, many single Foreign Service employees do have greater flexibility than their married colleagues and can take on an assignment without considering schools, spouse employment opportunities, and other issues that arise for those with partners and children.

Certain assignments are simply easier to manage when an employee is single, such as positions that require a lot of travel. Some FS employees aim to serve in hardship and/or unaccompanied positions while single, knowing that those assignments can become more complicated later when there may be more family concerns.

Many embassy communities can feel like a fishbowl, making it difficult to maintain privacy in one's personal life. Close-knit embassy communities often do welcome singles and include them as part of an embassy "family." But the type of embassy community varies from post to post, with larger posts in more developed countries tending to offer more anonymity. Smaller posts, especially hardship posts, tend to have closer embassy communities, where people are more likely to socialize together and look out for each other. The key to a fulfilling social life as a single in the Foreign Service is creating a support network at post from local friends, expatriates of a range of nationalities, and embassy colleagues.

Single parents in the Foreign Service must navigate the complexities of raising a child outside the U.S. Plusses include the ability to afford domestic help at most posts as well as access to (and tuition for) good international schools at many posts (though this will have an impact on what posts the parent bids on). Depending on the person and the post, single FS parents can find that building a social life can be difficult. Some will gravitate toward the family crowd to participate in activities that involve the kids.

As a general but not universal rule, being single in the Foreign Service presents more of a challenge for women than for men. Single men seem to be able to connect more easily with, and marry, non-American women overseas. Common wisdom has it that young, single male officers often come back from certain postings with a wife from that country. In fact, more than one-third of all Foreign Service spouses are foreign-born; and most, though not all, of those spouses are women.

Many countries of the world are still patriarchies where the male of the household is the primary breadwinner, so a working American Foreign Service single woman is simply not seen as a possible spouse by locals. Obviously this varies greatly from country to country, and the broader expatriate community can offer alternatives for the single woman.

Although FS single women may find active social lives and options for dating overseas, there is no way around the fact that it is still more difficult for a woman to find a partner to follow her around the world—which the FS life requires—than for a man. One alternative to the "who follows whom?" conundrum is for FS singles to marry each other, becoming a tandem couple. Tandems can bid on the same posts and can spend most of their careers together. As they rise in rank, they do face more limited job opportunities at the same posts, in part because one spouse cannot be supervised by the other. Tandems often find that at certain times, one person's career will take priority and compromises may have to be made in order to serve in the same location. Most tandems will spend at least one year apart, serving in different countries.

Today there are about 500 tandem couples in the State Department and an additional 81 interagency tandems, in which one spouse works for another foreign affairs agency. While a degree of creativity is required to ensure two successful careers, many couples find the tandem arrangement works quite well.

One of the unique and challenging aspects of being single in the FS overseas and dating in the local community is that it can be difficult to ascertain whether someone's interest in you is truly an interest in you, or if it is motivated by the hope for a free ticket to America as your spouse and, eventually, U.S. citizenship. Common advice FS singles hear is to avoid dating people who would be likely to be denied a tourist visa (those who would have a difficult time proving that they intend to return to their home country). While this makes trusting one's instincts even more important than when dating Stateside, the opposite side of the coin is that singles, particularly single men who may have had trouble socializing in the States, can find that dating overseas comes more easily. (Still, as students are told during consular training, "remember, we don't get better-looking just because we move overseas.") One consideration for single officers interested in dating while overseas is that, for security reasons, there are reporting requirements and restrictions on dating foreign nationals from certain countries. This is one factor to keep in mind when bidding on assignments.

Domestic Partners

Foreign Service employees who have same-sex partners have long sought to obtain benefits for their partners comparable to those enjoyed by spouses. Known as Members of Household (MOH), these partners were not given access until recently to benefits other family members received, including evacuation support, use of embassy medical services, or embassy employment and travel support.

A (NON-TRADITIONAL) TANDEM IN INDIA
By Clayton Bond

Ted arrived home at 2 a.m., after completing a reporting cable on Secretary of State Condoleezza Rice's meeting with Indian Prime Minister Manmohan Singh. He tried to slip in quietly, knowing that I had to be up at 3 a.m. to start my day working on the visit. Ted's cable, covering a meeting that ended at 10:30 p.m., had to be with the Secretary's party before the delegation's 8 a.m. departure for Pakistan. The embassy was working round the clock, arranging such events as the ambassador's breakfast for the Secretary and the chairman of the Joint Chiefs of Staff, who had just arrived from Islamabad. It was 2009, a week after terrorists killed nearly 200 people, including six Americans, in India's financial capital of Mumbai. Shuttle diplomacy was in full swing.

I arrived at the hotel at 4 a.m. and checked on the lounge that we managed to reserve at no extra cost for the delegation's breakfast, making sure everything was set up properly. As a general services officer (GSO) working on this visit, my job was to help ensure that all the venues were ready, all the logistics in order. After checking on the breakfast area, I conferred with the hotel management to go over billing arrangements again, to make sure they understood whom to charge directly for lodging and incidentals, and whose bills should be sent to the embassy. I also guided members of the Secretary's party to the breakfast area, reminded them about settling their room service and other incidental charges with the hotel, and showed them where to leave their luggage, which would be swept by security before being loaded into a van and delivered to the plane.

During a visit by a Secretary of State, every embassy officer is fully deployed. We had only 72 hours to prepare for this visit, which was sandwiched between two other high-profile visits. Since the attack on Mumbai, Ted, as political counselor, had participated in a number of secure video teleconferences, including one chaired by President George W. Bush.

The president and his advisers faced a dilemma: how to defuse tensions between two nuclear-armed neighbors, while leaning on Islamabad to dismantle the terrorists' infrastructure—but not so hard that the fragile civilian government would collapse. As the president's schedule determined timing, these meetings occurred sometimes at midnight India time, sometimes at 4 a.m., and the embassy's senior staff was starting to fray around the edges from a lack of sleep. After his late night cable-writing, Ted had to be up and fully prepared to brief Admiral Mullen at 8:15 a.m.

Tandem couples—where both are Foreign Service employees—save the U.S. government money. As far as we know, we were the first "non-traditional" tandem to be officially housed together, saving the taxpayer as much

as $100,000 during our India tour. The
ambassador, deputy chief of mission, and
entire embassy community welcomed us,
with hardly a ripple of controversy about
our unusual status. And although Indian
society tends to be socially conservative,
the New Delhi elite appeared to have no
difficulty adjusting to an openly gay couple at the American embassy. At one
party, I responded to the usual question
from an Indian guest: "Are you here with
family?" by saying, "I'm here with my
spouse." Pressed further, I identified Ted.

Clayton Bond (left) and Ted Osius in New Delhi.

Nonplussed, the elderly matron smiled and advised, "You live your life."

Ted and I met in Washington in 2004, at a monthly business meeting of
Gays and Lesbians in Foreign Affairs Agencies (GLIFAA), an officially recognized organization representing the concerns of gay and lesbian personnel and their families. Ted was then running the Korea desk and I was
serving as a watch officer in the State Department's 24-hour Operations
Center. We were married in Vancouver in June 2006 and had a commitment
ceremony in Ted's home state of Maryland the following month.

In some ways, it's easier for us than for couples where only one is a
Foreign Service employee. Still, tandemhood has its challenges, as when Ted
was assigned to be deputy chief of mission in Jakarta. Because I cannot be
in Ted's chain of command, I sought and obtained an in-cone management
position in Singapore, a 1.5-hour flight across the Malacca Straits. Just as the
Bureau of South and Central Asian Affairs worked hard to assign us together
in New Delhi, the East Asian and Pacific Bureau made great efforts to assign us to adjacent posts. While we hope that the federal government will
take further steps to support non-traditional families, we recognize that we
have come a long way since GLIFAA was founded in 1992.

*Following internships as a Pickering Fellow in the State Department's Office of
Environmental Policy and in U.S. Embassy Gaborone's political and economic
affairs section, Clayton Bond entered the Foreign Service with the 104th A-100
class on September 10, 2001. Prior to his posting in New Delhi, he served in
Washington, D.C., and in Bogotá, Colombia. He is a management officer. Clayton's
spouse, Ted Osius, joined the Foreign Service in 1989 and has served in Manila,
Philippines; the Vatican; the U.S. Mission to the United Nations in New York
City; Hanoi and Ho Chi Minh City, Vietnam; Bangkok, Thailand; and
Washington, D.C. Ted is a member of the Senior Foreign Service.*

Beginning in 2001, members of household were defined in the *Foreign Affairs Manual* as "those persons who have accompanied or join an employee assigned abroad and who the employee has declared to the chief of mission are part of his or her household, who will reside at post with the employee, and who are other than legitimate domestic staff." While posts were encouraged to welcome and offer assistance to the MOH, there was no guarantee of services or benefits.

Over the years, the situation gradually improved, with more and more overseas posts moving to provide tangible assistance to Foreign Service members of household. Effective in July 2009, the same-sex partners of FS employees of all five foreign affairs agencies were given the status of Eligible Family Members (EFM), the official term for spouses and children of Foreign Service personnel. This represented a major change and opened up a number of benefits to these family members for the first time, including access to many more jobs inside the mission. However, under the new regulations the term "domestic partner" still does not encompass opposite-sex partners, who, as long as they remain unmarried, are categorized as members of household and not EFM.

Foreign Service Children

Foreign Service kids—FS brats, as many fondly call them, and as many proudly call themselves—experience a world of opportunity, quite literally. Culturally comfortable with people of all shapes, colors, and sizes, they are at home in a global, diverse setting—but sometimes have a hard time coming back to a homogenous community in the United States. As Third Culture Kids (another common designation), they are never quite sure how to answer the question, "Where are you from?"

WAKING UP IN VIETNAM
By Benjamin Winnick

The three years I spent in Vietnam shaped my perceptions and world view more than any other experience in my life. I encountered prejudice and learned about being a minority. I witnessed poverty and saw the developing world firsthand. And I learned how culture shapes life, work, and behavior.

At my high school, the International School of Ho Chi Minh City, Americans were a minority. Most students were Vietnamese or Korean, among more than 20 nationalities. I encountered prejudice against America for the first time, though not from Vietnamese students. The prejudice came primarily from Western students, driven by objections to America's foreign policy but extending to its culture, history, and people.

I was not just Ben; I was "the American." I was torn between my own disagreement with U.S. foreign policy, loyalty to my country and its historic
values, and my desire to be accepted. There were also tensions among other
groups, particularly between Koreans and Europeans. After enduring these
tensions for over a year, I took action. During my sophomore year, I spearheaded the creation of the "Students for Tolerance Committee" to raise
awareness and reduce hostility at school.

My school experiences were complemented by invaluable lessons about
poverty and its problems that I learned from living in a developing country.
In Vietnam, I saw families living in metal shacks. I saw people use the Saigon
River as a toilet, drink its water, and bathe and wash their clothes in it. I saw
children working in fields and begging on the streets. Although I witnessed
these events daily, my most direct experiences of poverty and cultural differences came from volunteering at Bien Hoa Orphanage.

The orphanage showed me the hardships orphans face. The air inside
was filled with the stench of urine, feces, warm milk, mucus, and sweat.
There were rooms filled with dozens of tiny mewling babies. When we, a
group of nine volunteers, held the babies, we could feel their heavy, impaired breathing. Caring for so many tiny children was a Sisyphean task.
Only two caregivers worked at a time, and they concentrated on me-
chanical tasks such as laundry, cleaning, and bottle-feeding. They had little time to play with the children. We alleviated some of the strain but
even as we held, rocked, fed and played with them, there were unattended
children screaming for attention. I would console one child, but as soon
as I diverted my attention to another baby, the child I had just put down
would resume howling.

At Bien Hoa, I learned that when people are concerned with survival, it
is difficult to be altruistic. The women who worked at the orphanage seemed
more concerned with keeping their jobs than with the children's welfare.
They rarely let the children go outside because they feared that any injury,
even a scratch or bug bite, would jeopardize their employment. When one
of our teachers donated a pair of shoes, a woman on duty took them for
her own child. When someone is in poverty, short-term gain is a higher priority than moral correctness. Perhaps moral correctness is a luxury reserved
for those whose immediate needs are satisfied.

The orphanage also taught me the challenges of working with people
from a different culture. Culture is more than diet or apparel; it influences one's way of life and work. In America, people dispose of things
without hesitation, but the women at Bien Hoa were raised to conserve.
Whenever we tried to change a diaper that was not bursting, they would
stop us. Although we saw children suffering from diaper rash, defying

the women would have been terribly disrespectful. So, although we changed diapers when we could, we never openly disobeyed the women who worked there.

Thanks to Vietnam, I better understand the meaning of diversity. I recognize that culture shapes attitudes. I am able to function in foreign or new environments. I have more insight into prejudice and the way it excludes and divides people. I also recognize the serious need that exists in the world and our duty to do something about it. I still have a lot to learn, but living in Vietnam opened my eyes.

Benjamin Winnick grew up in the Foreign Service. His father works for the State Department. Ben spent his first three years of high school in Ho Chi Minh City and his senior year in Paris. He has also lived in Moscow, New York City, and Bethesda, Maryland. After high school, Ben went on to study at the University of Pennsylvania. A version of this essay, which was selected as the 2008 AFSA Merit Scholarship Best Essay, appeared in the July/August 2008 Foreign Service Journal.

For kids, moving frequently can be a source of stress. As babies and toddlers, they may "act out" the anxiety of being in a new place with no way to verbalize their feelings. As they grow older, they become more concerned about leaving friends behind. This peaks in the high school years, and many Foreign Service parents find themselves turning down assignments, or taking others they might not have previously considered, in order to accommodate their kids. Where and when FS teenagers will attend high school becomes a primary concern for families with children at that stage of life; some choose to plan for Washington assignments to cover the high school years.

Depending on the individual child, moving from one country to another can be exciting or painful. Some handle change better than others, just as adults do. What is a novel and inspiring expedition for one child is a social or academic nightmare for another. Often the experience provides a little of both. The good news is that many international schools have such transient populations that there are often many new kids coming in at all grade levels.

Foreign Service children are covered by their parents' "orders" (supported to live at each post) until they are 21 years old, at which point they are considered adults. Once they are on their own, they often look back on their childhood with fondness for the many adventures they had growing up in the Foreign Service. They tend to have a broader perspective than many of their American peers. Some try to replicate their experience growing up by joining the Foreign Service, Peace Corps, or other international organizations. Others settle down—usually in the United States—and are happy to plant roots and never move again!

A CROSS-CULTURAL FRIENDSHIP
By Rachel Midura

I am the 16-year-old daughter in a Foreign Service family. Guatemalan *huipiles* (traditional hand-woven blouses) adorn our walls, and Zambian baskets sit on our shelves. I can't remember a time when it was different. Yet I did not realize how unusual my life really was until after I became friends with a girl named Lana.

We had relocated to Prague just months before the new millennium, to a house within walking distance of the international school. Lana was in my fourth-grade class. She was Serbian and spoke halting English, but I was more than capable of filling any gaps in the conversation. I was drawn to her calm demeanor, and later delighted by her quick wit. When she invited me to her house, I was happy to accept.

The trip proved to be an adventure. Instead of her parents driving us—the only mode of transportation with which I was familiar—we headed to the nearest bus stop. After getting off the bus, we dodged cars in a bustling main street, and hiked past apartment buildings and grocery stores. By the time we reached her front gate, I felt a heady rush of adrenaline at having done something so *independent*.

Lana's austere house brought me down to earth. I remember thinking, where are all her things? Eventually I made the connection between the starkness of her home's interior and the news footage I had seen of bombings and rallies in Belgrade. Lana and her parents were refugees: they had what they needed for a decent life, but very little beyond that.

I don't know what Lana thought of me, but she must not have seen the shallow, naïve kid I felt like in that moment, because the afternoon went perfectly. We entertained ourselves in the same way our grandparents had—no television, no video games—and that became the standard for our afternoons. Once, we spent hours writing secret messages with burnt-out matches, then passing them from her lower balcony to the one above. Another day we built a pillow fort that stretched through three rooms.

For four years, Lana and I explored Prague together. When we cut through just the right patch of trees, we would come out on a rocky cliff overlooking the city. There, while we dangled our legs and basked in the rare sunshine, I explained the United States to her and she explained Milosevic's Serbia to me. We rode our scooters to the Hotel Praha pool, the grocery store, and the park.

Lana told me once about an American bomb that had landed near her house, and I was deeply shocked at this connection to a previously abstract event. I was angry that bombs happened to real people, not just faces on CNN.

On September 11, 2001, it was Lana who helped me understand the magnitude of what had occurred. We sat outside on the dewy grass and discussed how it felt to be hated. Together we tried to comprehend why complete strangers would want us dead, all because of what seemed like ancient history. While I had never had to face such animosity before, Lana was familiar with being written off as an "arrogant Serb."

Now I'm back in the U.S., in high school in a comfortable suburb near Washington, D.C., and Lana is back home in Belgrade. As an American teenager, it's easy to turn up my iPod and tune out the world. It is easy to overlook the news from Baghdad in favor of celebrity gossip.

Lana and I have stayed in touch. We talk on the phone, covering the meaning of life, the Kosovo situation, as well as my homecoming dress. For the past two years, we've been planning a trans-Europe backpacking trip. Though we face the hurdles of school, finances, and a couple of thousand miles, we are both enchanted by the idea of exploring together once more.

Rachel Midura wrote this essay as a high school junior living in Reston, Virginia, and is now in college at the University of Virginia. Born in Guatemala, she has accompanied her parents (FSO Christopher Midura is with the State Department and the author of the Kosovo story on p. 196) to Zambia, El Salvador, and the Czech Republic. This essay was originally published in the January 2008 Foreign Service Journal.

The Realities of Family Member Employment

One of the greatest concerns for FS families is employment for spouses and partners. Given the unique and transient lifestyle of Foreign Service employees, there will always be serious considerations and compromises to be made by spouses trying to build their own careers.

A 1957 State Department publication, *Suggestions for Wives from Other Foreign Service Wives*, offered the following advice: "Being married to a man in the Foreign Service gives you the satisfaction of using your mind and developing your capabilities in working more closely with your husband than would be true in some other occupations. You can be a great help to your husband in his career, and can live a rich and rewarding life by helping him in serving our country."

Back then, FS wives were considered unpaid government employees and their representational contributions were included in their husbands' evaluations. A 1972 State Department directive ended that practice, giving spouses more freedom to host or not host representational events—but not, in many countries, the freedom to find employment.

While job options have grown, many spouses and partners are still frustrated by the challenges associated with maintaining a career while accompanying a Foreign Service employee overseas. Most Foreign Service spouses and partners are well-educated and, in many cases, just as professionally qualified in their own fields as the FS employee. A 2006 survey conducted by the State Department's Family Liaison Office found that 75 percent of FS family members had college degrees and 38 percent had advanced degrees.

Family member employment is a key issue—though not always a top priority—for the foreign affairs agencies, because it is directly tied to their ability to recruit and retain the best employees. Still, those coming into the Foreign Service today should understand that the foreign affairs agencies will probably never be able to ensure that all family members who want good jobs can get them at every post.

Most FS spouses and partners who are not part of a tandem combination will not have "normal" careers, but can, with a combination of the right skills and the right postings, have a career, or at least a series of rewarding jobs in their chosen fields, if those fields are ones that lend themselves to Foreign Service life. Most spouses will not be able to avoid certain gaps in employment: Foreign Service life dictates frequent moves, as well as sometimes lengthy transition periods for training and home leave.

Data from 220 posts compiled by the Family Liaison Office for the November 2009 Family Member Employment Report, known as the FAMER, showed that the total number of Foreign Service spouses overseas was 9,743. Of those, 7,901 (81 percent), were women and 1,842 were men. The total number of spouses working overseas was reported to be 3,765. Of those, there were 2,470 working inside the mission and 1,295 working outside. The FAMER is a useful tool for bidding research; it is accessible through the Family Liaison Office intranet site and linked to the FS bidding tool.

The Family Liaison Office is an excellent place for Foreign Service family members to find career management advice and employment information. Once at post, the best places for information on employment are the Human Resources Office and the Community Liaison Office, which is the branch office of the FLO in just about every embassy. FLO advocates on behalf of family members and works with management to initiate and expand employment programs. FLO tries to keep tabs on spousal employment opportunities and realities and collects and shares job listings and other information related to employment for family members.

BEST-BET PROFESSIONS. Maintaining a career while serving as a Foreign Service spouse or partner depends on attitude, flexibility, transportable skills, strategic bidding, and luck. There are certain professions that do lend themselves to the mobile and not always predictable FS lifestyle. A basic list (not in rank order) might read like this: teaching, consulting and project management, public health, training, information technology, Web design, Web-site management or any other Internet-based occupation, translating/interpreting, writing and editing, accounting and finance, art and design, and home-based businesses.

Writers don't tend to earn a lot of money, but writing can be a rewarding profession that is highly portable. And the Foreign Service life can offer an endless stream of inspiring material. Some of the spouses who seem most at peace with Foreign Service life are the writers. "Nowadays, being overseas, especially in a posting with reliable Internet connections, is perfect for a writer—you can't help having all these incredible experiences that you want to put on paper, and even the bad days are fodder for essays and articles," says Francesca Kelly, a writer, editor, professional singer, and FS spouse and mother.

The field of public health can offer a highly flexible career path, as well, with employment or consultancy options with international organizations, USAID or organizations with USAID contracts, and with nonprofits. Public health professionals with expertise in traditional international health areas such as child survival, maternal health, and family planning have done well in developing countries, but find that jobs in more-developed countries are scarce. Technical skills in health education, epidemiology, needs-assessment, and program design are also in demand in many developing countries.

Although jobs on the local economy often do not pay well, salaries for positions with international organizations such as the United Nations, international and U.S.-based NGOs, and U.S. or multinational companies are generally not based on the local economy. Thus, the pay can be quite high and, within limits, tax-free.

Many spouses and partners are finding ways to take their jobs with them when they go overseas, arranging contracts with their U.S.-based employers for work that can be done remotely via the Internet. Some have found success with this approach even with federal government positions.

Those who arrive at post without the local language can find that a significant barrier to employment on the local economy. The Foreign Service Institute offers classroom language classes to family members on a space-available basis, but many spouses are unable to study before heading to a new post for various reasons, including lack of space in a class, the need to continue working, or childcare issues. FSI can also offer Rosetta Stone language materials online to family members through the FSI LearnCenter.

The State Department's Global Employment Initiative (GEI, previously known as the Strategic Networking Assistance Program) was launched in 2002 to assist family members seeking work on the local economy. Starting with eight offices, as of 2011 it had expanded to provide services to 65 posts. Run by the Family Liaison Office, GEI provides career advising services through global employment advisers. The advisers assist clients in their job searches and help with career development and planning, résumé writing, and honing interview skills. In addition, GEI establishes relationships with multinational corporations, organizations, and nongovernmental organizations in order to facilitate possible employment connections for family members hoping for a job on the local economy.

Many FS spouses choose to stay home with children for a number of years. Foreign Service spouse Jan Fischer Bachman notes, "If you want to stay home with kids, the FS makes it possible because of perks like free housing. The stay-at-homers-by-choice are probably among the happiest group of FS family members."

THE BILATERALS. A bilateral work agreement is an official agreement between the U.S. government and the host country granting permission for U.S. mission family members to seek employment on the local economy. It is established through a formal exchange of diplomatic notes. As of 2010, the United States had signed bilateral agreements with 111 countries. The list can be found at the State Web site's Family Liaison Office section.

In certain countries where there is no signed agreement in place with the State Department, there is a de facto reciprocal work arrangement that also allows family members to legally work on the local economy. In those cases, permission is established by precedent, and there is an established practice for family members to apply for and receive work permits. In 2010, there were 43 countries with de facto arrangements in place. This leaves about 20 countries in which the U.S. has a mission but no work agreement, making those the most difficult places for spouses to find employment outside the mission.

The Family Liaison Office supports efforts to establish bilateral agreements and de facto arrangements with all countries, but it is the post itself that takes the lead on negotiating an agreement with the foreign ministry of the host country.

JOBS IN THE MISSION. While there are fascinating and enriching opportunities for work outside the mission in many countries, these jobs can be difficult to find and not an option at some posts. Employment inside the mission is often the preferred option for family members, for reasons that include security, ease of commute with a family member and, for some, federal retirement benefits that can be accrued and carried from post to post.

Embassy jobs frequently held by family members include community liaison, office coordinator, consular associate, information management assistant, general services assistant, office manager, administrative assistant, housing coordinator, newsletter or Web-site editor, and security escort. Many of these jobs are part-time.

About 25 percent of all family members overseas work inside missions, and 13 percent work outside, according to 2010 data from the Family Liaison Office. As of 2010, more than 65 percent of family members who were working overseas were working inside a U.S. mission, and a majority of family members express a preference for work inside missions rather than outside.

There are a number of hiring mechanisms used by posts to hire family members. Creation of the State Department's Family Member Appointment (FMA) system in 1998 was one of the most important developments in family-member

A SPOUSE AT WORK IN THE MISSION
By Aryani Manring

When I heard we were moving to Indonesia for our first posting, I was beside myself with excitement. I grew up in Jakarta and my mom still lived there, so our first Foreign Service assignment wouldn't be so foreign after all. What would be new, though, was living overseas as a dependent of a U.S. government employee. When my husband joined the Foreign Service, I had been ready for a career transition myself, so I was looking forward to seeking new work overseas. But what were my options? I wasn't sure what to expect. As it turned out, I got a rewarding job at Embassy Jakarta that offered great professional development opportunities and, ultimately, confirmed my desire to join the Foreign Service.

Indonesia and the U.S. had no bilateral work agreement, which meant that opportunities to work on the local economy were severely limited. While we were still in Washington, I contacted the embassy's community liaison office coordinator (CLO) and signed up for the weekly e-newsletters, which included embassy job vacancies for "eligible family members" (EFM). I visited Jakarta for family reasons a month before our official transfer and made an appointment to meet the CLO. She introduced me to the human resources officer so I could learn more about specific job vacancies.

I was able to interview for an embassy position over the phone once I was back in Washington, and landed a yearlong spot in the political section as the human rights officer, covering for a Foreign Service officer who had curtailed and left post early. I was responsible for drafting the embassy's contribution to the annual reports to Congress on Indonesia's protection of human rights, and I worked with Indonesian activists and government counterparts to promote U.S. human rights-related policies. In a country which, at that time, had recently emerged from an authoritarian past, human rights were a sensitive topic.

As with any new challenge, it was trial by fire at first. In some meetings, I waded through acronym soup. But it went well. And thankfully, I already knew how to speak Bahasa Indonesia. I stayed with the job in the political section for two years, gaining confidence in my ability to communicate in the language of my fellow State Department colleagues.

I was lucky. Thanks to my colleagues and supervisors, I was treated as a full member of the embassy team from day one. In Jakarta, eligible family members employed in the mission were awarded nearly every opportunity afforded our FSO colleagues: reporting trips to remote parts of Indonesia, the chance to work on a high-level visit, public speaking opportunities, and more. And I wasn't the only one.

Other family members also found great work opportunities within Embassy Jakarta. In the economic section, four EFMs worked full- and part-time on issues ranging from biosecurity and health to regional economic issues and the environment. Two positions in the economic section were job-share positions, in which each person worked about three days a week. One political section EFM streamlined a complex process of vetting thousands

Aryani Manring with FSO spouse Scott Kofmehl in Bali, Indonesia.

of Indonesian security forces who were potential recipients of U.S. training. In the public affairs section, another family member handled all exchange programs, filling in for a Foreign Service officer who had departed post early. In the consular section, EFM consular assistants responded to public enquiries about various issues, assisted with applicant intake, and performed other duties. Family members were also office management specialists, nurses, escorts, English teachers for local embassy employees, and more.

Jakarta had a very inclusive "Entry-Level Professionals" (ELP) group that was open to EFMs, specialists, and generalists from any U.S. agency. The group organized a speaker series that brought in outside speakers to give lunch-time talks to the embassy community. Speakers ranged from filmmakers and food critics to anthropologists and a retired Indonesian ambassador to the United States. And, more than once, embassywide initiatives that did not fall squarely into any section's portfolio fell to the ELP group. For instance, the ELP group helped organize an anti-corruption themed rock concert with one of Indonesia's most famous bands at the ambassador's residence for hundreds of university students and embassy contacts.

Outside the embassy, other EFMs in Jakarta received funds from the J. Simon Kirby Foreign Service Trust to create their own professional development opportunities. One person received her certification to teach English as a Second Language and taught English to the embassy motor pool staff. EFMs were a critical part of Embassy Jakarta's community.

I should caution that Embassy Jakarta illustrates what is probably a best-case scenario for EFMs. Every U.S. mission is different, and not all posts have as many opportunities for family members. Jakarta's management team made establishing diverse EFM positions a priority.

The State Department, more broadly, is expanding opportunities for EFMs through initiatives such as the Professional Associates Program. Thanks to positive experiences in Jakarta, I decided that joining the Foreign Service was a great option for my career and family. I took the exams and fortunately, received an offer to join as we were preparing to depart Jakarta. Two weeks after my last day at Embassy Jakarta, I was sitting with my new A-100 class in Foreign Service orientation.

Aryani Manring was born in Seattle and grew up in Seattle and Jakarta, Indonesia. She worked as an eligible family member in Embassy Jakarta's political section from 2007 to 2009, and joined the Foreign Service in August 2009. In 2010, she headed out to her first assignment, as a consular officer for Embassy Mexico City. Her FSO husband, Scott Kofmehl, was also posted to Mexico City's consular section.

mission employment. It was an effort to standardize what had been highly inconsistent and localized employment programs for spouses. Those hired through this process are eligible for benefits including annual leave and retirement, which accrue with each subsequent FMA job. This hiring mechanism is providing spouses and unmarried U.S. citizen children ages 18 to 21—and, as of 2009, same-sex partners as well—employment benefits never before available to them in mission jobs.

The State Department established the Professional Associates Program in 1994 to open up unfilled junior officer positions to eligible family members; it now also covers unfilled mid-level Foreign Service positions in the "hard-to-fill" category. (HTF positions are those that lack sufficient qualified Foreign Service bidders.) Every year, State management sends out a bid list of HTF jobs open to eligible family members and Civil Service employees. These positions are filled as Family Member Appointments and come with retirement and other portable benefits.

The Expanded Professional Associates Program was established in 2009 to provide additional professional-level, full-time employment opportunities overseas for family members and to fill critical positions with well-qualified personnel. EPAP gives these family members an opportunity to work in Foreign Service entry-level positions in the following career tracks: political, economic, public diplomacy, management, general services, human resources, financial management, office management, information management, and medical.

Another hiring mechanism for jobs inside U.S. missions is the Personal Service Contract. Such jobs generally do not include benefits and are not considered long-term positions. USAID uses the PSC for many local-hire openings in overseas missions. Inside and outside the embassy, some of the best, most professional, opportunities for family members are in the field of international development, working with USAID as well as U.N. agencies and international nonprofit organizations.

Opportunities for family members inside U.S. missions vary widely from post to post, and even from year to year at any given post. Much depends on the management team at post, as well as on budgets and Foreign Service staffing. The key players determining the employment situation at a post are the ambassador and deputy chief of mission, the management officer, and the community liaison office coordinator. As American personnel cycle through from year to year, these players and dynamics change, as do the needs of each post.

Foreign Service family members seeking upwardly mobile career paths should probably not look to the embassy for employment. While it may be possible to find similar types of jobs at different posts, usually a family member looking for an embassy job has to take what is available, which will at best be a continuation of a type of work done at another post, and almost certainly not an advancement up a career ladder.

State management knows that there is a connection between recruitment and retention and family member employment opportunities. However, most agree that there is no silver bullet. Each host country has different issues influencing work opportunities. Each Foreign Service spouse and partner is also unique, with his or her own priorities, goals, skills, and employment interests. The Family Liaison Office's challenge is to provide family members with the information and resources they need to make informed employment decisions and manage their expectations in the process.

PART III

A Day in the Life of the Foreign Service: One-Day Journals

There are no typical days in the Foreign Service. One of the most challenging, and rewarding, aspects of Foreign Service work is that the activities of the job are intimately connected to the situation on the ground in the host country. If you're the administrative officer and a coup occurs, your job can change in an instant from negotiating a building contract to implementing an evacuation plan. If you're the political officer, you'll go from a meeting with parliamentarians to covering demonstrations on the street. And if you're the consular officer, you'll go from interviewing visa applicants to networking with the American community throughout the host country to keep them informed as the situation develops.

Most days do not come with a coup or another emergency situation, but even the most "normal" days on the job are not routine because of where the job is being done—in another country. With this in mind, we asked Foreign Service employees around the world to chronicle one day on the job. The selection of days illustrates the diversity of Foreign Service work in terms of positions, locations, and activities.

Go on the road in Siberia with Consul General Tom Armbruster as he meets with local officials, students, environmentalists, and an American prison inmate. Join Political Officer David Becker visiting a community development project in Cité Soleil, Haiti. Travel to a remote village in Burkina Faso with Economic and Commercial Officer Pamela Hamblett. And attend an adoption ceremony with Consular Officer Esther Pan Sloane in Guangzhou, China.

From the public affairs officer meeting with local English teachers in Dushanbe, to the human rights officer investigating prison conditions in the Democratic Republic of the Congo, to the office management specialist distributing action items to embassy officers in Stockholm, these are the stories of everyday life in the Foreign Service.

A Day in the Life of ...
A CONSULAR OFFICER

CONSULATE GENERAL CHENNAI, INDIA
By Kris Fresonke
OCTOBER 2008

8:55 A.M.   Visa interviews have been going on for an hour and there are still a hundred people in the lobby waiting for their turn. Officers sit at several windows, conducting interviews through microphones, a sheet of bulletproof glass between officer and applicant. There is a buzz of American English and Indian English in hectic conversation. My shift is about to begin.

9:00 A.M.   I raise the blinds on Window 2 to find an applicant already there, sliding his folder through the slot. It contains his passport and application form. In about two minutes of conversation, I determine that he is who he says he is; has a legitimate travel purpose; and has sufficient ties to India to ensure his likely return. I issue the visa and thank him.

9:05 A.M.   I conduct the same interview 99 more times during the next four hours. The U.S. consulate in Chennai is a "visa mill," an off-putting term for a truly vital service: issuing visas in areas of high demand. Other high-volume visa posts include Mexico, Brazil, and China. Visa officers at high-volume posts work long hours at a difficult task, interviewing potential travelers and judging speedily whether or not the travel is lawful and valid. In Chennai, we usually have a dozen visa officers "on the line," who conduct an average of 1,200 to 1,400 interviews per day in total. We've even done 1,800 in one day. Without our work making legitimate travel possible, the American economy would instantly feel the adverse effects. Without our care in deterring fraud, the United States would face significant dangers.

10:00 A.M.   An applicant wishes to travel to the United States to buy machinery. He cannot explain what machinery he wants to buy, why he wants to buy it, or who is selling it to him. This set of answers alone makes my refusal a simple matter; I then cross-check some of his application information. Two other applicants have been issued visas using the same data, which means a vendor has been selling the same package of fake business documents to several different people. I send him to the fraud prevention unit so my colleagues can get more information on this scheme.

10:30 A.M.   It's a heavy fraud day. This applicant claims he works at a major IT company (we learn later that they fired him), that he will work for a big U.S. company (we learn later that he illegally paid $3,500 for the documents), and that he has the sponsorship of a local business association (we learn later that he bought their stationery on the street). He is smiling and jovial throughout the interview, trying not to lose face in front of the visa officer.

10:50 A.M.   Up come moms and dads. Dozens of them. The high-tech industry has brought so many Indians to the United States on work visas that legions of Indian parents are setting out to see for themselves what their successful children have made of their lives. I interview 10 sets of parents, all retirees traveling abroad for the first time. More than one couple bless me for issuing their visas.

12:45 P.M.   I speak with a *shilpi*, a stone carver who adorns Hindu temples with images of the gods. The vocabulary he uses to speak about his work has not changed in centuries. Immediately afterward, I speak with a software engineer, whose technical terminology changes every few months. These two workers offer a microcosm of India: a high-tech future and a deep-rooted classical past, right next to each other in the visa line.

1:00 P.M.   Lunch break. I eat at my desk and read e-mails, and then order a few Christmas presents online.

2:04 P.M.   I'm late getting back to my window, and in those few minutes I miss the fraud unit interview nearby with the man buying machinery—an eventful exchange, because the applicant faints and crashes to the floor. From terror? From skipping breakfast? We send him home.

2:35 P.M.   Another applicant is "buying machinery." The cases are almost identical. Visa denied.

2:55 P.M.   We finish 1,200 interviews today. I conduct more than 100 of them, with a refusal rate of 20 percent, average for Chennai. Next I review documents sent to me by work-visa petitioners. I'm trying to determine whether the sponsoring companies are real entities with actual work available, or whether they're just a cover for billking illegal "petition fees" from applicants, who sometimes end up trapped in nonpaying jobs.

4:40 P.M.   I am late for a meeting I'm supposed to lead. We are starting a Virtual Presence Post for Bangalore. A local staff member and I are writing Web pages related to this neighboring city—about visas, cultural events, American citizen services, and business promotion.

5:20 P.M.   I am scheduled to introduce a film, "The Sting," at the Madras Film Society. Having spent my day untangling fraudulent documents and scams, I laugh remembering the confidence tricks in the complicated plot of this movie.

6:15 P.M.   The director of the film society greets me as I arrive, and even though I'm a repeat visitor, he places a garland around my neck. It's made of jasmine and cardamom and smells fabulous, a whiff of an eastern bazaar in the middle of a shabby movie hall. As protocol in India demands, I thank him and immediately take the garland off (it's considered uncouth to keep it on, as if you think you deserve the honor).

8:00 P.M.   The audience clearly loves the convoluted plot of "The Sting," and afterward a movie fan asks me, "Are all classic American films about outlaws?"

9:20 P.M.   The consulate car drops me at home, and I enter a dark house, my family asleep. My husband has left a plate of our cook's remarkable South Indian cooking in the fridge, so I reheat it, open a Kingfisher beer, and eat dinner on the balcony. Outside, a bull and farmer are clip-clopping down the street as SUVs and rickshaws speed past them. I can smell chai, cooking oil, and incense. The bells at the local temple are ringing. At moments like this, visas are just one small part of the Indian landscape.

Kris Fresonke joined the Foreign Service in 2007, and Chennai was her first assignment. She transferred in 2009, accompanied by her husband and two children, to an assignment as a political officer in Ljubljana, Slovenia.

A Day in the Life of ...
A PRINCIPAL OFFICER
CONSULATE RECIFE, BRAZIL
By Diana Page
APRIL 2008

7:45 A.M. The consulate van heads south down Brazil's coastal highway. I'm on a public diplomacy mission to Palmares, a town of 56,000 in the heart of Brazil's old sugar plantations. Our public affairs officer and her Brazilian counterpart are accompanying me on a trip to honor an outstanding public high school and to speak about the upcoming U.S. elections. The consulate in Recife—a city of more than two million and capital of Pernambuco state in the northeast region of Brazil—once downsized almost out of existence, has been revitalized; we now have six FSOs and more than 30 local staff. Getting outside the major cities is fundamental to reaching a broader public, and we're doing more of these trips.

Green cane stalks—potential ethanol—cover the hills along the road to Palmares. Conditions for the seasonal cane cutters are miserable, not that different from the shameful days of slavery, which ended in Brazil in 1888. The U.S. Department of Labor recently finished a survey of child labor in northeast Brazil; working with USAID, the consulate is supporting education campaigns to combat both child labor and trafficking in persons.

10:15 A.M. We reach the high school, which shares space with a technical college. All the corridors are open-air, with covered walkways to shield students from the tropical sun and rain. Hundreds of students fill the walkways and form two lines as the principal comes to meet us. He leads us between the rows of uniformed teenagers, who applaud enthusiastically. The principal tells us that the last diplomat to visit Palmares was the French consul—in 1898!

Just as we reach the auditorium, the mayor and his entourage turn up. A local radio reporter asks the reason for our visit. I say that we heard that these students topped the state educational test scores, and want to recognize their achievement. The mayor has questions about the difficulty of getting a U.S. visa. No matter where we go, no matter what the topic of debate, the visa question arises. Nothing else is as important to most foreigners as access to the United States. The number of applicants at the consulate has doubled in the past two years, and we are short of staff. The wait just for a visitor visa interview has reached two months. I explain this to the mayor, who asks for my card, so he can contact me "just in case." I know this means a phone call soon, and then I'll explain that even as "the consul" I cannot bend U.S. laws and regulations to favor those who feel entitled to special treatment. Actually, I enjoy explaining this aspect of American values, although I don't convert many politicians.

11:00 A.M.   I begin my address to the students by asking if they know any of the candidates running for president of the United States. "Obama!" a young man yells out, and the students clap. Given how little international news coverage is aired on Brazilian TV, it surprises me that these students in rural Brazil follow our primaries. Later, they launch into hard questions, such as whether the U.S. invaded Iraq to secure its oil reserves.

We encourage the students to compete to become one of the 35 "Youth Ambassadors" from Brazil chosen every year to go to the United States for two weeks. Open to low-income, public high school students with a working knowledge of English, good grades, and demonstrated community service, this program brings future leaders into direct contact with Americans, both in Washington, D.C., and small-town American high schools.

1:30 P.M.   Before we leave, the school principal offers us a city tour and talks about the dismal economic prospects for his students. His vision of teaching students new environmentally sustainable technologies is impressive. We decide to nominate him for one of the embassy's international visitor programs in the U.S. for educators.

3:00 P.M.   As our van heads back, my cell phone rings. My office manager asks if I can get to Recife in time to meet the Pernambuco governor before his plane leaves for Brasilia at 5:30. At the ambassador's request, I have been trying to find out if the governor would be available to accept a special invitation to visit the aircraft carrier USS *George Washington* when it passes Recife on its way to Rio de Janeiro for joint exercises with the Brazilian navy. I am to deliver the invitation personally, thus conveying its importance.

5:15 P.M.   We head directly to the airport's executive hangar. But it was the governor who had good news to give me. He's just heard from General Motors that the company will locate a major logistics center in Recife's port facilities. When I tell him about the invitation to fly out to the Navy carrier, he accepts immediately.

6:00 P.M.   I arrive at my official residence, a ninth-floor apartment overlooking the ocean. Ships are anchored off the port, beyond the reef that gave Recife its name more than 400 years ago. The carrier is out too far to see.

Diana Page served as principal officer in Recife from 2005 to 2008, then transferred to Washington, D.C., for an assignment at the State Department's Foreign Press Center. Prior assignments include Buenos Aires, Argentina; Georgetown, Guyana; Mexico City, Mexico (twice); Sarajevo, Bosnia-Herzegovina (on a peace monitoring mission); Santiago, Chile; and Brasilia, Brazil. Before joining the Foreign Service in 1990, she was a Peace Corps Volunteer in Bahia, Brazil. She also spent 15 years as a journalist covering Latin America.

A Day in the Life of ...
AN ECONOMIC OFFICER

EMBASSY DHAKA, BANGLADESH
By Carter Wilbur
APRIL 2007

6:30 A.M.   The first thing I do this morning, like most mornings, is call my wife on her cell phone. For the past few months, Sarah has been living in a village about 30 miles north of Dhaka. She is working on a master's degree in public health through an international nongovernmental organization's university. We both had five months of Bengali-language training before coming to Bangladesh, so she is able to function reasonably well for this field research phase of her program. She comes home on weekends, but we like to keep in touch during the week, too.

7:15 A.M.   After breakfast and a quick scan of the local and U.S. headlines on the Internet, I head off to the embassy. Some days I walk to work (10 to 15 minutes); other days I take the car (15 to 20 minutes in traffic). Regardless of which way I go, I pass crowds of young, colorfully dressed Bangladeshis heading off to jobs in the garment factories.

7:45 A.M.   I check e-mails and cables for anything that may be of general interest or affect any of the issues I cover, which include commercial advocacy on behalf of U.S. companies, as well as environment, science, technology, and health (ESTH) topics. (A fairly small post, Embassy Dhaka does not have a Foreign Commercial Service officer.)

9:00 A.M.   Once a week, we have an "all hands" political/economic section staff meeting in the atrium. Fueled by pots of coffee and strong, sweet tea, American and Bangladeshi staff go around the table giving updates on our issues. I discuss topics both as the ESTH officer and as the commercial officer.

10:00 A.M.   I head out to meet with poultry industry association representatives to discuss the ongoing outbreak of avian influenza. I will visit several poultry farms in the nearby countryside that have reported infections, being careful not to spread infection or contaminate myself. The U.S. government has several programs, mostly through the U.S. Agency for International Development, but also with the Foreign Agricultural Service (FAS) and others, to help the Bangladeshi government contain and manage the outbreak in coordination with the United Nation's Food and Agricultural Organization. It is pretty easy to get cooperation from all sides. The United States benefits, because the faster we stop these outbreaks the less likely they are to get out of control and spread to the United States. Bangladesh benefits, because many residents depend on "backyard" poultry to supplement their income or protein intake. Much of what I learn and observe will be reported back to Washington and to neighboring posts.

1:00 P.M.   Back at the embassy, I work on drafting and revising the Bangladesh portion of the Special 301 Report, an annual global review of how countries are doing in protecting intellectual property rights. Worldwide, copyright piracy is a scourge that costs both American and Bangladeshi industries (music, film, software) millions of dollars a year. Many Bangladeshi musicians have trouble making a living, because their CDs are pirated immediately upon release and sold for less than $2 each. So stopping piracy is not only an economic issue, but key to protecting Bangladeshi culture. I work with the Trademarks and Copyrights Office in Dhaka to try to increase enforcement, but the Bangladeshi government has many other priorities and scarce resources.

4:30 P.M. The official workday ends; I usually leave the office by 5 or 5:30, depending on whom I run into on the way out. I'm throwing a birthday party for my wife over the coming weekend, and many of our friends from the embassy and local community will be there. A lot of the entertainment in Dhaka is self-created: dinners at each other's

Carter Wilbur, center with notepad, at a poultry farm in rural Bangladesh accompanied by an embassy intern, local staff member, and several villagers.

homes or at one of several good restaurants, board-game nights, and sports (tennis, ultimate Frisbee, or running). We enjoy our community here, a mix of Americans from the embassy, expatriates from all over the world, and Bangladeshi friends.

6:00 P.M. After a quick jog in the park across the street from my home, I relax before heading off to a working dinner for visiting U.S. cotton exporters, wearing my commercial officer hat. Bangladesh's garment industry uses a lot of cotton, so the embassy's Trade Center (which serves the basic functions of a Foreign Commercial Service office, but is run by the political/economic section), FAS representative (a Bangladeshi agronomist), and I all work together to facilitate imports from the United States to meet their needs.

9:00 P.M. Bangladeshi dinners tend to start late, and I arrive during mocktail hour (a cocktail hour with juice, tea, and coffee instead of alcohol, since this is a majority-Muslim country), which is followed by a buffet dinner. I learn about global market conditions in the cotton industry and how they may affect Bangladesh's garment industry, and I make new contacts in the shipping, garment, and finance markets.

11:00 P.M. On the ride home, I make notes on what I learned for possible inclusion in an economic report. This was an unusually long day, but a productive one.

Carter Wilber joined the Foreign Service in 2005 as an economic officer. Prior to that, he served at various times as an Army officer, an attorney, and a businessman. His first FS posting was to Dhaka for a rotational assignment as an economic/commercial officer and vice consul. Next he and his wife, Sarah, and their new baby headed to a posting in Lilongwe, Malawi. In 2010, Carter was assigned to the economic section of Embassy Kabul, Afghanistan, an unaccompanied posting.

A Day in the Life of ...
A CONSUL GENERAL

CONSULATE GENERAL VLADIVOSTOK, RUSSIA
By Tom Armbruster
MARCH 2008

6:00 A.M.   I awake on the Number Five Train, *Okean*, which I boarded last night at 7:30 p.m., bound for Khabarovsk from Vladivostok. The birch trees and small settlements that line this stretch of the Trans-Siberian railway come into view. Although this land is still home to some 300 wild tigers and even a few endangered leopards, no wildlife is evident this morning.

6:30 A.M.   After my morning "shower" using the sink in the communal bathroom, the train attendant comes by with *chai*, Russian tea in a glass with a silver holder. The steam fogs the window as we approach Khabarovsk, the second-largest city in the Far East. Just a few kilometers from town, more factories appear, some obviously from the Soviet days that are in disrepair or abandoned, and some just beginning to bustle. Closer still, there are rail cars on neighboring tracks loaded with huge logs bound for wood-processing factories in China.

8:00 A.M.   My Russian assistant and I arrive in Khabarovsk and are met by our driver, who drove from Vladivostok the previous day, an eight-hour trip. From the train station we drive to the Parus Hotel on the banks of the Amur River. At the hotel, I meet the U.S. Marine attaché who has come from Moscow to participate in our first meeting of the morning.

10:00 A.M.   We arrive at the prison, home for many months to an American citizen charged with murder. As usual, we spend the first 30 minutes showing our documents, making frantic phone calls to higher officials, and eventually convincing the Russian security guards that, yes, we have an appointment, and yes, we *will* be seeing the American citizen. With that smoothed over, we hand over magazines and food that prison officials will screen and then pass on to the American.

10:30 A.M.   We are taken to Investigation Cell One, and the American prisoner is ushered into a booth across from us. He looks good and, as in past visits, is informative about prison conditions, interested in news from the outside world, and specific about his few needs and requests. We provide information about the new U.S.-Russia prisoner exchange program and its implications for his case, letting him know that he must decline to appeal the case if he decides to apply for an exchange.

11:30 A.M.   We say goodbye, knowing that we'll be back in a few months but unsure of what he will decide. Ultimately, our job is to inform and provide options. The American prisoner will have to make his own decision.

12:30 P.M.   There are other people involved in the American's case: his lawyers and another U.S. official who has been in Khabarovsk following the case. We meet to compare notes and see if there is anything else we can do to advocate for him.

1:00 P.M. We have lunch in a typical Russian-style restaurant, where they serve *kvass* (lightly fermented beer made from black bread), *blini, borsht*, and caviar, ubiquitous in the Russian Far East.

2:30 P.M. From American citizen services we switch to business development. The Khabarovsk Airport is making a pitch for American freight forwarders to use their airport as a hub for Asian operations. Airport officials argue that costs are lower and logistically, Khabarovsk can serve all of the cities that Seoul, for example, serves. The case is persuasive, and we promise to provide their briefing to the major document and package companies in the United States.

Tom Armbruster and friends ice fishing on the Amur River.

4:00 P.M. Our small group walks along the Amur River with Russian environmentalists. The river's water quality has suffered greatly from contamination by Chinese industries and chemical spills, and Russian nongovernmental organizations want help improving it. Experts from Portland, Oregon, have already provided water monitoring equipment and advice. The river is a beautiful, wide waterway that is frozen over now, but is obviously a great recreational asset in summer. Even in winter, ice fishermen take advantage of its bounty. Just upriver, we can see the museum that will host a poster show we are sponsoring in the spring, a display of U.S. and Soviet war propaganda. We hope that event will allow us to meet some of the surviving Russian World War II heroes.

5:00 P.M. We arrive at a local university to meet with students who are members of the local USAID-sponsored "Jessup team." They will attend the Jessup International Law Moot Court Competition, the world's largest moot court competition, with participants from over 500 law schools in more than 80 countries. They will participate in a mock trial in the United States involving a fictional international law incident. In this case, a tanker with hazardous materials runs aground on an island. Who has juridication? Who is liable? For students living in a city with serious environmental challenges of its own, this is a great exercise. Their rehearsal, in English, is impressive, and I wish them well in America.

6:30 P.M. We take a quick spin around the city's outdoor ice rink. Kids and adults of all ages show why Russians win so many figure skating titles. Some seem more at home on ice than on land. I manage not to fall.

8:00 P.M. We have dinner at the new hockey arena. Unfortunately, there is no game tonight, but the spaghetti is pretty good in the restaurant overlooking the rink. The arena is a great new addition to the city. I go over tomorrow's itinerary: a visit to Komsomolsk-on-Amur, where Boeing is working with the Sukhoi Aircraft company to build a regional jet that will help make Vladivostok and Khabarovsk a little less remote. It's one of the best examples of what the United States and Russia can do when we cooperate, like space cooperation and our combined efforts in World War II. We'll be up early for the drive. Who knows? Maybe we'll spot a tiger on the way.

Tom Armbruster is from El Paso, Texas. He joined the Foreign Service in 1988, and was the U.S. consul general in Vladivostok from 2007 to 2010. Previous postings include Helsinki, Finland; Moscow, Russia; Nuevo Laredo, Mexico; Washington, D.C.; and Dushanbe, Tajikistan, where he was deputy chief of mission. Temporary-duty assignments have included Kabul, Afghanistan, and the U.S. mission to the United Nations in New York City. Following Vladivostok, he moved to New York City for a tour as the diplomat in residence for the New York region. He and his wife, Kathy, have two children.

A Day in the Life of ...
AN ECONOMIC AND COMMERCIAL OFFICER

EMBASSY OUAGADOUGOU, BURKINA FASO
By Pamela Hamblett
OCTOBER 2008

7:00 A.M.   I arrive at the embassy early to answer e-mails that arrived from Washington during the night.

7:30 A.M.   I meet with my three locally employed staff to discuss the day's work plan.

8:00 A.M.   I return to my office to put some finishing touches on a cable. I have not been at my desk for five minutes before the protocol officer calls to say that a last-minute invitation has arrived for an important ceremony that will be attended by the prime minister. Within minutes I am on the way, trying not to watch as the driver negotiates the crowded, chaotic streets of Ouagadougou.

8:45 A.M.   We arrive at the Burkina Faso Tourism Expo. I am greeted by officials who escort me down a red carpet, flanked by 30 horsemen dressed in local garb; somewhere nearby, a brass band plays.

9:30 A.M.   The prime minister arrives, and everyone stands as he enters the plaza. The ceremony is filled with

Women in Dayassemnore, a village in Zoundwogo Province, perform a local dance in honor of the embassy visit.

speeches, songs, and colorful dances; I almost forget the 100-degree heat. After the ceremony, the prime minister invites us to tour the exhibit hall with him. We follow en masse from one exhibit to another. At the insistence of my hosts, I pause to have my picture taken with a terrified fox and a cranky-looking pelican.

Embassy vehicle in the riverbed.

11:15 A.M. Back at the embassy, my development assistant is anxiously waiting. (There is no USAID presence at post, so I oversee development projects here.) We have plans today to visit a small village near the Ghana border to evaluate a potential development project to be funded by the Ambassador's Self-Help Fund. We must complete the 300-kilometer roundtrip before sunset, because embassy policy says we cannot be on the roads outside Ouagadougou after dark due to hazardous driving conditions and banditry on the roads.

1:10 P.M. We rendezvous with our guide at the border town of Po, where the paved road ends and our trek through the bush begins. The guide explains that we will have to cross a few small streams, but adds that since the rainy season is nearly over, this shouldn't pose a problem. As we leave Po, the dirt road quickly becomes a dirt track, which eventually becomes nothing more than a donkey path. At this time of year, the vegetation is over 10 feet tall; it scrapes along the side of the vehicle as we bump ever deeper into the bush.

1:35 P.M. We have no problem negotiating the first two streams, but the third appears to belong in the "small river" category. Although the water is probably not more than a foot deep, the steep banks make me question if anything but a donkey cart has ever traversed this route. Our driver seems nonplussed by the situation as he guides the car down the steep bank and across the river. Things seem to be going well until we reach the opposite shore, which is so steep we slide backwards, the rear tires becoming hopelessly mired in the sandy river bottom. Much to our surprise, our guide calmly pulls out his cell phone and explains our situation to someone on the other end. He reassures us that help will soon arrive and suggests that we proceed on foot.

1:50 P.M. As we walk down the dusty path surrounded by towering fields of millet, I hear drums and singing in the distance. The guide's phone call has alerted the villagers of our arrival, and they want to give us a warm welcome. As we continue along the path, we meet villagers on their way to rescue our vehicle, and soon an informal receiving line forms on the narrow path.

2:00 P.M. We arrive at the village and are invited to sit beneath a large baobab tree. As the meeting begins, one of the elders explains that they need money to dig a well because during the long dry season, they have no water to grow crops and often go hungry for months at a time.

2:45 P.M.   As we hear the details of the villagers' plan, I suddenly feel something land on my right shoulder. Turning my head, I find myself eye-to-eye with a huge black spider with spindly legs and bright green stripes. There is nothing in the world I find as horrifying as spiders, but I fight to keep my composure by telling myself that it just wouldn't do to have a U.S. diplomat jumping up and down screaming like a maniac. So I nonchalantly reach back and calmly flick it off my shoulder, only to have it land on the gentleman next to me! I am still contemplating what to do about the spider when the village chief approaches me holding the traditional gift of a live chicken. I thank him for his gracious gesture, and soon we are on our way back to the spot where we had last seen our car—this time accompanied by the entire village.

3:10 P.M.   When we reach the river, I am relieved to see that the villagers have extricated our SUV from the riverbed, and it is safe and sound on the opposite shore. With the car on the other side, we need to cross the riverbed on foot. So, shoes in one hand and chicken in the other, I carefully wade across the stream, climb into our vehicle, and bid our kind hosts goodbye. On the two-hour return trip I have plenty of time to reflect on this memorable day that began with the prime minister and ended with me barefoot, carrying a live chicken.

Pamela Hamblett is the economic/commercial officer at Embassy Ouagadougou. Before joining the Foreign Service in January 2007, she spent 20 years in public relations in the private sector. Hamblett is a single mother with a teenage daughter.

A Day in the Life of ...
A CULTURAL AFFAIRS OFFICER
EMBASSY DUSHANBE, TAJIKISTAN
By Anne Benjaminson
JULY 2008

7:40 A.M.   Another crazy drive to work. My husband, Greg, who works in the political/economic section, is behind the wheel today. The good part of driving in Dushanbe is the lack of traffic. The bad part is that this seems to encourage people to use the entire road. Miraculously, we arrive in one piece.

8:00 A.M.   I arrive in the public diplomacy section and face a mountain of e-mails. Due to our

Anne Benjaminson congratulates students of the embassy's English Access Microscholarship Program.

nine-hour summer time difference with Washington, messages from my colleagues in D.C. tend to build up overnight. Today, many concern an upcoming visit from The Moth, a New York–based storytelling group, as well as the impending arrival of four Fulbright students from the United States, our largest-ever Fulbright group. I check up on visas for the storytellers and arrival dates for the students, and then rush out for a quick countdown meeting with everyone involved in next week's one-day visit by acting Central Command (CENTCOM) Commander General Martin Dempsey.

Benjaminson (in cap) talking with rural Tajik children at a Youth Enrichment Program camp.

8:30 A.M.   Everyone involved in the visit attends the countdown meeting. I suggest the delegation use downtime to visit the State Antiquities Museum in Dushanbe, which houses the largest Buddha statue remaining in Central Asia. While most Tajiks are Muslim, the country has a rich Buddhist and Zoroastrian past that predates Alexander the Great's arrival here. The embassy received a grant several years ago that helped renovate the Buddha, and it's a highlight for visitors to Tajikistan.

9:30 A.M.   Colleagues from the political section and a visiting officer from Washington join me for a meeting with the prosecutor general's office about the Open World Program. Sponsored by the Library of Congress, Open World is one of our largest exchange programs with Tajikistan. This year, we sent more than 50 Tajik professionals on 10-day visits to the United States. We've been trying to send some of this office's employees to the United States for months, but the prosecutor general hasn't been allowing them to travel. We explain the advantages of the employees' participation, and are pleased when the meeting ends with an assurance that the individuals will be permitted to travel in the fall (which they are).

11:00 A.M.   Our summer intern is heading out to recruit local storytellers to perform with The Moth. We brainstorm about people we know, including a former zookeeper and a piano teacher who told us a great story about playing for opposition soldiers during Tajikistan's civil war. We also decide that our intern should talk to employees of Dushanbe's famous Shah Mansur Bazaar, known as the Green Market, to see if anyone wants to share stories. Tajikistan has a rich oral tradition, and we're looking forward to showcasing it alongside American storytellers.

12:00 P.M.   I'm happy to find pasta sauce made from my recipe on the menu in our cafeteria. I serve on the board of the American Employees Association, and one of our goals has been to teach the cafeteria staff recipes that are popular with Americans. My colleagues seem to be enjoying it.

2:00 P.M.   I chair the selection committee for participants in an upcoming exchange. We always have far more qualified applicants than there are places available, and this program is no exception. As I page through applications from doctors, I'm struck by how few materials and training opportunities are available to them here in Tajikistan. Last winter, many had no power in their hospitals and clinics for months, but they still managed to treat patients and deliver babies. Many professionals have left the country, but those who remain are extremely dedicated to their work despite the immense challenges they face. It feels good to give them a chance to meet colleagues in the United States and learn more about simple preventive health measures that could save lives here.

4:00 P.M.   Local English teachers participating in a three-week training we're sponsoring in Dushanbe drop by the office. They show me a newsletter they've published about their experience, and ask if I can visit their class next week to talk about exchange opportunities for teachers. Their English has improved markedly since they started the program, and their enthusiasm is through the roof.

5:15 P.M.   Time to get some exercise! An officer in our Defense Attaché Office is also an aerobics instructor, and she teaches classes after work several times a week. Even when I'm feeling lazy, it's hard not to go when the class is 50 feet from my office. While I'm in the class, my husband plays soccer outside with embassy colleagues.

6:30 P.M.   Sweaty but happy, we head home and shower and change in time to meet friends for dinner. Expatriates working for nongovernmental organizations comprise our regular group, and we try to have dinner together every Friday night. After dinner we head to the plaza in front of Dushanbe's opera house, which turns into a barbeque and beer garden in the summer. It's a great way to end the day.

Anne Benjaminson, from New York City, joined the Foreign Service as an economic officer in 2004. Her first assignment was a consular position in Budapest, Hungary. From Tajikistan, she moved in 2008 to a job in the Embassy Kabul economic section, followed by a tour in the State Department Economic Bureau, Office of Aviation Negotiations. A graduate of the University of California at Berkeley, she speaks Russian, Hungarian, and Spanish, as well as some Tajik/Dari.

A Day in the Life of ...
AN ECONOMIC/ENVIRONMENT, SCIENCE, TECHNOLOGY, AND HEALTH OFFICER
Embassy Tegucigalpa, Honduras
By Jason McInerney
NOVEMBER 2007

4:45 A.M.   Okay, I'm up. An embassy car will pick me up in 15 minutes. I shower quickly and do a final check of my backpack. I've traded in my suit for cargo pants and a collared shirt, sturdy hiking boots, bug spray, and plenty of socks. Water bottles, earplugs, and a change of clothes complete my gear.

On the way to the Rio Platano Biosphere Reserve.

5:00 A.M.   The doorbell rings and I head out into the fading coolness of early morning. My driver and I are headed to the military side of the international airport. Honduran President Manuel Zelaya has invited all the ambassadors serving in Tegucigalpa to join him on a two-day visit to see his nation's efforts at protecting a remote rain forest. It was a last-minute invitation and our ambassador is unavailable, but Deputy Chief of Mission Jim Williard remembered I'd been trying to arrange a reporting trip to the rain forest. Would I like to go? As an economic officer in charge of environmental issues, I jumped at the chance.

6:00 A.M.   We arrive at the airport. A few of the guests are already there, and many more stream in over the next three hours. There are Cabinet-level officials from the government of Honduras, an assortment of foreign ambassadors or their deputies, and media representatives. I chat with the minister of forestry, learning how population growth and the relentless conversion of forest to pasture and then to farmland puts pressure on protected areas.

9:30 A.M.   The presidential airplane is an old, white C-130 transport plane. Earplugs in hand, I toss my bag onto the luggage pile and board via the rear ramp. Conversation fades as the engines rev up and we lift off. It is impossible to see out the passenger window, so I jot down some notes from earlier discussions and then catch a little sleep.

10:15 A.M.   Bump, bump. It's a good landing, considering the dirt airstrip. We're halfway to our destination. We're on a rarely used military runway, and there are no facilities besides a water truck, a tarp to protect us from the intense sun, and two colorful, ancient buses that will transport us to the other end of the runway. Three helicopters appear over the horizon. Two more helicopters appear later, and all five will make multiple trips, shuttling us to the jungle.

1:30 P.M.   We jump onto an ancient Huey helicopter and take off. The "RPM Limit" warning light flashes red for most of the flight. I try to ignore it and focus on the scenery. Flying at low altitude, we can see farmland transition to forest, though the forest contains several permanent-looking, and illegal, logging settlements. We land, hop out, and head to camp.

2:05 P.M.   This rain forest is not what I expected. For one thing, we're fairly high up, so it's warm but not hot. There are pine trees here alongside their subtropical cousins, and no triple canopy in sight. I leave my backpack on an old army cot in one of the large green canvas tents and head to the lunch tent. We're all hungry and dig into the meal of rice and chicken. I meet a German from a nongovernmental organization who has spent many months meeting with residents of the illegal logging communities inside the forest, with government officials, and with other NGOs. He's an expert and a great source of information.

Jason McInerney after crossing the Platano River.

3:30 P.M.   The guests are getting restless. Finally, President Zelaya arrives via helicopter and greets us in turn. Tomorrow, the military will lead us on a hike through the rain forest. Today, improbably, we are treated to a PowerPoint presentation, set up inside an army tent, showcasing how the Honduran Army patrols the jungle and protects it from illegal loggers. It is a monumental task, especially for a country this poor. Nevertheless, the deforestation rate is comparatively low for Central America, so the military presence is having some effect. During the presentation I jot down notes from the conversations I had during lunch. Back at the embassy, I will write a report on what I've learned.

6:30 P.M.   I trade in my notebook for a flashlight and descend a dark, muddy trail. Dinner is being served in a tent near the river. Colorful lights ring the dinner tent, lending a festive atmosphere slightly at odds with the remainder of the excursion. Although the focus of this trip is the rainforest, I am also responsible for covering the Honduran energy sector, and value the opportunity to meet and speak with the newly appointed energy minister after dinner. Later, I meet the Japanese deputy chief of mission and several high-ranking Honduran military officers.

10:45 P.M.   A Honduran band sings folk songs inside the dinner tent. President Zelaya and a few members of his Cabinet join them. It is not for show; Zelaya is from Olancho, cowboy country, and he knows the songs by heart. Slowly the guests begin to trickle back to their tents. One logistical casualty of this hastily planned trip was sleeping bags. There are only a few, and they go to the president and his entourage. The night air is cold, so I use my spare clothes and mosquito net as blankets. Other guests, similarly without sleeping bags, grumble about the cold as I drift off to sleep.

After serving in the U.S. Air Force, Jason McInerney joined the Foreign Service in 2003. He has served in Naha, Japan; Tegucigalpa, Honduras; Washington, D.C.; and San Jose, Costa Rica. He and his wife, Miluska, have two children.

A Day in the Life of ...
AN OFFICE MANAGEMENT SPECIALIST

EMBASSY STOCKHOLM, SWEDEN
By Lynn C. Stapleton
NOVEMBER 2008

7:00 A.M. I like to get in early, so that I can get situated and get a handle on the day before the phone calls start, new e-mails jam the inbox, and new tasks send me off in multiple directions. I flash my badge and make my way through the various checkpoints to enter the embassy. I stop to collect the mail and newspapers for the political and economic sections, and check my personal mailbox.

We only get mail when the huge diplomatic pouches arrive; sometimes twice a week, sometimes every other week. I disarm the alarms for our floor, put my lunch in the refrigerator (our cafeteria is being renovated) and turn on the printers.

7:15 A.M. I sit down to work my way through unclassified e-mails, which include embassy business and meeting requests and confirmations from Swedish government officials, usually from the Foreign Ministry. Then I go through the classified e-mails, a much smaller number, and move on to incoming cables. These include messages from the State Department

Lynn Stapleton (right) greets a Swedish participant at the embassy's EU presidency torch-passing event.

directing us to "démarche" (inform) key Swedish players about the U.S. position on various issues, including recent events; or to request that Stockholm take specific actions in alliance with the United States. Cables may also include requests for information on local events or demographics. Other cables of interest, but which require no action on our part, are those from far-flung U.S. embassies back to the department reporting on their activities. These make for interesting reading, but I have to be careful not to get too caught up in them.

I add the "action" cables (those that require action and a response) to a spreadsheet and bring them to the attention of the responsible officers. The volume of cables is quite large. The responses that we generate inform the decisions that our government will make on specific courses of action. We add value by being the local eyes and ears that can give context to events. Even in countries that may not be on most Americans' radar, events unfold that have far-reaching implications for American interests.

8:30 A.M. My colleagues start arriving, new tasks are assigned, and the phone starts ringing. Sweden is gearing up to assume the European Union presidency. The political counselor has just returned from the "torch passing" in Prague, where

France has handed over the presidency to the Czech Republic. Sweden is now a part of the "troika"—past, present, and future presidents. Today we have a high-level visitor from Washington, is here to help us prepare; we anticipate a lot of VIP visitors and an increasing number of instructions from the State Department.

9:00 A.M. The visitor leaves for meetings with our contacts at the Swedish Ministry of Foreign Affairs, meetings that I have been arranging over the past four weeks. I manage the flow of information about the additional short-term staff we are requesting to assist us with the increasing work flow to come during Sweden's E.U. presidency—a variety of folks from graduate student interns to contract State Department retirees. I update my spreadsheet tracking upcoming staff housing needs.

11:30 A.M. Two nurses from the health unit have started a 30-minute lunchtime "no-matter-the-weather" walk in a beautiful area next to a large park. We pass

Lynn Stapleton in her Stockholm office.

the Japanese, Finnish, Turkish, and British embassies as we proceed down the wooded path to the water. We walk briskly as we discuss our unfolding days. The Swedish nurses always give me good information on things to do in Stockholm.

12:00 P.M. Lunch is followed by a staff meeting with the political and economic section officers, the political and economic counselors, and our four-member Swedish staff. We are fortunate to be able to draw on a lot of local expertise here, and it helps that most Swedes are fluent in English.

3:00 P.M. I finally receive a response to a historical question I have been researching for the political counselor regarding the existence of a long-forgotten agreement between the United States and Sweden. I was asked to locate a copy of the agreement and have been in touch with various presidential libraries in the United States and with the Library of Congress. The document in question has been discovered in Washington, D.C., and a generous State Department librarian has agreed to take a drive to retrieve it for me. Her e-mail, with the document attached, is a welcome sight after months of research. I share this with the political counselor and draw up a memorandum for the deputy chief of mission, who will then instruct us on how to use this new information in upcoming meetings with the Swedish government.

5:00 P.M. I ride the public bus home. It is crowded with deaf students from the school at the end of the bus line. We make our way along busy Strandvagen, which follows the harbor in central Stockholm, a daily sight that I enjoy. Twenty minutes later I arrive at my apartment. My husband, Tom, and I walk to the indoor farmer's market to wander the food stalls and collect food for dinner.

10:00 P.M.   I am tired after another full day. Every day is different. I enjoy reading a Swedish design book—a newfound interest—before heading to bed.

Lynn Stapleton joined the Foreign Service in 2008. Stockholm is her first post. She received a B.S. degree in economics from the University of California, and A.S. degrees in medical technology and court reporting. Prior to joining the Foreign Service, she worked as a freelance court reporter with a specialty in medical/technical expert litigation, in Virginia, California, London, and Buenos Aires. She and her husband, Tom, a retired Morgan Stanley executive, have four grown children in the United States.

A Day in the Life of ...
A COUNSELOR FOR PUBLIC AFFAIRS

EMBASSY NOUAKCHOTT, MAURITANIA
By Heather Carlin Fabrikant
JANUARY 2009

8:00 A.M.   I'm weaving in and out of Nouakchott traffic. Roads, where they exist, are slender and crowded by sand. Goats and donkeys jostle with cars and humans for the right to transit. Today is the second anniversary of Saddam Hussein's death, and flyers announcing the public screening of a documentary celebrating his life hang all around the city. The sun blares through my dirty windshield as I find my way east past the Congressional Palace on the way to work. It is in this building, with its green spires and majestically futuristic look, that President Sidi Ould Cheikh Abdallahi was held captive for several months this fall. Abdallahi—Mauritania's first democratically elected president—was deposed on August 6, 2008, just hours after I arrived in the country for my first assignment as a U.S. diplomat. Ever since then, life has been a whirlwind, and today will be no exception.

8:12 A.M.   I call the security officer to confirm the details of a rumored protest over the current situation between Israel and Hamas in the Gaza Strip. We have a professor of English in town from the United States, and protests like yesterday's— the most violent the country has ever seen—will prevent her

Lunch at Nouakchott English Center with, left to right, English teachers Jack and Bah, Cultural Affairs Assistant Babaly Sy, English Language Fellow Jordan Early, Peace Corps Volunteer Angela Coffee, and English teacher Boubacar Kane.

Nouakchott artists' portraits of Barack Obama.

from conducting her lectures at the Teacher Training College for the second day in a row. Mauritania is the only Islamic republic that has diplomatic relations with Israel, and its diverse population is insisting that the military junta cut these ties. I learn that more than 300 students have already congregated at the college, and that we must cancel today's lecture. By tapping into the English-teaching network, which includes the Peace Corps and local universities, we piece together a "Plan B" for our scholar.

9:15 A.M.   During our weekly section head meeting, I thank the security office and remind the whole team about the 11 a.m. meeting to discuss our plans for an event marking the inauguration of Barack Obama, just two weeks away.

9:30 A.M.   As acting consular officer while the regular consular officer is on vacation, I draft a "Warden Message" to the American community in Mauritania, warning them to avoid politically dangerous areas during these protest days.

10:15 A.M.   I bring Mauritanian novelist Bios Diallo to a meeting with our chargé d'affaires. Diallo, a writer and journalist with the national television network, is here to discuss his role as moderator for our inauguration event panel discussion.

11:05 A.M.   I meet with embassy volunteers to plan our inauguration event. President-elect Barack Obama is very popular here; local artists have painted bright oil canvases of him wearing traditional clothing. For the big night, we are turning the embassy's tennis court into an amphitheater. The swearing-in will be projected live in Arabic, French, and English. The chargé will give a speech, which I must draft, focusing on peaceful democratic transitions. The information management, community liaison, and security officers walk through the court envisioning all the details, from how to route the cables to where to lay out the traditional pillows and mattresses, the seats for our guests.

12:30 P.M.   I meet 10 local English teachers at the nearby Nouakchott English Center for a lunch in honor of our visiting professor. We feast on *tiébou djenn*, a popular West African dish made of marinated fish with eggplant, sweet potatoes, cabbage, fish eggs, and squash, spread over fried rice. Over the traditional mint tea, I stand and briefly thank the director and teachers for their continued support as a partner of our Access Scholarship program, which teaches English to 80 young Mauritanians annually. As one cup of tea soon becomes the ceremonial three, I ask the teachers their views on potential presidential candidates (all believe that the coup perpetrator, General Mohamed Ould Abdel Aziz, is a—or *the*—likely presidential candidate), the protests ("unprecedented"), and whether diplomatic relations with Israel will be cut ("never").

2:30 P.M.   The information officer sends his draft of the daily media summary report for editing. Since it is a widely read publication, we are careful to ensure that the correct meaning of the original French/Arabic is accurately conveyed in the English summary.

4:45 P.M.   I receive a call from the chargé advising me to be on call in the evening in the event that Mauritania breaks its ties with Israel, as this could cause larger local assemblies and the need for an official embassy response.

5:00 P.M.   Mauritanian hip-hop legend Mohamed Lemine is waiting for me in the lobby to discuss the possibility of collaborating with our visiting jazz and hip-hop artist for a jam session in honor of Black History Month.

5:30 P.M.   I call our English Language Fellow to check on our visitor's meeting with the nascent Mauritanian English Teacher's Association. I put the finishing touches on two proposals I have been working on, and send press coverage back to Washington of last week's embassy-hosted reception for five new Mauritanian recipients of Fulbright grants.

7:00 P.M.   In Mauritania, there are few restaurants where one can have wine with dinner. We choose *L'Endroit* (The Place), which is rustic and calm, with a sand floor and a tent roof. The menu is on a large blackboard that is carried to your table. Here I join our visitor, the English Language Fellow, and several Peace Corps Volunteers for a conversation about our homes in the United States, Mauritanian politics, and the challenges of teaching English. It is important for me to keep a finger on the pulse on English-language activities and maintain contacts in the field. Plus, I enjoy their company.

9:00 P.M.   I arrive home at the end of a long day and, as I have, countless times since my arrival, marvel at my luck to be serving my country in such interesting times. I nestle in bed with a book as the now-familiar sound of goats bleating nearby lulls me to sleep.

Heather Carlin Fahrikant joined the Foreign Service in 2008, after a career in refugee affairs that took her to West and Central Africa, the Middle East, and Central America. A native of Washington, D.C., she received a B.A. in world history from the University of Pennsylvania and an M.A. in international relations from the Graduate Institute of International Studies in Geneva, Switzerland. Nouakchott was her first Foreign Service post.

A Day in the Life of ...
A CONSULAR OFFICER

CONSULATE GENERAL HO CHI MINH CITY, VIETNAM
By James P. Du Vernay
JANUARY 2009

5:15 A.M.   As I step out into the cool, predawn Saigon morning, a stream of motorbikes and honking city buses is already trickling by. A motorbike taxi driver calls out to me, but I decline and begin my daily run before a torrent of vehicles clogs the streets in earnest. Down at Van Hoa City Park, next to the former presidential palace, I carefully maneuver around the far more numerous tai chi and badminton enthusiasts.

7:45 A.M. During the five-minute walk from my downtown apartment to the consulate, my gaze meets that of the friendly vendor selling beverages from her sidewalk café. While she prepares a glass of fresh-squeezed orange juice for me, I also buy two ears of steamed corn on the cob from another vendor selling from a basket mounted on his bicycle. The corn and juice together cost less than one dollar.

8:00 A.M. The workday begins calmly, as local and American staff steadily arrive. After five months here, I have grown accustomed to the challenging daily schedule of an entry-level consular officer at a post experiencing surging demand for both immigrant (IV) and nonimmigrant (NIV) visas, as well as American Citizen Services. We start by responding to e-mails and reopening complicated cases from the previous day. Officers prepare themselves for the sustained mental effort required for hours of careful interviewing. Meanwhile, out in the waiting areas, hundreds of applicants complete intake procedures and wait anxiously for their visa interviews.

8:30 A.M. All officers are "on the line," and the consulate hums with the energy of more than a dozen simultaneous interviews. In the NIV section, we are in the middle of high season for student visas. Each day we meet wave after wave of hopeful young people striving to prove their student intent and qualifications. Consular officers must quickly discern which applicants are truly interested in pursuing education and which are simply looking for an easy way to enter the United States. Drawing on an understanding of the local context combined with knowledge of the complexities of immigration law, we have about three minutes to accurately adjudicate each case.

12:00 P.M. The NIV section completes its final interviews for the morning. We work through a full appointment schedule, and every officer has interviewed at least 50 applicants so far today; one officer interviewed 76. Although many applicants did not qualify for a visa, I met a few impressive and interesting ones, such as the student returning to Dartmouth on full scholarship and the scientist accepted to a Ph.D. program in the United States. More interviews await us in the afternoon, but for now, I relax over lunch at a local restaurant with the four local staff members I supervise. I am one of only two Westerners in the place. We enjoy the local specialties, including beef noodle soup, spring rolls, and fresh fruit shakes. Throughout the meal, my colleagues patiently indulge my desire to practice speaking Vietnamese.

1:00 P.M. Back at my desk, I review notes and add the last changes to a PowerPoint presentation. The NIV section chief has asked me and two other entry-level officers to talk about student visas at a large college fair this afternoon.

2:00 P.M. Reflecting the burgeoning interest in U.S. higher education, more than 400 students and parents crowd the standing-room-only reception hall for our presentation. After our prepared remarks, we respond to questions for 15 minutes before we have to leave. I feel like a celebrity as we determinedly move toward the exit through the crowd of people requesting business cards and trying to ask more questions.

3:00 P.M. We return to the consulate and join other officers in processing the day's remaining immigrant visa cases. Working at a consulate that ranks as one of the busiest immigrant visa-processing posts in the world, we pull together as a team to manage the heavy workload. IV work differs considerably from NIV work; cases usually require a careful examination of complicated paperwork and investigative analysis of claimed relationships, especially at a high-fraud post. Some cases can take months or even years from start to finish.

6:00 P.M. I head over to the consul general's residence with a few colleagues for a reception. In support of a visit by members of Congress, the consulate is hosting a reception so members of the delegation can meet important contacts from the local government and business community. Assigned the role of greeter, I welcome guests, help them check in, and introduce them to the consul general. Later, my job is to mingle, speaking with guests about their work and ours, as well as generally ensure they enjoy the reception. During the evening, I meet several interesting contacts and have the opportunity to discuss politics with a congressman from Illinois.

9:00 P.M. I return to the consulate, and then head home. Once again, I feel thankful to post's housing board for assigning me to an apartment so close by. At home, I complete an assignment for my Vietnamese class the next morning. Like most days, this particular Thursday has proven long and full. Between the visa interviews, the college fair, and the reception, I spoke to hundreds of local people. Although tired, I look forward to another day on the visa trail. First, however, it is time for a much-needed good night's rest.

James Du Vernay joined the Foreign Service in 2007 as a management officer. Ho Chi Minh was his first post, followed by a tour as staff aide to the U.S. ambassador to Pakistan at Embassy Islamabad. He continues to enjoy the early morning fitness routine he developed in Ho Chi Minh City. He speaks French, Spanish, Italian, Vietnamese, and Urdu. James grew up in New Jersey and is single.

A Day in the Life of ...
A COMMUNITY LIAISON OFFICE COORDINATOR
EMBASSY BUENOS AIRES, ARGENTINA
By Candace Brasseur
JANUARY 2009

6:30 A.M. I can't sleep anymore; it's a Friday and today's workload is on my mind. The Community Liaison Office is coordinating a volunteer day trip to the *banco de alimentos*, a Buenos Aires food bank, scheduled for Monday in honor of

Martin Luther King Jr. Day. We are also finalizing details for Tuesday's inaugural celebration event, which we are coordinating with the public affairs office. The embassy community will have the opportunity to view Barack Obama's swearing-in on a large screen. We are also scheduling the entertainment and spouse events for an upcoming 30-member congressional delegation (CODEL) visit.

7:15 A.M.   I sip a *café con leche* while reviewing and finalizing the proposed CODEL schedule on my home computer, so it will be all set when I arrive at work.

8:20 A.M.   I commence the 40-minute walk to the embassy, passing by the cemetery where Evita Peron was laid to rest, countless museums, and parks. The beauty of this city never ceases to amaze me, especially early in the morning on a summer day. I am surrounded by dog walkers, each with at least 10 dogs. I'm part of the pack, and I love it.

9:00 A.M.   I arrive at the embassy, feeling fortunate to be an American as I pass the huge line of people hoping for visas to our country. No matter the public opinion of the United States, our line remains longer than at any other embassy in the city.

9:05 A.M.   At my computer, I'm ready to e-mail the CODEL schedule to the control officer. I press the button to turn on the computer. Nothing. Not a good sign.

9:20 A.M.   My co-community liaison office coordinator (CLO), Mary Henry, is off on Fridays, so I am using her desk while the information management officer works on my computer. I recall how kind and welcoming Mary was when I first arrived one year ago. Little did I know I would end up as co-CLO with her. I could not ask for a better partner; she never fails to impress me with her acumen, patience, practicality, and sense of humor—a must for this job.

10:15 A.M.   The computer is fixed. I do a quick e-mail scan: responses for the upcoming events, responses to a childcare survey, requests and questions from both spouses and employees, and the latest CODEL update. Apparently everything has changed overnight: all that planning I thought was done is now null and void.

12:00 P.M.   I am on the phone with the CODEL control officer, discussing the changes and requests in detail. I send an e-mail to see if a spouse tour of the ambassador's residence can be scheduled for Saturday. I make phone calls and begin to iron out the adjustments. It starts to come together again.

1:30 P.M.   Someone from maintenance enters, mentioning the inaugural event and *un problema*. The words I catch are "*pantalla*" and "*cortada*." (Please don't tell me there is a tear in the projection screen!) We go down to check it out. It turns out to be the curtain (*cortina, not cortada*) in front of the screen that is torn. We can push it aside; crisis averted.

2:00 P.M.   Back at my desk, there is an e-mail frenzy regarding the difficulties of scheduling a tour on Saturday. Local staff does not work on Saturdays; should we pay them overtime? I assure everyone that the tour does not have to take place on Saturday.

3:00 P.M. The revised CODEL schedule is almost done. A newcomer stops by, asking whether he should live in the city or the suburbs with his wife and two teenage children. We discuss the pros and cons of both, and I send off some e-mails connecting him with families with high schoolers from both locations.

Embassy Buenos Aires hosts inauguration celebration, January 20, 2009.

4:00 P.M. Fire drill. While we're all walking to the ambassador's garden to be accounted for, an FSO mentions that the move to this post has been the toughest transition for his family. I make a mental note to call his wife next week to see if we can help. On the way back to the office, I see locals sipping *mate* in the park. They certainly have the right idea, always taking the time to enjoy life.

5:00 P.M. The embassy officially closes at 5:45 p.m., but I'll be here longer, as usual. A few more people come by with requests.

6:00 P.M. The building is empty and I spend the next two hours responding to e-mails without interruption. One is from a former CLO for Embassy Beijing. The first line reads, "It ain't easy being CLO." I laugh: only another CLO can truly appreciate all we do. Then, right before I am about to leave, I open a farewell message from Secretary Condoleezza Rice thanking all State Department employees for their service. I feel proud to be part of this community serving the U.S. overseas.

8:40 P.M. I make it home just in time for dinner and my sons' evening ritual of watching old "MacGyver" episodes dubbed in Spanish. If only I could run the CLO office with just a paper clip, a battery, and a stick of chewing gum.

Candace Brasseur is married to Lieutenant Commander Michael Brasseur, U.S. Navy, who was deployed to the Middle East for one year. She stayed on in Argentina as CLO during his absence, and subsequently transitioned to the position of assistant cultural affairs officer as part of the Professional Associates Program. Although her family has moved eight times in seven years, this was her first overseas job. She has an MFA in film from Columbia University. In Buenos Aires, she conducted dissertation research on the English Access Microscholarship Program in Argentina, working toward a Ph.D. from New York University. She passed the FSOT and QEP and will be taking the oral assessment in 2011.

A Day in the Life of...
A POLITICAL OFFICER

EMBASSY KINSHASA, DEMOCRATIC REPUBLIC OF THE CONGO
By Tracy Whittington
JUNE 2007

7:00 A.M.   I slept poorly under the mosquito net, so I wake up disoriented and late. For a moment, I can't remember where I am—but definitely not home in Kinshasa. I'm in a hotel in the eastern Congolese city of Bukavu, where I've traveled with our human rights desk officer, Stuart, for a reporting trip. Thankfully, we're in a better hotel than my last visit, where I woke covered in flea bites, had one bucket of cold water for showering and flushing the toilet, and suffered from food poisoning the whole time.

8:00 A.M.   I meet Stuart for breakfast at the hotel restaurant overlooking Lake Kivu. It's much cooler here than in Kinshasa, but there's always the nagging awareness that Kivu contains massive methane deposits, so any earthquake will send it all to the surface and kill everyone within a hundred-mile radius. But how likely is that, really? I concentrate on the fresh passion fruit on my plate instead.

8:30 A.M.   Our guest, Murhabazi, arrives. (Like many Congolese, he uses just one name.) One of our best contacts in eastern Congo and a former participant in the State Department International Visitor Program, he runs an integration center for rescued child soldiers. Over breakfast, he updates us on the latest political developments in the province.

9:30 A.M.   After breakfast, we load a few boxes of donated clothes into his truck. He asks if we have any books. Bukavu, population 450,000, has no libraries and no bookstores.

10:00 A.M.   A United Nations colleague takes us to the local prison. Our mission is to investigate the conditions leading to the recent escape of 20 prisoners. The prison director meets us outside the crumbling building, along with a military intelligence officer and a parade of lesser officials ready to accompany us.

11:00 A.M.   We inspect dirt-floored cells and take photos of rotting ceilings. We make notes about the lack of medicine and the malnourished prisoners cooking scraps of food in fires on the ground in the courtyard. We ask to see the cells used by military intelligence, thinking we'll be rebuffed; but the prison director throws open the doors to the closet-sized spaces.

11:30 A.M.   Far from hiding the miserable human rights situation, the prison director leads us from violation to violation. He begs us for money to feed the prisoners and tells us they escaped when he let them out into the hills to look for food.

11:45 A.M.   I call a colleague at the embassy to tell her about a possible candidate for an Ambassador's Self-Help Fund grant—a nongovernmental organization that works with the prisoners in the jail to grow crops.

12:00 P.M.   The prison director ends the tour by showing us the cell where he, his wife, and his six kids live. We buy the kids soda from a street vendor and give our e-mail addresses to the surrounding officials, who will later write and ask for money, jobs, and visas.

1:00 P.M.   Back at the hotel, we meet with a well-respected local pastor to discuss human rights violations in the surrounding villages. He shows us graphic photos of recent machete massacres by rebels.

2:30 P.M.   We drive high into the hills surrounding the city to Panzi Clinic, which specializes in treatment for the victims of Congo's sexual violence epidemic. Dr. Mukwege explains the progress made in treatment of fistulas, a condition caused in many countries by early childbearing, but here in the DRC caused by violent sexual assaults. His hospital has pioneered the medical training for this treatment, the grim benefit of an endless supply of patients.

3:30 P.M.   Dr. Mukwege takes us on a tour of the hospital, ending at a grassy field where more than 200 patients have gathered. A few tell their tales. One elderly woman saw her sons tortured and killed before she herself was raped. She starts sobbing, and I wrap my arms around her and want to cry myself. Dr. Mukwege tells them we will record their stories for the Human Rights Report, an annual report to Congress from the State Department tracking human rights around the world. They sing to us in Swahili, and we walk away silent and overwhelmed.

5:30 P.M.   We drive back to the hotel as the day ends. In Central Africa, days and nights are equal length, and the sun always sets by 6 p.m. As we're bounced through rutted roads, we hold on and discuss reporting cables to draft after the visit.

5:45 P.M.   I take a few minutes to call home and check in with my husband in Kinshasa, 1,000 miles away.

6:00 P.M.   We host a dinner with local journalists and the United Nations press officer to discuss the recent murder of a Congolese journalist. Stuart wants to know if the journalists are afraid for their own safety. The conversation, entirely in French, grows lively and lasts through the meal.

8:00 P.M.   I end the day with a quick walk through the hotel gardens to Lake Kivu. Lights twinkle in Rwanda on the other side of the lake, and I try to reconcile the paradise-like location with its endemic human destruction. I dangle my toes in the water, but know better than to swim. The lake is reportedly filled with parasitic worms that cause bilharzia, a chronic illness in the region.

9:00 P.M.   Back in my room, I read an American news magazine that does not mention Congo and think about ways to get my reporting to people in the State Department who can affect policy.

9:30 P.M.   I fall asleep and have nightmares.

Tracy Whittington, formerly Tracy Naber, joined the Foreign Service in 2005. Her first posting was to Kinshasa as a political officer responsible for the human rights portfolio. In 2007, she transferred to a consular position at Consulate General

Montreal. In 2009, she moved on to the State Department Operations Center in Washington, D.C., and heads next (in 2011) to a public diplomacy assignment in Bolivia. Before joining the Foreign Service, Tracy was a Presidential Management Fellow, and then a Civil Service employee at the Defense Information Systems Agency in Denver. She grew up in Wyoming and worked in Colorado for 10 years. She met her husband in A-100 class. They married in 2009, so she is now part of a tandem couple.

A Day in the Life of ...
A POLITICAL OFFICER AND ARMS CONTROL DELEGATE

U.S. MISSION TO THE ORGANIZATION FOR SECURITY AND COOPERATION IN EUROPE
VIENNA, AUSTRIA
By Hugh Neighbour
JANUARY 2009

7:00 A.M. I review the Austrian newspaper over breakfast and then catch the public bus to the U.S. OSCE Mission.

7:55 A.M. At the office, I check for instructions from Washington.

8:30 A.M. I attend the daily senior staff meeting run by the deputy chief of mission.

8:40 A.M. I make calls and send e-mails to OSCE delegates from Germany, Czech Republic, France, and Turkey. Then I consult with other members of the U.S. arms control delegation (USDel)—military officers, a senior political appointee from the Defense Department, and State Department FSOs and Civil Service arms control experts. Some are from Washington on rotations usually lasting three to six weeks, and some are in Vienna long term. Many have substantially more arms control experience than I do. I fine-tune a U.S. statement for today's meeting.

9:10 A.M. En route to the Hofburg, the historic Austro-Hungarian former palace where OSCE meetings are held, we discuss who does what today.

9:30 A.M. Today's meeting is the weekly Joint Consultative Group (JCG), dealing with implementation of the 30-nation Conventional Armed Forces in Europe (CFE) Treaty, considered a cornerstone of European security. First we proceed to the coffee bar. In multilateral diplomacy, success usually comes out of agreements brokered before formal meetings. USDel members talk to several delegations, not just about today's meeting, but also about upcoming issues. I speak to four country representatives separately, and in a discussion with my Russian counterpart, tell him, "You know Russia was in contravention of the CFE Treaty again, and one of the NATO allies will call you out today. The United States will support that ally." The Russian replies, "I know, thanks. My reply will defend Russia's interests."

10:00 A.M.   I still feel a burst of pride as I take the seat behind the microphone at the United States nameplate, despite almost two years here. The rest of the USDel is within whisper or note-passing range. The Czech chairman convenes the meeting precisely on time.

10:15 A.M.   Germany reports that Russia has refused a CFE inspection, and urges Russia to meet its treaty obligations. As planned, Britain, France, the U.S., Turkey, Portugal, Italy, Romania, and others back Germany.

10:45 A.M.   Russia countercharges that the U.S. and NATO demand Russian actions in exchange for only promises. After quick consultations within the USDel, I reply to Russia, as do several allies. Debate ensues.

11:30 A.M.   The meeting adjourned, we return to the coffee bar. Members of USDel thank helpful allies and listen to concerns, each of us speaking to several other delegations. We're prepping for tomorrow's weekly 56-country Forum for Security Cooperation (FSC). Working group topics include small arms and light weapons, and cyber security. My Russian counterpart and I review issues for tomorrow's FSC. We wryly observe we'll cross swords over the situation in Georgia.

12:00 P.M.   To follow up on yesterday's 34-country meeting on the Open Skies Treaty (that governs unarmed aerial surveillance flights), I chat with the Belarusian delegate. He succeeded me as chairman of Open Skies meetings. USDel experts are working to update the treaty to allow new sensor technology. Open Skies is a success; everyone wants to keep it contributing to openness, transparency, and cooperation.

12:15 P.M.   Another American and I have a lunch meeting with delegates from Estonia, Latvia, and Lithuania in a coffee bar near the Hofburg. The Baltic States are not in CFE, so they want a readout on this morning. The conversation turns to cyber security, a big concern for Estonia.

2:00 P.M.   Back at the office, we go over impressions of today's meetings, including how working groups went. I make a quick phone call to Washington and answer e-mails.

3:00 P.M.   I arrive at Canada's mission for what we call "tea," but is actually the weekly meeting of 26 NATO arms control delegations. With only allies present, some of the toughest discussions all week forge complementary and/or common approaches on open issues.

4:30 P.M.   Back at the U.S. mission, I approve a cable report on today's JCG meeting (written up by one of the "rotators" from Washington) and prepare for tomorrow's meetings. Then I make calls to the Georgian and British delegations.

7:30 P.M.   I leave the office and head home.

10:00 P.M.   I do a final check of the BlackBerry; happily, no need to phone Washington.

Hugh Neighbour joined the Foreign Service in 1982 after service as an officer in the U.S. Navy. A career political officer, he was posted to Panama, Britain, Australia, Germany, Sweden, Bolivia, the Fiji Islands, Austria, and Washington, D.C. He retired from the Foreign Service in late 2010 to pursue other opportunities.

A Day in the Life of ...
A FOREIGN SERVICE SPOUSE

EMBASSY SAN JOSE, COSTA RICA
By Kelly Schierman
AUGUST 2008

4:30 A.M.   The neighborhood roosters have started crowing even earlier than usual today. Probably not a bad thing, because the school bus is supposed to come at 6:15, I think. The bus driver called last week to confirm the time, but we did not have a language in common, so I'm not sure what he said. I do know that school starts at 7:20. We groggily haul ourselves out of bed and, while my husband gets ready for work, I get our three boys ready for their first day of school in a new country.

6:15 A.M.   The bus does not come.

6:30 A.M.   The bus does not come.

7:00 A.M.   I call the bus driver, who seems to be promising to be at our home in five minutes.

7:30 A.M.   The bus still does not come. I call the school; the receptionist promises to contact the bus driver.

7:32 A.M.   Since I speak hardly any Spanish—although learning is quickly becoming a top priority—I use my best

The Schierman kids waiting for the school bus in San Jose.

gringa Spanish to ask the guard of our *condominio* (gated community) to call a taxi for me. He tries. "Sorry, Señora, I cannot get an outside line on this phone." Hmmm, I hope there's never a fire.

7:40 A.M.   Back inside, I start to call a taxi and suffer a moment of panic: there are no street addresses in Costa Rica. How do I tell the taxi driver where to come? I find instructions to my house given to me by the embassy for just such an occurrence. They are in English. I decide to call the school again.

7:45 A.M.   I am interrupted by the embassy driver who has come to pick up my husband for work, except that my husband has already left with a colleague. I ask the driver to call a taxi company for me. He tries, but the phone numbers I have do not work. He has the consul general in the van with him, so he is eager to be off. I reluctantly wave goodbye.

8:00 A.M.   I call the school again and am informed that my children's bus has already arrived, obviously without my children. I take a deep breath, repeat the Costa Rican national mantra—"*Pura vida*" (literal meaning: "pure life;" practical meaning: "hang loose")—and remind myself that I will laugh about this later.

8:05 A.M.   I finally find a working number for a taxi company and somehow make myself understood; the driver shows up five minutes later in a battered 1972

Ford Pinto. No seat belts. My oldest son takes one look at the car and asks how I know it's a taxi and not someone who is going to kidnap us. Frankly, I don't have a good answer. But we all get in the car anyway, and I show the driver my carefully copied directions to school.

8:30 A.M.   We arrive at school, where my two oldest boys get out and bravely wave good-bye. Then, in my best Spanish, I try to give Alejandro, the taxi driver and my new best friend, directions to the preschool for my youngest son. We make it.

8:50 A.M.   Alejandro brings me home. I have a very strong cup of coffee and kick myself repeatedly for not having studied Spanish before now.

9:30 A.M.   My embassy sponsor takes me to the grocery store. I purchase something that I hope is sour cream, but it's in a plastic bag and the picture is not instructive. I wonder how the stroganoff will turn out this evening.

12:00 P.M.   Alejandro and I pick up Benjamin at preschool.

12:30 P.M.   Benjamin and I eat lunch, and I make him take a nap. I lie down with him, of course.

2:00 P.M.   We wake up when the roofers arrive. The eight-foot-square skylight in my living room leaks gallons; I've been using the trash can from our welcome kit to catch the water.

2:15 P.M.   It sounds like the roofers have dropped a ladder—or possibly an elephant—on the roof. There may be more leaks to fix now.

3:00 P.M.   The bus driver calls. He has my children, but can't find my house. The afternoon rains have started and the noise on my tin roof makes it sound like I am inside a jet engine, so I can't hear (or understand) a thing he's saying. A bilingual student finally takes my instructions; I pray they will be relayed to the driver.

3:15 P.M.   The bus pulls up and drops off my children.

5:30 P.M.   My husband arrives home from work and, after a hurried supper (it was sour cream, after all), Alejandro picks me up and takes me to the school for "Welcome to School" night. The meeting is conducted largely in Spanish, so I understand very little, but it's nice to meet some of the parents.

7:30 P.M.   An embassy family drops me off at a friend's house after the meeting. My husband and I served with Jeanne and David in Tel Aviv eight years ago, and it's good to see them again. Jeanne is the community liaison office coordinator and is hosting a community service project in her home. I have a wonderful time helping out, visiting with Jeanne and David, and meeting others from the embassy community.

9:00 P.M.   Jeanne takes me home, and I look forward to tomorrow morning. Who knows? The bus might even show up!

Kelly Schierman is a former State Department technical specialist who has lived in Frankfurt, Tel Aviv, Jakarta, and Zagreb. She currently calls Costa Rica home, and is frantically studying Spanish with her three boys and husband, Gary, who works in the IT section of Embassy San Jose. You can read more of her adventures on her blog, "The Embassy Wife," at http://kellyarmstrong.pnn.com.

A Day in the Life of ...
A POLITICAL/ECONOMIC SECTION CHIEF

EMBASSY CONAKRY, GUINEA
By Shannon Nagy Cazeau
DECEMBER 2008

1:30 A.M.   Two days before Christmas, I awake suddenly from a deep sleep, scrambling for the ringing phone. A political party contact apologizes for disturbing me, and then tells me that President Lansana Conté, who has ruled Guinea for more than 24 years, died a few hours ago. He says that an official communiqué will soon be broadcast over national television.

1:40 A.M.   My phone rings again. It is our defense attaché (DATT). He, too, apologizes for waking me, though he hasn't, and tells me this may be the real thing. I move to the living room so as not to wake my husband and three-year-old daughter, who crawled into bed with us sometime during the night. I call the chargé d'affaires, and we discuss whether or not we believe this is the real deal. Conté was in poor physical condition, and we have been hearing rumors of his death for months. We agree that a pending official government declaration warrants a call to the Operations Center. She asks me to wake up our deputy chief of mission and public affairs officer.

2:00 A.M.   President Conté's death is official. The head of parliament announces that he will be assuming the presidency, as provided for in the constitution. The DATT reports that various military elements are starting to mobilize. My husband comes out of the bedroom, and I tell him what is going on. Having grown up in Haiti, he is a veteran of coups. He, too, recognizes that sleep is over for the night and settles in at the computer.

2:30 A.M.   Phone calls continue back and forth for the next few hours as embassy officers exchange information received from contacts.

5:40 A.M.   The DATT reports that 30 military troops seized control of the national radio/television station, which is located directly across the street from the embassy.

6:00 A.M.   An embassy announcement via radio (we all have hand-held radios at home for such emergencies) informs us that only section heads and key reporting officers should come to work. My daughter and 20-month-old son are just waking up. "Did Santa come yet?" my daughter asks. She is disappointed at the answer, but then excited because Dad is going to stay home with her for the day instead of going to work. He also works at the embassy.

6:45 A.M.   On my way to work, I see dozens of heavily armed soldiers milling in front of the radio station. Jubilant, they ignore my car as I pass by. When I walk into the embassy, a wave of heat assaults me. Our central air conditioning system broke for good a few days earlier, and it is now approaching 100 degrees in our offices.

7:30 A.M.   The military has seized control of the government and suspended the constitution. My staff, two locally employed Guineans, who were told not to come to work, start calling in with information as they get it. The economic officer and the Presidential Management Fellow make it to the embassy safely, just as the military across the street starts blocking traffic. I task our Fellow with keeping a crisis log of events and ask our economic officer to focus on information gathering. I will write the reports and make sure the front office is getting what it needs.

8:00 A.M.   I work quickly to gather information and get a first report to the State Department. I send it out just as Washington is starting to wake up. We have an Emergency Action Committee meeting to evaluate the security situation. Our management officer informs me that the generator at my residence is almost out of fuel, and he is not sure they will be able to deliver any today. I call my husband and advise him to turn off the generator for a while so that we will have electricity tonight. There is now a tank across the street at the radio station. We continue to receive reports of various military movements, but no reports of injuries or deaths.

12:30 P.M.   The now-displaced government condemns the coup and maintains that they are still in power.

1:45 P.M.   More than a hundred heavily armed soldiers have installed themselves across the street at the radio station.

2:00 P.M.   We are focused on information gathering and reporting back to the State Department as quickly as possible. We are all dripping sweat because of the 100-degree heat. I spend the day writing, talking on the phone, and going from meeting to meeting. There will be time for analysis of what this all means for our foreign policy later, once things have settled down. As calm descends on the city, I am told that the embassy was able to deliver fuel to my residence after all.

6:00 P.M.   I send in my last report of the day to the department, saying that the coup appears to have been successful, and that a military officer has proclaimed himself the country's new president. I drive home, escorted by an armored embassy vehicle.

6:30 P.M.   Oblivious to my exhaustion, my kids are excited to see me. They chat animatedly about Christmas and the upcoming visit from Santa Claus, now less than two days away. I am glad that I wrapped presents over the weekend and don't have to do it tonight. My phone continues to ring throughout the evening as information pours in. I keep a notebook handy.

8:30 P.M.   I put the kids to bed and then go to bed myself. I fall asleep almost as soon as my head hits the pillow. Tomorrow is Christmas Eve. It is going to be a busy day.

Shannon Nagy Cazeau, a political officer, joined the Foreign Service in 2001. Prior to Guinea, she served in the Philippines and Benin. She is married and has two young children. As an Eligible Family Member, her husband has found work at each of their assignments. In Conakry, he worked as a small-grants project coordinator.

A Day in the Life of ...
A POLITICAL OFFICER/
STABILIZATION COORDINATOR

HAITI STABILIZATION INITIATIVE
EMBASSY PORT-AU-PRINCE, HAITI
By David Becker

MAY 2009

6:20 A.M.   An embassy armored shuttle pulls into my driveway, and I start another day as the counselor for stabilization for Embassy Port-au-Prince. The embassy opens at 7, and we try to end the day at 3:30, because the traffic on the few usable roads is horrendous later in the day. My colleagues comment on the "Cité Soleil uniform"—cargo pants, open-necked shirt and, most importantly, hiking boots—that I wear on days when I am going into that famous slum. Cité Soleil sits on a former mangrove swamp about six inches above sea level, so dug latrines are few and far between. There is a pervasive smell in some parts, and you watch your step.

After the 2004 U.S. military intervention, followed by the 11,000-soldier United Nations peacekeeping force (MINUSTAH), politically connected gangs were still running Cité Soleil until, about 18 months ago, gang-led kidnappings and killings forced the government to ask MINUSTAH troops to intervene. After nearly two months of running gun battles, the U.N. force controlled the zone, but had no way to peacefully solidify the gains. Enter the Haiti Stabilization Initiative (HSI). The Defense Department funded a team of dedicated State officers, working with the U.S. Agency for International Development and other international donors in an attempt to use "guns to butter," full-spectrum, civilian-led stabilization efforts to reopen Cité Soleil to international assistance after years of isolation.

8:00 A.M.   Before jumping into our armored Suburban, I say hello to the Red Zone team of local guards and Rob, our designated security officer for this trip. Rob worked in Haiti for a nongovernmental organization and speaks Creole, which means he can listen to the comments of the crowds and warn us if there's trouble as we check on projects.

8:30 A.M.   Accompanied by our USAID team member, we meet Matt, a former Peace Corps Haiti Volunteer who represents the International Organization for Migration (IOM), an intergovernmental agency that we fund by passing Defense Department funds to USAID, which then puts the funds into an existing contract with IOM for small projects in the hot zones of Haiti. Convoluted? Yes, but it was the quickest way to get things going after intervention. Speed is our mantra—we live or die on our ability to quickly reinforce positive events.

We tour a marketplace that IOM built as part of a deal to get vendors off the streets, especially off the main highway that we are building. The new road goes through the middle of the slum, opening it to economic activity, and making it harder for gangs to control access. The mayor supported the market project, because he hopes to collect municipal revenues from the vendors when things improve.

9:00 A.M. Matt introduces us to a group of local residents from the neighborhood, and we ask them about projects. We support volunteer community leaders who have asked for small projects because, after years of quasi-war, Cité Soleil has no real grassroots leaders or local organizations left except the gangs. We encourage people

Becker hearing from local leaders in Cité Soleil.

who will set a different example and indirectly face down those still-dangerous groups. Successful projects fill neighbors with pride and reestablish ties of trust as they dig ditches and lay paving together. In the poorest slum in a country with 80-percent unemployment, the cash wages from the projects don't hurt either.

9:45 A.M. We move on to inspect the U.N. base in central Cité Soleil, which is being rebuilt with HSI funds as a Haitian police station. All police were run out of Cité Soleil in 2004, so this project is highly symbolic for rebuilding the trust and cooperation of the population. But it took almost a year to get agreements and a proper title to the land, so we are behind schedule. Months ago we negotiated an understanding that MINUSTAH forces will not pull out immediately after police arrive, but they are impatient for police to take over the security duties. HSI is MINUSTAH's "exit strategy" for the neighborhood and, in a sense, for the country. Cité Soleil is a bellwether for Haiti.

11:00 A.M. We check in with the local police commander, who has only 30 officers for the entire zone. He has a special advantage, however, because he is from Cité Soleil. The security side of our guns-to-butter approach is to train local police who can work with the same community organizations we are slowly building on the development side. This is a change in Haitian National Police philosophy and style, and our partners in the narcotics affairs section have their work cut out to sell the idea. But this police commander gets it intuitively, and he walks where few others will. We fund a couple of U.S. police advisers on site to help this transition.

1:00 P.M. I have lunch with Dr. Herns Marcelin, a Haitian social anthropologist working at the University of Miami who studies violence. We hired him originally for surveys in Cité Soleil to measure progress and changes in the environment. We then enticed him into working there with the nascent Community Forum, an association of community groups trying to set overall priorities and reach out to donors with a plan for the future. This is not easy in an environment where 30 percent of the population does not have enough to eat each day, and where 80 percent cannot read or write. We back this organization discreetly—it must be a true community effort, not a U.S. government effort.

2:30 P.M.   Back at the office, I make some calls to businessmen we are courting for scholarship funds for a vocational school in Cité Soleil that we resuscitated from near-bankruptcy. I take a look at a draft of the weekly e-mail newsletter that we send to a wide audience. We do not do a lot of traditional reporting, but we keep interested parties informed through these regular messages.

Becker (center) giving interviews to Haitian media at new Cité Soleil police station.

3:00 P.M.   I meet with the embassy press attaché to brief her on our latest communications products. Because the image of a violent, chaotic Cité is burned into the minds of most Haitians, we produce everything from posters to a French-language newsletter extolling the changes. She tells me that the HSI documentary, produced in-house, is nearly ready and will reach 50 small Haitian cable TV stations. It may well be aired at midnight, but it will still be better than nothing, and it costs very little.

3:30 P.M.   Back on the shuttle, I read e-mails on my BlackBerry and make calls to set up meetings for the next day. Tonight I will attend a reception at the Canadian embassy, which will give me a chance to talk up the program. Maybe I can get them to contribute.

Postscript: A year after the January 2010 earthquake: Cité Soleil was relatively unscathed by the earthquake—tin shacks do not collapse easily, and can be propped back up again when they do. HSI-funded police stations, roads, bridges, schools, and canals all survived. The real threat was from about 300 gang members who escaped from the damaged national prison. So far, the newly strengthened community has resisted efforts to return to gang control. Police and U.N. forces remain. NGOs that could not work in Cité Soleil prior to 2008 are still present.

David Becker is a political officer who joined the Foreign Service in 1983. He has spent 15 years in countries with serious internal and external conflicts, including El Salvador, Honduras, Guatemala, Colombia, and Ethiopia. He has also served in Burkina Faso, Washington, D.C., and Miami (where he was detailed to a telecommunications company), and spent two years as political adviser to the combatant commander of the U.S. Transportation Command, in rural Illinois. In August 2010, he transferred to a position as a research fellow at the Center for Complex Operations at the National Defense University in Washington, D.C., where he looks at lessons learned from Haiti and other low-budget, civilian-led stabilization efforts. He is married with three daughters.

A Day in the Life of ...
A PUBLIC AFFAIRS OFFICER

PROVINCIAL RECONSTRUCTION TEAM
BAGHDAD, IRAQ
By Michael McClellan
MAY 2007

6:00 A.M.   Ka-boom! The Baghdad morning wake-up call—one lone rocket lands near the Republican Palace, home of Embassy Baghdad. It doesn't happen every day, but often enough to keep us edgy, as we never know where it will hit. I get out of bed, grab a quick shower, and get ready to head over to the DFAC (military-speak for dining facility) for some breakfast.

6:30 A.M.   I don my body armor and Kevlar helmet, although it will probably hit 120 degrees today. There have been plenty of incoming rockets and mortars lately, so I don't go anywhere without them.

7:30 A.M.   After a stop at my office in the palace to check one of my four e-mail accounts, I suit up again for the 15-minute walk to the Provincial Reconstruction Team (PRT) office near the main gate of the Green Zone, the five-square-mile heavily fortified area also known as the International Zone. Army Sergeant Steven Undercoffer and I usually walk over together, both for the camaraderie and the protection he affords me. He's a trained medic and fully armed, so when I'm with Steve, I feel safe. As we walk along the road—peppered with shrapnel holes, small craters, and the detritus of past shellings—we're reminded constantly of the danger. Always looking ahead, we've mapped out every foot of this road; if the incoming alarm goes off, we've got anywhere from three to six seconds to get under cover, so we're always alert and ready to dive as we discuss the day's schedule.

8:00 A.M.   After a quick staff meeting at the PRT office with my colleagues from State, the military, Department of Justice, and USAID, we're off to work. Since this is a Thursday, we have our weekly meeting with the press office of the Baghdad Provincial Council.

10:00 A.M.   Four heavily armored Humvees (High Mobility Multipurpose Wheeled Vehicles) are lined up on the street with a half-dozen U.S. soldiers milling around waiting for us. Inside one of the Hummers, a young GI reads his Bible; in another, the driver reads a comic book. My life depends on these young men and women, who are less than half my age. After a briefing on the route we will take, we load up, put on goggles and Nomex fire gloves (like the NASCAR drivers wear!), buckle in, and head off into the "Red Zone" (the rest of Iraq, everything outside the Green Zone) for our meeting.

Driving through the crowded streets of Baghdad, I see children playing in the parks, old men sipping tea under trees, busy cafés, and women shopping. I yearn to walk those streets freely, as I did in Sana'a and Cairo, chatting with the people and enjoying the local culture; but this is a war zone, and public diplomacy here is different.

As we pull up to the provincial council building, the Humvees line up for a quick exit. Soldiers get out first to scan the area and the surrounding buildings and then, finally, give me the "all clear" to get out of the vehicle. Stepping out, I scan the hundreds of balconies overlooking our parking lot, thinking how easy it would be for a sniper to take a shot at me, and then quickly hurry into the building. I am one of only two civilians in this group, and I'm unarmed—so it's easy to tell who's being protected.

11:00 A.M.   Our counterparts are waiting in the press office. We doff our helmets and body armor, sweet tea is served, everyone exchanges pleasantries, and we get down to business. Long meetings are not a smart idea in a war zone; you don't want to give your enemies time to identify your location and move in an attack squad. We wrap it all up in under 45 minutes.

Public diplomacy is normally thought of as "telling America's story to the world," but that is not our objective here. Instead, we focus on capacity-building: helping the Iraqis to tell their own story, open up lines of communication between the public and their elected leaders, and understand the values of openness, free speech, transparency, and good governance. My Iraqi-American colleague checks on the council newspaper we're funding to see how they're doing with production and content. We talk to the spokesman about training in Jordan for council spokespersons from across Iraq. We also discuss good-news stories that the council should publicize to further the shared goal of generating faith and confidence among Iraqis in their elected leaders and the democratic process. Rather than tout what the United States is doing, we focus on the Iraqi government's accomplishments.

11:45 A.M.   The sergeant guarding the door sticks his head inside and tells me it's time to go. He's in charge. I've been in the Foreign Service longer than he's been alive, but he's the boss of the convoy, so we quickly end the meeting, pile on the body armor and helmets, and head for the Hummers. I am grateful for a quick and uneventful drive back to the Green Zone.

12:00 P.M.   We return to the DFAC for a heavy lunch, designed for young men in their 20s who burn 10,000 calories a day in the desert heat, and then back to the embassy office in the palace. The day is only half over, yet I'm already exhausted from the heat, the body armor, and the general tension under which we all work.

2:00 P.M.   My position is split between the PRT and the embassy public affairs office, so I spend most afternoons at the embassy. As the primary grants officer, I've got grant proposals to review. We use them to encourage the work of Iraqi nongovernmental organizations. Payments are invariably made in cash. I drive over to the Al-Rashid Hotel to meet a grant recipient and give her a bag with roughly $30,000 in it. Her armed bodyguard accompanies her to the meeting, but knowing she is risking her life to do TV programs promoting dialogue between religious groups strengthens my resolve to help her and the many other Iraqis who are determined to rebuild their country. After hot tea and Turkish coffee, the meeting concludes and she is on her way, the bag of cash tucked discreetly in her purse.

4:00 P.M.   A couple incoming rockets hit right outside the palace, knocking a chunk out of the fountain. We dive under our desks, wait for the "all clear," and

Michael McClellan (standing, center) with a Baghdad security detail, also known as "the public diplomacy team."

then get back to work. I pick up the large piece of shrapnel I found near the palace that I keep on my desk as a reminder of the inherent dangers in this work. It came from the mortar shell that hit a bus, killing three people and injuring several others. There is no diplomatic immunity in a war zone. Diplomacy in a war zone is not the usual Foreign Service assignment, but such assignments are becoming increasingly common. We have a vital role to play in conflict zones and, personally, my year in Baghdad has been the most rewarding assignment of my career. Would I do it again? Absolutely. The friendships I have made, the work we have accomplished, and the heroism and dedication of the Iraqi people I see up close mean far more to me than the extra pay and perks that such assignments bring.

6:00 P.M.   I head over to the dining facility for dinner with one of the civilian contractors working for the State Department. After loading up our trays and taking seats that are away from the windows and doors, we discuss initiatives we hope to undertake with the PRTs in other parts of Iraq. Thankfully, dinner passes without incident.

8:00 P.M.   Wrapping up work, it's time to head back to my "hooch" (trailer), where I relax with some Armed Forces Network TV and a book. *Inshallah*, the night will pass quietly.

Michael McClellan is from Bowling Green, Kentucky. A member of the Senior Foreign Service, he joined in 1984, serving first with the U.S. Information Agency and then with the State Department as a public diplomacy officer. He has served in Sana'a, Yemen; Cairo, Egypt; Moscow, Russia; Pristina, Kosovo; Hamburg, Germany; Dublin, Ireland; and Addis Ababa; Ethiopia. In 2009, he transferred to a posting as diplomat in residence at the University of Michigan's Gerald R. Ford School of Public Policy.

A Day in the Life of ...
A COMMERCIAL COUNSELOR,
FOREIGN COMMERCIAL SERVICE

EMBASSY MEXICO CITY, MEXICO
By Michael Lally
JANUARY 2008

8:00 A.M.   My embassy colleagues and I attend a small breakfast with members of the American and Mexican business community, hosted by our deputy chief of mission. The intimate setting allows private-sector representatives to share their perspective on the global economic downturn and suggest measures the embassy can advocate with the Mexican government to alleviate the effects of the market slowdown. Our countries' economies are highly integrated, with more than $1 billion in trade every day.

9:15 A.M.   The commercial officer, locally employed staff, and I meet in a local hotel lobby to brief a representative of a medium-sized American manufacturer, in town for discussions with potential distributors. We have scheduled a good set of meetings for the firm through our Gold Key program, a kind of matchmaking service we offer for American businesses seeking local partners. We brief the firm's representative on negotiating techniques with Mexican firms and provide advice on how to attract Mexican customers. The company rep tells us of decreasing orders in the U.S., making his Mexico trip very important. Our staff will accompany him to the meetings.

10:00 A.M.   We host a pre-event press briefing for 20 U.S. and Mexican reporters on a major infrastructure conference we are hosting to highlight hundreds of road, power, environmental, and other construction projects announced by the Mexican government. Our marketing plan is going well, with more than 200 American and Mexican firms signed up and more than 400 one-on-one meetings scheduled. Our public diplomacy colleagues ensure that the right reporters are in the room so our effort can be picked up in the next news cycle. On the way back to the embassy we hit ferocious traffic, but that gives me time to catch up on e-mail on my BlackBerry. Our minister counselor writes from the U.S. that she just spoke to about 100 U.S. firms at an event organized by our Trenton, New Jersey, office; we will need to follow up with several of the firms on potential sales in Mexico.

11:00 A.M.   I join the ambassador for a meeting with the CEO of a Midwestern firm encountering problems with the local authorities near its manufacturing facility in central Mexico. We agree that the best solution is to send a letter from the ambassador to a key local decision-maker, followed by phone calls to potential advocates. Given the fragile situation at the plant, the ambassador wants the letter to go out today, so I write the draft during a break between meetings.

12:00 P.M.   Our office hosts a webinar on Mexican water and wastewater projects to be tendered in 2009-2010. Several of our U.S. Export Assistance Centers (we have 100 offices in the United States) helped market the event to American firms in their communities. Thanks to them, and to webinar technology, more than 70 American firms join the program from their desktops. Our consulates in Guadalajara, Monterrey, and Tijuana join the conversation and offer advice on the specifics of their local markets and water projects to be bid on in their territories.

Michael Lally leads a February 2008 press briefing on the U.S.-Mexican commercial relationship for Mexican business journalists.

2:00 P.M.   My colleagues and I have lunch with contacts from the Presidencia (Mexican White House) to go over plans for the infrastructure event. We coordinate the attendance of several Mexican ministers and discuss plans to sign several agreements to fund feasibility studies in the airport, environmental, and power sectors. This funding, provided by the U.S. Trade and Development Agency, helps give U.S. firms the inside track on potential tenders as these projects are fully developed.

3:30 P.M.   We provide a business briefing to visitors from 10 Texas companies, in town on a trade mission. After the overview, we field a series of questions on the exchange rate, negotiating contracts, security, and other topics. The ambassador, a native Texan, drops by to shake hands and give advice on doing business in Mexico.

4:30 P.M.   We hold a countdown conference call to go over details for next month's visit by Secretary of Commerce Carlos Gutierrez. Our office is working with the security and advance teams to generate a minute-by-minute schedule of his events, as well as a summary of key business issues to raise with his Mexican counterparts.

5:30 P.M.   A U.S. telecommunications firm requests an urgent meeting to discuss its complicated regulatory situation in the Mexican market. Working with our partners in the economic section, we provide the latest updates on personnel changes in the relevant Mexican ministry and discuss the points to make at our next meeting with the new Mexican department head.

6:30 P.M.   A local Mexican industry association hosts a reception focused on the IT sector. The room is rich with firms seeking new technology for the telecommunications, manufacturing, and automotive industries. I chat with several of them to learn about their business and find out what they need from potential U.S. suppliers. As I drive home, I estimate that we made five to seven good contacts with solid Mexican companies.

8:00 P.M.   Dinner with the family at home is followed by homework with my five-year-old daughter (now learning her ABCs). My wife, who works in the embassy's consular section, updates me on home and office matters.

9:00 P.M.   I quickly read the U.S. and Mexican business press, including on-line publications, and then review my calendar to prepare for tomorrow's agenda.
10:00 P.M.   Lights out.

Michael A. Lally, who is from the Bronx, N.Y., joined the Foreign Service in 1993. His previous assignments include Kyiv, Ukraine; Almaty, Kazakhstan; Baku, Azerbaijan; and Philadelphia, Pennsylvania. From Mexico City, he transferred to Ankara, Turkey, where he is the commercial counselor. He and his wife, whom he met in Kyiv, have a daughter. Michael was recently promoted to the Senior Foreign Service.

A Day in the Life of ...
A REGIONAL MEDICAL OFFICER

EMBASSY MOSCOW, RUSSIA
By Larry Padget
FEBRUARY 2009

7:45 A.M.   I finish my morning workout while, at home, my children head out of the door in the darkness and snow to get on the school bus. We live on the Embassy Moscow compound. The gym is fantastic and close by, so I've got no excuse not to work out.

8:30 A.M.   I make the 30-second commute from my apartment to the office and quickly check e-mail. I usually answer 50 or more e-mails every day on a wide range of both administrative and medical questions. Moscow has one of the State Department's largest medical units in the world. As the regional medical officer (RMO) here, I am the primary care provider for the Foreign Service community across several countries (Russia, Belarus, and Finland); the in-house medical consultant for the executive offices of the embassies I cover; an arbitrator of finances for the medical program; and a disaster medicine doctor ready to evacuate a critical patient when necessary. Primarily, though, I am a family doctor—a personal physician. I make house calls, sometimes thousands of miles away, so I spend quite a bit of time in dodgy airports.

9:00 A.M.   A few days a week, I attend morning meetings, but today I'm in the clinic. The only provider in the clinic today during walk-in hours, I see five patients. Today is the usual mix of diarrhea, upper respiratory infections, and back pain.

11:00 A.M.   Today I'm seeing two pregnant patients and filling out the paperwork that will enable them to return to the U.S. to deliver in their hometowns. Typical clinic visits include general medicine patients (diabetes, hypertension, etc.), newborn and pediatric screening exams, and routine physicals. Moscow in the winter can be tough, so I often see depression or illness related to the short, cold days and long nights.

12:00 P.M. I walk back to my apartment to pick up my wife, Alison. We take the Metro to the Bolshoi Theater to pick up tickets for a ballet, "Don Quixote." Cultural life here is great; there is always something wonderful to attend.

1:00 P.M. Back at the office, I am now an administrator, running a self-insured company, making recommendations to the senior diplomatic staff in the embassy, going to meetings, and managing money. I am also scheduling travel to three of the posts I cover: St. Petersburg, Yekaterinburg, and Minsk.

Dr. Larry Padget and his family in Red Square.

3:00 P.M. I'm off to a local hospital to check in with an embassy employee who was admitted yesterday and may need additional surgery. A significant part of my job here is overseeing the medical safety of my patients. Is it safe for the patient to have surgery at post? Where is the best place with the best care? Do I need to call in a medical evacuation team? If so, to where?

As a Foreign Service doctor, I am also a medical sociologist. The Chinese, Mongolian, Finnish, Russian, and Belarusian medical systems with which I've worked have often been vastly different from what I knew in the United States. Other countries have different ideas about what causes illnesses and how they should be treated, or not treated. RMOs practice a unique type of diplomacy. I try to get the best evidence-based care for my patients while being sensitive to local medical practices. Conflicts and negotiations over a patient's privacy, individual patients' rights, and care expectations often do occur, but all the physicians I've met abroad care deeply about their patients.

6:00 P.M. I head home to my family and dinner.

8:00 P.M. The phone rings. It is the Marine security guard. I need to quickly go down to the medical unit and put a splint on a patient with a probable fracture. I will put a cast on her in a few days, once the swelling goes down.

10:00 P.M. Off to bed.

Dr. Larry Padget joined the Foreign Service in 2006. In addition to Moscow, he has served in Beijing, China, and in the Office of Medical Services in Washington, D.C. He is a graduate of Southwestern Medical School in Dallas, Texas. Before joining the State Department, he was a U.S. naval flight surgeon and had a private family practice near Austin for 10 years. His wife, Alison, has a Ph.D. in nutrition and won the 2007 Secretary of State Award for volunteerism abroad. They have two young children.

A Day in the Life of ...
A PUBLIC AFFAIRS OFFICER
CONSULATE GENERAL GUANGZHOU, CHINA
By Ed Dunn
JANUARY 2009

7:00 A.M.   I jump into a cab to head to work early, aiming to beat Guangzhou's notoriously unpredictable traffic. Balancing my coffee mug so I don't spill on my suit coat, I contemplate how the only thing you have control over here in China is waking up and putting on your clothes—after that, it's all a crap shoot. Guangzhou is my second Foreign Service posting, and no two days are alike in this job. As the assistant public affairs officer, I work for the public affairs officer (PAO) alongside seven locally engaged staff to implement a wide-ranging public diplomacy program. There are only two Americans in the section, so we don't split the information officer and cultural affairs officer portfolios; here, we get to do both jobs. I am also the Virtual Presence Post officer for Nanning. In our small section—housed in the centrally located Garden Hotel—entry-level officers gain exposure to the whole range of public diplomacy activities in a dynamic environment in an important region of China.

7:30 A.M.   I arrive at the office and turn on the TV to check out the international and local news while sipping coffee and scanning cables.

8:00 A.M.   It's time to go over press guidance from Washington and respond to any program-related e-mails that came in overnight. For the first of many times during the day, I check the consulate Web site. I ask our webmaster to make content updates that reflect program priorities. All the while, the TV news continues in the background so that if something breaks I'll know.

9:00 A.M.   Today we have an International Information Program (IIP) speaker in town, so the PAO and I split the day's events. He will sit in on the morning presentation, and I will move forward with our upcoming U.S. presidential inauguration event planning. While the PAO is with the speaker, I work to update the past week's activities in an online database so we can quantify our work and let Washington know what we're doing. For better or worse, metrics have a direct impact on whether we're going to get funding for more projects.

10:00 A.M.   I contact another entry-level officer (we're called ELOs) from the consular section to discuss the Weekly Forum presentation that she gave last week, a talk called "American Cuisine as a Facet of U.S. Culture."

10:15 A.M.   Public affairs work requires maintaining momentum on numerous programs concurrently, so I check in with our local staff member in charge of alumni programs to discuss a proposal to fund a series of professional development seminars for the upcoming fiscal year.

11:00 A.M.   My Virtual Presence Post officer hat on, I touch base with the embassy's transformational diplomacy officer in Beijing (she's the officer in charge of the VPP program) to provide an update on the past month's activities in the Nanning-Liuzhou-Guilin corridor in Guangxi province.

12:15 P.M.   I speedwalk to my favorite local Hunan hole-in-the-wall to pick up a quick six-*renminbi* (87 cents) lunch-box loaded with red peppers.

12:30 P.M.   Over lunch in the PAO's office, we discuss our upcoming outreach trips to the other provinces of the consular district—Fujian, Guangxi, and Hainan—and make plans to take upcoming speakers (who will talk about financial regulation, environmental law, minority rights, and American music culture) on the road with us. We briefly discuss follow-up on our pending English MicroAccess Scholarship proposal and local reporting on the consul general's press roundtable on the U.S. presidential transition and inauguration. The coverage has been good, and we want to provide clips to Embassy Beijing for the front office and the public affairs office.

1:00 P.M.   Checking in with our local staff on today's print media, I start summarizing Chinese-language news stories into English for the weekly *Southern Window* media reaction, which gives U.S. officials in Beijing and Washington a snapshot of South China media views on issues of importance to the U.S. government.

3:00 P.M.   I call a local caterer about next week's inauguration event to try to persuade them to provide food for twice as many people for the same budget. I gather relevant materials in English and Chinese to distribute at the upcoming events.

3:30 P.M.   Heading into our multipurpose room, I'm pleased to see a group of about 30 students, academics, and media contacts assembled for the Weekly Forum. Continuing our series on American culture, I give a talk on "Popular TV in the U.S.—Who's Watching What?"

5:10 P.M.   I scan the America.gov site and print out portions of new IIP e-journals to read in anticipation of our upcoming Weekly Forum series on Black History Month. Then I check next week's public affairs schedule so nothing slips through the cracks.

5:45 P.M.   I pack up to try to beat the traffic home, always to no avail. Instead of waiting for a cab only to sit in traffic (Guangzhou, a city of more than 11 million people, has serious rush-hour traffic), I decide on a tasty Turkish dinner at the Sultan, one of the many fantastic restaurants within a block of the Garden Hotel.

7:00 P.M.   Having avoided the worst of the rush-hour traffic, I hop in a cab and head back to the Consulate Tower apartment building in Shamian Island, a historic area that used to be home to many foreign trading houses. Many entry-level officers live in apartments here.

7:45 P.M.   I sit down to watch the news and check my BlackBerry for the umpteenth time. Once Washington wakes up, the e-mails start flying in.

9:00 P.M.   I get on the Internet to check personal e-mail and Facebook to see what other FS friends are up to around the world. Picking up the BlackBerry for the last time today (honestly), I check tomorrow's schedule.

Ed Dunn, who was born and raised in Edina, Minnesota, received his bachelor's degree from Emory University and a graduate certificate from the Johns Hopkins SAIS-Nanjing Center before joining the Foreign Service in 2006. Previous assignments include Islamabad, Pakistan, and Washington, D.C., where he served as a watch officer in the Bureau of Intelligence and Research and, most recently, as a Pakistan desk officer. Ed is single.

A Day in the Life of ...
A CONSULAR OFFICER

CONSULATE GENERAL GUANGZHOU, CHINA
By Esther Pan Sloane
JULY 2008

7:00 A.M. The sun peeks blearily from behind the usual gray scrim of fog and pollution as I walk through the grounds of the White Swan Hotel, next to the Consulate Tower apartment building where many Americans assigned to ConGen Guangzhou live. The Pearl River is slow-moving and thick with debris and other mysterious items, but between the tugboats plying its waters I can see the heads of intrepid swimmers. Local people have swum in the river for years and are not going to let industrial contaminants or the mud-colored water stop them.

7:10 A.M. I step into the White Swan shuttle, which will take me the 45 minutes across town to work, thinking about the day ahead. I have to respond to a few adoptive parents who want to know why their cases have not been processed more quickly. Many American couples coming to China to adopt are in their 40s or older, and most have tried to have children for years. As the adoption process gets longer—currently three years and counting, from handing in the initial application to bringing home a baby—nerves understandably get frayed.

8:00 A.M. At the office, I nod to the guards, walk through the quiet main room, and sit down at my computer. A desperate father has written an eloquent letter asking us to squeeze in an appointment so he can bring his infant daughter home before the Jewish holidays. I make a note to do it, and write him back with the good news. The most rewarding thing about working in adoptions is being able to help Americans in a very personal and direct way.

10:00 A.M. As the morning progresses, I do the paperwork for the 35 families we will be seeing this afternoon. Their files are laboriously compiled collections of tax documents, home studies, local birth certificates, police statements, and orphanage decrees. Many of the families we are processing today submitted their documents two or more years ago, and have been waiting since then to be assigned a child by the Chinese government's Bureau of Adoptions. And it's only getting harder: While our post processed nearly 8,000 adoptions in 2006, we will do less than half that number in 2008. The supply of children available for foreign adoption is dwindling. The Chinese government tells us that more Chinese are adopting domestically, but some sources say the orphanages in rural areas have as many children as ever. Whatever the cause, the result is that fewer Chinese babies are being adopted by American and other foreign families each year.

1:00 P.M. After lunch, I answer more inquiries from parents and their congressional representatives. Adoption work is high-profile, and we get a lot of attention from Capitol Hill. We assemble the packets of official documents for the families and then print the visas for our newest little compatriots, who will become American citizens upon entering the United States with the visas we give them today.

4:00 P.M. The best part of the day arrives: the adoptions ceremony. I walk out to the main waiting room, greet the assembled families, and chat with them about where they're from and what they do. Then I administer the citizenship oath and congratulate them on their new families. Speaking to parents from all over the United States and seeing the joy and relief on their faces as they hold their long-desired babies in their arms makes everything about the job worthwhile.

5:30 P.M. The consulate closes, and I hop a cab across town to the Garden Hotel, where the public affairs section is located. Tonight I am volunteering for a public affairs event, moderating a discussion on American politics following a screening of "The War Room," one in a series of political films that the consulate is showing. In Guangzhou, every officer is encouraged to be a part of our public outreach program, what former Secretary of State Condoleezza Rice called "transformational diplomacy," and what Secretary of State Hillary Rodham Clinton calls "smart power."

7:00 P.M. After a quick dinner at a local Vietnamese restaurant with a colleague, I'm back at the hotel, and the students start arriving for the film event. We have a lively and varied discussion about presidential candidates Barack Obama and Hillary Clinton. There's enormous interest in the election among Chinese young people, and I enjoy answering their questions about the democratic process.

9:30 P.M. As we pack up and usher everyone out, I get in a cab for the half-hour trip home. It's been a long day, but it's always energizing to finish it by reaching out to Chinese young people.

Guangzhou was Esther Pan Sloane's first Foreign Service posting. Before joining the Foreign Service in 2006 as a public diplomacy officer, she worked as a journalist, foreign policy analyst, and theater director. From China, she and her husband and young son headed to London for her second tour.

A Day in the Life of ...
A POLITICAL OFFICER

PROVINCIAL RECONSTRUCTION TEAM DHI QAR, IRAQ
By Jon Dorschner
MARCH 2008

6:00 A.M. I wake up to clear skies. For the past week, dust has blown nonstop through our base in Dhi Qar province, at times so thick it obscures the sky and diffuses light into blood orange. This week's sandstorm appears to be over.

PRT Dhi Qar meeting. The man in the posters is Husayn ibn Ali, a martyr for Shia Muslims, whose picture is ubiquitous in the Shia areas of Iraq.

I am the political officer and public affairs officer for this Italian provincial re-construction team (PRT), staffed by Italian aid professionals and contractors from the U.S. and Germany, and housed in long prefabricated buildings in what used to be an Air Force base. My housing is typical—one room, empty except for a cot, a detached closet, and a folding chair.

Since I am going on a mission with the 82nd Airborne, I've gotten up a little earlier than usual. My clothes, flak jacket, and helmet are laid out on the folding chair. After dressing, I load the protective gear into the back of my truck and head for the DFAC (dining facility) to eat sausage, a powdered egg omelette, and lots of potatoes and bacon, washed down with coffee and juice.

6:30 A.M.   After breakfast, I drive my truck into a parking lot at the edge of the runway, put on my protective gear, and walk through the high reinforced concrete walls into the company briefing room to join the non-commissioned officers and officers for the pre-mission brief. We go over procedures, use of radios, frequencies, our route, and the schedule, and discuss what to do if we receive hostile fire and how to respond if a vehicle breaks down. After all questions are answered, the company commander gives us a short pep talk, and we file out to our assigned Humvees.

We are accompanying the battalion commander, who will formally open a medical clinic constructed by the 82nd in a poor neighborhood of a nearby town. I will take photos and later write up a story about the project for the Arabic-language newspaper I established for the PRT. I will also send it to the public affairs section of Embassy Baghdad, where it can be featured on the embassy Web site.

7:30 A.M.   Once the gunners have strapped themselves into the gun turrets, we slip our headphones and mouthpieces over our helmets, and our 10 Humvees drive off the base in single file, kicking up a big cloud of dust. We stop just outside the gate, pick up the colonel's interpreter, and turn onto the highway. The trip is quiet. The lead vehicle alerts us to Iraqi vehicles parked on the shoulder of the road ahead, while the gunners swing back and forth in their turrets, always on the lookout for danger.

10:00 A.M.   Once we arrive, the troops fan out from the vehicles and set up the perimeter. They open the doors of our Humvees and escort us to the ceremony. The Iraqi doctors (both male and female), local politicians, and the influential tribal sheik whose construction company performed the work, wait outside the brand new clinic to greet us. The doctors show the colonel and the rest of our delegation through the rooms. We see the new pharmacy and meet the pharmacist. We check out the new X-ray facility and meet the technician. Afterward, we file into a nearby room to listen to speeches. The doctors bring us Iraqi soft drinks and chips.

The colonel welcomes the clinic as a sign of progress and praises the doctors for their dedication, thanking them for helping bring medical care to a deprived neighborhood. He points out that the site was formerly an abandoned field and that the local residents used to have to go far away for medical care. The clinic director is grateful for the American assistance and pledges that he and his staff will maintain the clinic and provide good care to their patients.

1:00 P.M.   We drive to the mayor's office in the heart of town. The soldiers reestablish the perimeter and escort us inside, where we shed our protective gear and ask the mayor about his town. Expressing appreciation for the American projects and the help provided by the soldiers, the mayor points out that his town has always supported the government in Baghdad and worked closely with international troops. The colonel congratulates the police chief for working with the international forces and making the town safer. After drinking the obligatory tea and eating cookies, we put our protective gear back on, the soldiers grab their rifles stacked against the wall, and we head to the Humvees for the drive back to the base.

3:30 P.M.   My Humvee pulls up in front of the PRT compound. I bid farewell to my buddies in the 82nd, get out, go to my room, take off my body armor, and collapse onto my cot. On the PRT, we work seven days a week, often long into the night, so we grab sleep whenever we can, and then go back to work.

6:30 P.M.   After a nap, I head back to the office, download the photos, and write the story. Tomorrow, the Iraqi newspaper editor will translate it into Arabic for the paper, and I will send it to Embassy Baghdad for distribution to journalists and others curious about what we are up to in this far-flung PRT.

Jon Dorschner joined the Foreign Service in 1983 as a political officer. He holds a Ph.D. in South Asian studies, and has taught international relations and South Asian studies at the U.S. Military Academy at West Point. His Foreign Service assignments have been to Dhaka, Bangladesh; Islamabad, Pakistan; New Delhi, India; and Washington, D.C., where he was the India analyst for the State Department's Bureau of Intelligence and Research, and the political/military adviser for the South Asia Bureau. He and his wife, Nilu (originally from Jamshedpur, India), have two children. After his Iraq assignment, he transferred to the economic section of Embassy Berlin.

A Day in the Life of ...
A CONSULAR OFFICER

CONSULATE GENERAL SHANGHAI, CHINA
By Jaimee Macanas Neel
APRIL 2008

6:00 A.M.   My husband, Jim, is already awake and getting ready for work. We're a tandem couple working together in Shanghai's consular section. Jim served in São Paulo, Brazil, and in the Office of the Coordinator for Counterterrorism at Main State before I joined the Foreign Service. This is my first tour, and it's been fun working together.

6:45 A.M.   Our five-year-old son Jimmy is dressed and watching "Sesame Street." (Thank goodness for the Armed Forces Network, bringing U.S. television to China via satellite!) Our Chinese housekeeper arrives and asks Jimmy what he wants for breakfast: cold cereal. Luckily, we were able to send boxes of cereal in our consumables shipment to Shanghai; otherwise, we'd be paying nearly $14 a box to buy it here.

7:00 A.M.   Jim and I walk out of our four-story townhouse to meet the consulate's shuttle bus. Some of our colleagues are already on board, discussing the day's various events and meetings.

7:40 A.M.   We arrive at the Westgate Mall on Nanjing Road. The consulate in Shanghai has offices all over the city; the consular section is located on the eighth floor of a downtown shopping mall. It's a cold morning, and the neighborhood tai chi group is stretching in front of the Gucci store. This morning they are exercising with swords instead of the usual fans or streamers. (Sometimes, instead of doing tai chi, they ballroom dance!) Nearby, the line of anxious visa applicants wraps around the mall entrance, hundreds of hopeful travelers hugging their applications and documents. I imagine many have already been waiting outside in the cold for more than an hour.

8:30 A.M.   I open the American Citizen Services (ACS) window for business. Jim and most of the other consular officers are working through the nearly 500 nonimmigrant visa interviews for the day. The steady flow of Americans begins: passport renewals, notarials, lost passports, and certificates of births abroad. My mind clicks into autopilot as I help customers: sign, stamp, crimp; sign, click, save; wash, rinse, repeat.

10:40 A.M.   A call comes in from a local international school reporting that an American teacher has died of a heart attack. I get as much information as I can from the caller, alert the ACS chief, and open a new case record. The local hospital will follow up with more details via fax.

11:15 A.M.   More routine citizen services at the window.

11:50 A.M.   The fax comes in regarding the recently deceased American. I locate the American's family contact information and check what time it is in

California. I go into my chief's office and close the door to make the call. I speak to the parents, express my deepest condolences, and carefully note their contact information. They want to travel to China immediately. I hang up the phone and ask one of our local staff members to draft a letter to the Chinese consulate in Los Angeles requesting an expedited visa for the family members. Luckily, the ACS room is quiet. We close up for lunch.

Jaimee Neel at her Foreign Service swearing-in ceremony, June 2006.

12:05 P.M.   As I head out, the NIV chief asks if I can help out on the interview line. One of our colleagues is out sick, and the hardworking officers on the line need lunch, too. I quickly log on to a computer next to my husband and take the next visa applicant.

12:08 P.M.   The applicant is a student with limited English skills. I begin my regular questions, "Why do you want to study in America?" Then I ask, "Who will pay for your studies?" He answers: "My uncle, Angel Santos." This should be interesting; the applicant's name is Wang Peng, and he's from a small village outside Shanghai. "Who's Angel Santos?" I soon discover that he met Mr. Santos on the Internet, raising serious concerns about whether the applicant is actually a student. More likely, he is going to the U.S. to work. The story does not add up, and I explain that the visa is refused.

12:30 P.M.   Lunch—yummy Shanghai dumplings—with my husband. We savor this opportunity to have lunch together every day.

1:45 P.M.   I'm in a consulate car heading to Shanghai's prison for foreigners. I review the files of the three Americans I'll be visiting today. We visit them once a month to check on their health and well-being, and to review the status of their cases. I'm bringing several letters, magazines, books and newspapers, and 30 Big Macs from McDonald's, a special request from one of the detained Americans.

2:30 P.M.   I arrive at the prison. Consular officers have been coming to visit these prisoners for several years now—one has been here for nearly nine years. The prison guards recognize me and my Big Mac delivery and escort me to the meeting room without delay. The magazines, books, and letters are examined for any "illegal" content or "sensitive information." I meet with each of the Americans for 30 minutes. They all seem relatively comfortable and are eager to talk about current events, news from their families, and minor complaints about overcrowding in their cells. They're glad to see me; I'm one of the only visitors they see each month. I take notes to prepare the cables reporting on the visits first thing in the morning.

5:30 P.M.   The consulate driver drops me off at home, since our apartment is on the way back to the consulate. Jimmy is so excited to see me home early. I give Jim a call and wish him luck at the Spanish consulate's reception tonight. He's still at the office, and tells me he's out of business cards. "Just use mine," I say. "They both read: J. Neel, Vice Consul."

Jaimee Macanas Neel joined the Foreign Service in 2006 as a public diplomacy officer. From Shanghai, her first posting, she moved on to Arabic-language training and then Cairo, Egypt, where her husband, Jim, is also assigned. Jaimee met Jim at Brigham Young University Law School. They are enjoying the adventure and challenge of taking their two children and two cats around the world. Prior to joining the Foreign Service, Jaimee was an inner-city schoolteacher and volunteered with orphanages in Brazil.

A Day in the Life of ...
AN AMBASSADOR

EMBASSY HARARE, ZIMBABWE
By Charles Ray
JANUARY 2010

5:30 A.M.   I wake up a half-hour before the alarm goes off and am up for the day. After 30 minutes of exercise, a shower and shave, I take my Pekinese for her morning "business." She and I then retire to my home office, where I check personal e-mail and do a little writing for my personal and official blogs. I also check Facebook and LinkedIn for updates from my contacts.

7:00 A.M.   Over breakfast, my wife and I discuss the day's social events, which include hosting a lunch at the residence for a visiting U.S. businessman.

7:45 A.M.   My driver picks me up for the 15-minute commute to the embassy.

8:00 A.M.   I check e-mails and cable traffic and go over today's schedule with my office manager. I then have a quick chat with the deputy chief of mission about overnight events and check the pulse of the mission to make sure there are no surprises lurking about the chancery.

9:00 A.M.   Time for the country team meeting. Each section and agency at post fills me in on what they have been doing for the past week. I fill them in on my views on the latest events in Zimbabwe and the instructions we've received from Washington. The meetings are limited to 45 minutes so people can get back to getting actual work done. I only hold a country team meeting once a week, but have individual meetings with many of our section and agency heads more frequently, particularly when the hardliners in government have been acting up; which, unfortunately, they have. There have been recent reports of officially sponsored youth gangs terrorizing villagers suspected of being sympathetic with the opposition party.

9:55 A.M.   I leave the embassy for a meeting with Zimbabwe's minister of agriculture. While the ostensible purpose of the meeting is to discuss the impact of the drought on the annual maize harvest, he spends the bulk of the time defending his role in the controversial land 'redistribution' program and complaining about the U.S. sanctions on certain members of the government who have been implicated in human rights violations. I listen patiently and politely, express my disagreement with his points, and agree to authorize working-level groups between his ministry and the embassy to discuss how we can help the farmers get through a hard year and still not violate the sanctions. The meeting ends on a cordial note. Walking me back to my car, the minister reminisces about his stay in the U.S. as a student in the 1970s.

11:00 A.M.   I'm back at the embassy for a brief meeting with the defense attaché about my planned trip to Europe to meet with the regional military commander

Amb. Ray with a student following a speech he gave at a local school in honor of Martin Luther King Jr. Day.

to discuss an initiative for having a personnel recovery expert as part of the country team. In this landlocked country, we need all the help we can get in an emergency, and recovering Americans who might be in distress in an isolated area of the country, or even in one of the cities, is what personnel recovery is all about.

11:45 A.M.   I depart the embassy for the residence to host a lunch for a visiting American businessman who is interested in my views on U.S. companies doing business in the country. A lively discussion ensues on the political and cultural obstacles he is likely to face. My political-economic counselor joins us, and explains how difficult it can be for foreigners to do business in Zimbabwe given the tendency of some officials to demand a share of any business that is doing well.

1:30 P.M.   I return to the embassy to meet with the USAID director for a discussion about a planned delivery of H1N1 flu protective suits for local medical personnel.

1:55 P.M.   I depart the embassy for a meeting with the deputy prime minister. A former trade union official, she wants to tell me about a program she is initiating for empowerment of rural women and seeks U.S. assistance and advice.

2:30 P.M.   I depart for a regularly scheduled meeting with European Union, Canadian, and Australian ambassadors to coordinate our assistance programs and review political developments within the country's coalition government.

4:00 P.M.   Back at the embassy, I review new e-mails and cables from Washington, now that the department's workday has started (Washington is seven hours behind us). One particular instruction for a démarche to the local government catches my eye. In a country that has just come out of hyperinflation, and has had difficulty conducting a census of its population, this démarche asking for statistics on traffic fatalities from use of cell phones while driving seems like a poor use of resources. I realize, however, that it is an important issue in Washington, so I instruct my political counselor to make his best effort to gather the information.

5:00 P.M.   I leave for the residence to freshen up, and then my wife and I attend a dinner hosted by the Italian ambassador.

10:30 P.M.   We get back to the residence, and I walk the dog once more. Then I spend a couple of hours on the computer catching up with family and friends, and working on another chapter of a mystery novel I'm writing.

12:30 A.M.   I fall into bed for what I hope will be five hours of uninterrupted sleep.

Ambassador Charles A. Ray is a member of the Senior Foreign Service. He previously served as deputy assistant secretary of Defense for POW/missing personnel affairs and director of the Defense Department's POW/Missing Personnel Office. Ray has also been a diplomat in residence at the University of Houston, and served as ambassador to Cambodia from 2002 to 2005. He was the first U.S. consul general in Ho Chi Minh City, Vietnam. Other Foreign Service tours have included China, Thailand, Sierra Leone, and the Bureau of Political-Military Affairs in Washington, D.C. Prior to joining the Foreign Service in 1982, Ray served in the U.S. Army for 20 years, retiring with the rank of major. He and his wife, Myung Wook, have two sons and two daughters.

PART IV
The Foreign Service in Action:
Tales from the Field

oreign Service professionals work on the front lines of history. If something important happens in a country, the Foreign Service is there, keeping the U.S. government informed, protecting American interests and, where possible, playing a constructive role. Yet because the Foreign Service role in world affairs is often played behind the scenes, few know about the dangers faced and the skills and courage exhibited every day by Foreign Service employees serving overseas.

In the aftermath of the 2004 Asian Tsunami, Consular Officer Mike Chadwick quickly converted his holiday in Thailand to a search endeavor to find and assist Americans amidst the chaos. Following a terrorist attack in Sharm el-Sheik, Egypt, Jacqueline Deley was on the scene to find out if any Americans were harmed. When Kosovo declared independence in February 2008, Public Diplomacy Officer Christopher Midura was there to bear witness to the historic event, while, at the same time, Public Diplomacy Officer Rian Harker Harris managed press relations in Belgrade during violent demonstrations following the declaration of independence.

The work of U.S. diplomacy is done without fanfare. Those who serve do not do it for glory or for publicity. Yet recognition for the courage and the sacrifices made every day by the Foreign Service is warranted, and these stories give a glimpse of the ways that the Foreign Service makes a difference in the world.

DEMOCRACY UNDER CONSTRUCTION

MALDIVES, 2006
By Anamika Chakravorty

Anamika Chakravorty

My first Foreign Service posting was as a political officer at Embassy Colombo, covering both Sri Lanka and the Republic of Maldives. It was 2006, and Sri Lanka had seen new outbreaks of open conflict in its three-decade-long civil war, while Maldives was an Islamic country making an arduous transition to democracy. One morning, two senior host-government officials phoned me in rapid succession. Under the circumstances, calls from highly placed individuals were unlikely to bode well.

As it happened, though, it was Maldivian officials phoning to report that a small group of protesters was carrying an American flag in the capital, Malé. "I'm so sorry," the callers said in strained tones. "But we believe … well, we think these people might be planning to burn a U.S. flag. We're terribly embarrassed. I hope you know this isn't representative of the attitude in Maldives, and this group doesn't have much support. We just wanted to alert you."

I was surprised, and also deeply touched. I know there are some governments that would tacitly support their citizens burning an American flag; others would happily supply matches and kerosene! Yet here were two foreign officials calling to assure an American diplomat that such behavior was not the norm for their country.

Knowing that Maldives—a country comprising more than 1,000 coral islands off the coast of Sri Lanka in the Indian Ocean—was struggling with unfamiliar aspects of democracy, such as balancing security concerns against freedoms of assembly and expression, I tried to provide a nuanced response that went something like this: "I appreciate your call, and as an American and as a diplomat, it makes me sad to hear someone might burn our flag. However, our own Supreme Court has ruled that to be an acceptable form of political expression. While I believe it is the resort of inarticulate persons who cannot express their message in a sophisticated way, they should have the opportunity to voice their views as long as they don't endanger others. I hope your government won't prohibit freedom of expression even though you disagree with the sentiment in question."

I hung up, wondering what would become of the protesters. The following day, a journalist contact got in touch and asked if I had heard about the fracas over the U.S. flag in Maldives. I asked what had happened. He explained that the police approached the protesters and asked whether they had an American flag. When they replied in the affirmative, the police asked if they had been planning to burn it. They said no. The group handed over the flag, and was allowed to continue the protest.

For Maldives, this was a step forward. It was not government permission for full freedom of expression, but at least it was a compromise. Protesters were not jailed arbitrarily, nor did they lash out at the police.

In October 2008, Maldives held its first-ever multiparty elections. Tears of joy came to my eyes when I read that they passed peacefully and there would be a smooth transition of power. A man I had visited under house arrest less than 18 months earlier was elected president!

I know that the work the embassy did—advocacy, high-level representation on human rights, sending expert speakers, documenting issues in the annual Human Rights Report, and supporting democratization in myriad ways behind the scenes—contributed to a positive shift for Maldives.

During my tour, I was fortunate enough to work with officials who joined their government for the same reason I had joined mine: to represent the loftiest ideals of fellow citizens and to bring about improvements when possible. I was also lucky enough to work with opposition leaders who risked their freedom and made great personal and professional sacrifices to advocate for their vision of full democracy.

I was honored to nominate one such activist as an International Woman of Courage in 2007, a woman who showed grace and strength in the face of adversity. I knew that Maldives, a country with a population of just 350,000 and no resident U.S. diplomatic mission, might not be on the State Department's radar. So I was delighted when the activist was selected as one of eight inaugural winners of the prestigious award.

Although I have since left the region for another assignment, I still keep up with news of the Maldives. I fell in love with my first portfolio. I had plunged into my work in Colombo with reckless abandon, putting in hours of personal time and answering calls at all hours of the day and night.

When dealing with contacts, I encountered cynicism, frustration, and infighting, as well as kernels of optimism, deep patriotism, strength, and true courage. Sometimes I, too, fell prey to pessimism or grew irritated at personalities or political developments. I talked about Maldives to anyone who would listen, and even to some who would not! I bored my friends with my zeal, but I also managed to win some converts who focused on Maldives and advocated for democratization.

Ultimately, in a global political climate fraught with violence and fear, Maldivians did not get a storybook ending. They got something even better: a new beginning, won through the hard work, persuasive skills, persistence, and fearlessness of committed citizens.

Anamika Chakravorty served as a political officer in Colombo from 2005 to 2007. Prior to joining the Foreign Service in 2004, she worked as a civic educator for the nonprofit Close Up Foundation. After Colombo, she served in Kingston, Jamaica, then as a watch officer in the State Department's Operations Center, and most recently, as the deputy political/economic counselor for United Nations affairs at the U.S. Mission to International Organizations in Vienna.

AFTER THE ASIAN TSUNAMI

THAILAND, 2004
By Mike Chadwick

When my wife and I flew from Singapore to Phuket, Thailand, for a three-day Christmas holiday in 2004, our only real concern was oversleeping and missing our plane home. The weather was perfect and the ocean was postcard blue. But our relaxing holiday ended early—at about 10 a.m. on December 26, 2004—when a massive tsunami broke over the west coast of Thailand, also smashing into Indonesia, Sri Lanka, and other countries bordering the Indian Ocean.

I was on the balcony of our hotel on a hillside overlooking Phuket Beach when the ocean began roaring like a jet engine. My wife joined me in time to see a surge of white water rolling in, seven or eight feet high. It smashed through the restaurant on the beachfront below, picking up everything inside and pulling it back out to sea in a tangle of junk. Our hotel was high enough up that we were safe, for which I will be forever thankful.

The tsunami knocked out power to the hotel and left us in an information blackout. Powerful waves kept rolling in, and the beach below, usually filled with bright umbrellas and food stalls, was strewn with wreckage. When the electricity finally returned, we saw the first news reports with estimates of hundreds, then thousands, of deaths. I called the embassy to say we were okay, and agreed to stay and help out. I didn't realize that I would be there for almost two weeks.

I started gathering information on American citizens by walking to the nearby hospitals in Patong, checking lists of the dead and injured. Early the next morning, I talked with the American citizen services chief in Bangkok, who had heard about a central site to which victims were being evacuated. My wife went to the airport to fly home to Singapore, and I headed out in search of Americans. A few wildly overpriced taxi rides later, I found myself at Phuket City Hall, where the Thai government had established a refugee assistance area. I grabbed a table in the room designated for foreigners, hung up a handwritten "USA" sign, and started assisting Americans as they arrived.

The room, usually an information center, was only about 30 by 60 feet. Within a day, consular staff from more than 30 countries had set up shop there. Survivors of all nationalities streamed in until there was no room to sit, so even the badly injured had to stand while others shoved past them. It was chaos. It was almost impossible to reach anyone outside Phuket. The cell-phone service companies set a two-minute talk limit as their lines were swamped; when I did get through to the embassy in Bangkok, I had only a few seconds to update them.

Soon more American personnel arrived from Embassy Bangkok. We divided the jobs: searching hospitals and morgues for American victims, assisting Americans who wanted to leave Phuket, sending lists of victims and survivors to Embassy Bangkok, and providing updates from the field so the State Department could make informed decisions about humanitarian aid and support.

Tsunami victims suffering from injuries and shock wandered around City Hall trying to figure out what to do next. The walls around them were covered with photos of the missing—tanned and smiling faces, posted in the hope someone might recognize them. Survivors pored over pictures taken at the makeshift morgues, hoping they

Aftershock waves continue to roll in after the tsunami hit Phuket.

would not find their missing friends and loved ones among the rows of distorted faces needing identification.

By the end, the tsunami had claimed well over 200,000 lives worldwide, including an estimated 8,200 killed or missing in Thailand. Many thousands more, both Thai and foreign, were injured, displaced, or left destitute. There were 34 Americans among the bodies recovered, and another 135 were still unaccounted for several months after the wave hit.

The stories told by survivors were heartbreaking: parents searching for lost children, people crying for friends they saw crushed by buildings, newlyweds who had watched their spouses swept out to sea. But there were also a few happy endings. One American told me he spent the first night after the wave sitting on a beach thinking his children had drowned, only to discover when he finally made it to our desk that they were on our list of survivors. They had been evacuated by boat.

Another American, whose European girlfriend had died in the tsunami, wanted to accompany her body home the following day but had lost his passport. We couldn't issue him a passport in Phuket, but we convinced the consular officials of her country to let him travel with only a copy of his passport photo page, which his family faxed to us.

The cooperation among the representatives of all countries was inspiring, while the kindness and generosity of our Thai hosts to their foreign guests in the midst of their own sorrow will stay with me forever. Sometimes it takes a tragedy to remind us of our shared humanity.

Mike Chadwick served as a consular officer in Singapore from 2003 to 2005, his first Foreign Service assignment. He joined the Foreign Service in 2003 as a public diplomacy officer. After Singapore, he served in Chisinau, Moldova, followed by a tour at the State Department in Washington, D.C. From there he went on to the consulate in Fukuoka, Japan, as the public affairs officer. He is married with one young son.

TEN FOR A DOLLAR

LIBERIA, 1996
By Michael Bricker

Monrovia in 1996 was a post with the distinction of having the highest hardship level and danger pay in the Foreign Service. The war-torn society faced obliterated infrastructure and the probability of yet another civil war. Embassy personnel, like all city residents, were under a 7 p.m. to 7 a.m. curfew, not a difficult one to manage because there was simply nowhere safe to go after dusk.

A country established in 1847 under the motto, "The love of liberty brought us here," Liberia was founded and colonized by freed American slaves and their descendants. The American influence could not be overstated: the national flag, the currency, and even the police uniforms were all modeled after those of the United States. But a palace coup in 1980 ushered in a period of economic and political instability and periodic civil war.

Among the many things that pulled at our heartstrings in Monrovia was the plight of the deaf orphan children. These children—deaf because their mothers had contracted rubella during pregnancy, and discarded by their families because of their disability—became children of the street. They once had a school and orphanage, but it was demolished in the previous civil war. The children were dressed in rags.

When I met them, I was amazed by how friendly they were. Their tragic circumstance bonded them into an unusual extended family where the oldest would help the youngest and teach them ad hoc sign language. One of the local ministers allowed them to sleep at night on the floor of a remote church and the cement slab of an unfinished building (so the girls and boys could sleep separately), provided that they cleaned up in the morning. From there, they fanned out each day to survive by begging and searching for food. In a battered country, they had few choices.

During the second year of my tour, in 1995, I took a trip back to the U.S. for a training program held in a small town in Virginia. My wife came along. One night after dinner we walked along a strip mall typical of small-town America. One of the few stores still open was a thrift shop, so we stopped in to take a look at the books. The shop had an inner section that contained children's clothing. What drew our attention was a handwritten sign that proclaimed, "Children's Clothes—10 for a Dollar." When the proprietor confirmed the offer, I said, "Ten cents each! Lady, close your doors, I'm buying the store." Not being from a wealthy background, I got a thrill just saying that.

Over the next few hours, the three of us packed up all the clothes into boxes. I made several trips to the hotel room, and then we spent the next several hours labeling the boxes. By morning we were ready to mail them to Monrovia, but first we had to find a private shipping service. There was no room for error or delay, as we were flying back to post the next day. After many trips to the shipping office, the last of the boxes was on its way. The shipping cost us more than the clothes, but it was still a bargain.

We were back in Monrovia for a few months before the boxes began to arrive, the final one six weeks after the first. I put in a request to rent an embassy truck and asked one of the deaf adults who knew the orphans to spread the word that we would be delivering clothes to the church the following Saturday. In a country lacking basic electricity and phone service, this was the surest means of communication.

That Saturday, we loaded the truck and drove an hour on dirt roads to the church. The minister and hundreds of children were waiting outside and greeted us warmly. They helped us unload the truck. As we were bringing the cartons into the church, one fell and broke open, and 50 or so pieces of clothing spilled out— jeans, blouses, and T-shirts. The children stood in astonishment—it was as if they were viewing the crown jewels. And in that moment it hit me with full force— regardless of any particular tribulation, my life is opulent when compared with that of many, if not most, of my fellow inhabitants of the globe.

From that day on, we have never thrown away any clothes that could be donated. One action, one person, can make a difference. The greatest gift is when you are, every once in a while, in a position to be that person.

Michael Bricker served in Monrovia from 1993 to 1996. He joined the Foreign Service as an information management officer in 1990. Aside from Monrovia, he has served in Seoul (twice), Warsaw, London, the U.S. Mission to the United Nations in New York City and, most recently, Vienna.

MADONNA IN KUNDUZ

AFGHANISTAN, 2008
By Matthew Asada

"Who's Madonna?" asked Wadood, an Afghan journalist friend, as we discussed music. Halfway around the globe from Rochester Hills, Michigan, I contemplated whether, and how, I should introduce one of my favorite hometown artists. Should the performer who had provoked the Catholic Church be introduced to this young Muslim man? Could one fully comprehend the hypersexualized American icon in a society where the sexes are segregated and women are covered? I could count on two hands the number of Afghan adult women I had seen without a burqa covering all but a bit of their eyes.

As the State Department representative on the German-led Provincial Reconstruction Team in Kunduz, I'd been living in a very male world for months. My job was to report on political and economic developments in Northeast Afghanistan, advance reconstruction priorities, and represent American foreign policy as well as culture. I was the only American diplomat in Northeast Afghanistan.

When I landed on the pockmarked airstrip the Soviets had paved before their 1989 departure, I was greeted warmly: "Hi. Abdul Mateen here." A young, bearded

Afghan man in jeans and a button-down shirt shook my hand firmly as I stepped down from the plane. Good-humored and armed with an easy smile, Abdul would prove indispensable as my political assistant, interpreter, driver, and jack-of-all-trades over the next year.

Matthew Asada at the Salang Pass that connects North Afghanistan with Kabul province.

I traveled extensively throughout Northeast Afghanistan with a freedom of movement that few other diplomatic personnel in the country enjoyed at the time. By car, plane, helicopter, horse, and foot, Abdul and I toured the desert plains, lush river valleys, and snow-capped mountains—from the American-built Afghan-Tajik bridge to the Soviet-built Salang Pass, and from the historic Greek ruins in Ay Qanoom to the Sufi poet Rumi's birthplace in Balkh.

As I constantly urged him to speed up so we wouldn't be late for an appointment, Abdul would instruct me on the flexible Afghan concept of time. As we passed the remains of destroyed concrete electricity poles and depressions in the newly laid asphalt, he recounted the story of the most recent improvised explosive device attack by the insurgents. During these long journeys I heard about the privileged position of educators under the communist regime, the anarchy and corruption of the civil war, and Abdul's hopes and dreams for his new wife and child under the Karzai government.

Together, we drank hundreds of cups of tea to get the story. Students shared their anxieties about university admissions. Traders bemoaned the lack of electricity and the shortage of rice in the marketplace. Government officials inquired about possible donor funding schemes for their latest project. Mullahs decried the negative influence of Indian soap operas on Afghan society.

This was the expeditionary diplomacy of which young diplomats dream: outside the embassy, among the people. I donned the local dress—a long pajama shirt with baggy drawstring pants—sported a tightly trimmed beard, and practiced my rudimentary Dari-language skills with everyone I met. I roamed the city bazaars, occasionally stopping for a glass of freshly squeezed pomegranate juice or hand-churned ice cream available only in rose-water flavor.

One evening in Kunduz, while my not-so-pious Afghan hosts shared a forbidden bottle of vodka (alcohol is prohibited in the country and the overwhelming majority of Afghans do observe this), we discussed the Afghan and Tajik governments' plans to open for traffic the long-awaited $49 million bridge between the two countries—built and funded by the United States. The next morning, Abdul and I raced to the bridge to join in the inauguration of what could become the backbone of a new Central Asian Silk Road. Our Afghan hosts slaughtered two goats and let the blood spill onto the new bridge. The Tajiks joined us on the Afghan side for a magnificent feast of lamb and rice—flavored with raisins, carrots, and pistachios—and ice-cold Pepsi imported from Pakistan.

As the closest U.S. official to the new bridge, I worked with Afghan and Tajik officials to maximize its usefulness—expanding open hours, encouraging pedestrian traffic, and facilitating working-level talks on the border crossing. Before the bridge, 30 trucks a day had been ferried across the river from Afghanistan to Tajikistan. Soon after it opened, more than 200 trucks were crossing each day, and the one-day record stood at 600.

Entrepreneurs responded to the new bridge and built gas stations, restaurants, and hotels at the border and in the provincial capital to accommodate the dramatic increase in trade. Amid the ruins of the dilapidated cotton warehouses and the remnants of Soviet military facilities, Afghans were building a new, commercially viable border crossing point that would be the region's economic bridge to the future.

The first international agricultural fair in Kunduz in June 2008 was another highlight of the year, both for the region and for me personally. I had suggested the idea to colleagues the previous December on a trip to Kabul. The U.S. Agency for International Development supported the Ministry of Agriculture in organizing the three-day event, which brought together 150 exhibitors—50 of whom had crossed the new bridge from Tajikistan to be there, several for the first time. More than 23,000 people attended the event, which passed without a single security incident. The fair was the talk of the town and the Afghan intelligence service, police, army, and fair security proved themselves up to the job.

The people I met in Northeast Afghanistan expressed appreciation for international assistance, optimism about the future, and curiosity about the United States. I worked to maximize opportunities for boys and girls to participate in high school exchange programs and laid the foundation for a cultural center in the city to encourage this interest in learning more about the United States.

I found many friends in Kunduz and throughout the region. Before my departure, Wadood gave me two CDs. "Here, these are for you. I thought we could trade—my favorite Afghan music for your favorite American music."

For a moment, I considered giving him my copy of Madonna's "Immaculate Collection." But while music is universal, and Northeast Afghanistan had made a lot of progress during the past year, I thought better of it. The Material Girl would have to wait for her unveiling.

Matthew Asada served as the State Department representative on the German-led Kunduz Provincial Reconstruction Team from 2007 to 2008. He joined the Foreign Service as a political officer in 2003. His first assignment was to Lahore, Pakistan, as a management officer. He then went on to Munich, Germany; Kunduz, Afghanistan; and then Kolkata, India. His most recent assignment was as a special assistant to the special representative for Afghanistan and Pakistan in Washington, D.C.

SURVIVING A TERRORIST ATTACK

YEMEN, 2008
By David Turnbull

It was September 17, 2008. I was only three weeks into my first Foreign Service tour, as a vice consul at Embassy Sana'a, and my stress level was high. Our consular caseload is complex, and I was still struggling to get my feet on the ground. However, it was the end of the week and I was in the best mood I had been in since arriving in Yemen. Today, I thought, would be different.

Years of false alarms had numbed me to fire drills. So when the high-low alarm went off in the embassy, I kept working. When it didn't stop, I turned to a colleague to ask what the noise was. Probably a drill. I looked around the room. Where was everyone? Then I heard the explosion.

The whole room shook and dust started to fall from the ceiling. My colleagues were all already under their desks. "Get down!" someone yelled. I scrambled to the floor, trying to get a grip on the situation. Before I could figure out how to fit myself into the small box of space between a file cabinet and my computer, the second explosion hit. "This is not a drill," wailed the overhead. No kidding! "Duck and cover. There have been explosions outside the embassy." I began to wonder if the half-inch of wood above my head would give me any protection. The metal file cabinets next to me were more comforting.

We were under our desks for more than an hour. We counted six explosions. Apparently there was gunfire, too, but we couldn't hear it through the bulletproof visa windows. Aside from a firefight raging outside, it was uncomfortably quiet. Where were the sirens? Why couldn't we hear anyone mobilizing? What was happening? Everyone stayed calm. We cracked jokes to ease the silence. Humor means you're still alive. Welcome to Yemen.

In the intervals between explosions, I tried to find the most comfortable duck-and-cover position and prayed. Then I checked in on some colleagues who were out of the office, sent a couple texts home to my loved ones just in case I didn't make it, and waited. Dying under a desk was not high on my list of ways to go. I put on the sneakers I had packed for the gym. If ever there was a time I might need that extra half step, it was now.

Around 11 a.m. we were ushered into a "safe room" by security personnel. For those who had been at the embassy for the March attack six months earlier, the entire procedure appeared routine. But this time it was worse: whatever was happening was bigger than mortars. I was in shock. I knew enough to get some water, but just sat dazed in the corner for about 20 minutes, not knowing what to do. When one of the nurses came over and started making small talk, I began to snap out of it.

Eventually all the people in the consular waiting room were brought to the interior holding area. No windows separated us now. The men and women headed to opposite sides of the room and waited patiently with the rest of us. Along with their babies. So many babies. Our local staff did a phenomenal job attending to the crowd. Everyone was remarkably calm. The children seemed blissfully ignorant. I watched a five-year-old take care of his little brother: they ate crackers, made a mess with M&Ms, and played. Periodically, the ambassador came in to update us; and as we watched through the doorway, a slew of military personnel mobilized with a surprising amount of battle gear.

In the meantime, I got hold of myself and realized I could be more useful standing up. I escorted people to the bathrooms and played secretary for our press spokesman, who was answering nonstop calls from the international media. I was impressed watching the section heads mobilize to manage the situation and get messages out. Equally impressive were the embassy medical staff, looking after our wounded guards (one of whom died before he could receive full medical attention). These were experienced diplomats in action.

Later in the day, we were evacuated from the embassy with a full military escort. The trip was harrowing, and I decided not to go home alone. A few of us went to a friend's house, recounted stories, and recovered. There, we sat in disbelief watching the same news stories over and over. Six men dressed as police officers had tried to blast into the embassy compound with two vehicle-borne improvised explosive devices and suicide vests. When they failed to breach the perimeter, they began firing their assault rifles and eventually detonated the explosives originally intended for all of us inside. As we watched these reports, my colleague's visiting mother whipped up an *iftar* meal for us (the meal to break the fast each day of Ramadan)—my first.

For a second, under the desk, I had thought, Why should I issue one more visa? But then I remembered all the people in the waiting room, huddled under cover too. I thought about our local staff, who had been working hard through Ramadan without a bite to eat or drink. I thought about the local guards out front, who check for bombs every day and rely on the protection of soldiers. I thought about the soldiers. I couldn't blame Yemen, and I couldn't hate these people. This attack was bad for all of us, Americans and Yemenis. The only difference was that now, because of this attack, I would have a choice—to stay or go home as part of the evacuation that would be sure to follow.

I awoke the next day, back in my bed. I read the news of the attack, claimed by al-Qaida in the Arabian Peninsula, for the umpteenth time. And it was clear— for better or worse, I wasn't going anywhere. This was the job I had fought for, and these are the places we need diplomats. No one ever said it was going to be easy.

David Turnbull served as a consular officer in Sana'a from 2008 to 2010. He joined the Foreign Service as a political officer in 2008 following a yearlong internship with the State Department. Sana'a was his first posting, and from there he went on to a position as the staff assistant to the U.S. Permanent Representative to NATO in Brussels, Belgium.

ONE RIOT, ONE AMBASSADOR

MACEDONIA, 1999
By Charles A. Stonecipher

One summer midnight in the Balkans, an American ambassador walked into a refugee camp to try to quell a riot and save the lives of Roma (gypsy) refugees under attack. He succeeded, and went home to bed. It wasn't diplomacy around big tables in grand rooms. The U.S. embassy had no responsibility to intervene, and few who were not there ever heard about it. But the actions of Ambassador Christopher Hill highlight the power of the individual Foreign Service officer's moral and physical courage.

At about 11 p.m. on June 5, 1999, my cell phone rang at home. It was Ed Joseph, an American working for Catholic Relief Services as a refugee camp manager at Stenkovac Camp, a few miles north of Skopje, the capital of the small, ethnically tense Balkan nation of Macedonia. Stenkovac housed tens of thousands of refugees from Kosovo, mostly ethnic Albanians. There was a riot going on, Ed told me, and it looked like people were going to get killed. A rumor had run through the camp that some Roma residents were Serb collaborators who had participated in a massacre of ethnic Albanians in Kosovo weeks earlier. A mob had formed in the camp to go after the two accused Roma families. The camp managers had just enough time to get to the scene, pull the Roma away, and get them inside the small building they used as an office. Two of the men had been very badly beaten and were only semi-conscious.

The building was surrounded by masses of angry people, pounding on the doors and barred windows trying to get at the Roma. If the mob got in, it was unlikely any of the Roma, including the children, would stand a chance. Ed was on the edge of the crowd by the front gate with other camp administrators, but their efforts to break up the crowd were not working. He did not know how long it would be before the mob would be able to smash its way into the building.

Ed knew that sending Macedonian police into the camp would only inflame the situation. We quickly ran through some ideas—NATO troops, Western European police officers from a training mission, a couple of others—but none had any prospect of working in time, if ever. The one trump card we could think of was the immense respect of the Kosovar Albanians for the United States, and for our ambassador in Skopje, Chris Hill, admired for his efforts to prevent the Kosovo conflict. Maybe he could calm the mob. It was a long shot, and we could not rule out the grim possibility that in the confusion Hill himself could be attacked or trampled. We could think of no other options, so I called Ambassador Hill.

Hill listened to my explanation of what was going on and our vague idea for his intervention, then simply said, "Yes, I want to get out there right away." Minutes later, Deputy Chief of Mission Paul Jones, Refugee Coordinator Ted

Morse, Ambassador Hill, and I were standing at the gate to the camp, looking at the milling mass of people surrounding the building that held the Roma. We were met by Ed, an interpreter, and a gaggle of worried but seemingly powerless camp elders. As I listened to the din of noise from the unseen center of the crowd, the plan we'd concocted on the drive out began to seem a bit light.

We had decided to start with the interpreter using a bullhorn to announce that Ambassador Hill was coming into the camp to address the residents. The people closest to us would be able to hear it, and we'd wait for their reaction. Hill would then enter the camp flanked by Ted and Paul, holding lights. I would troop along with both arms overhead, displaying a towel-sized American flag I'd grabbed on the way out of my house. Relying on the flag and Hill's face, we hoped to pass far enough into the crowd for him to be able to make a speech at a spot where he could be seen and heard by as many people as possible. If he was able to calm things down, I'd try to get vehicles up to the building and we'd load the families and get out as fast as we could. There was no Plan B. Ambassador Hill looked around, said he was as ready as he was going to get, and headed for the gate.

Initially, our biggest problem was visibility, but the people on the edge of the crowd quickly turned to face us, recognized Ambassador Hill, and let us pass. With each step farther into the crowd, though, it got hotter, denser, and darker. Paul Jones grabbed a plastic crate for a podium as we pushed on. Around us the crowd swirled but people's attention increasingly turned to us. When we were about midway to the building, Hill stood on the crate while the interpreter continued announcing, "Ambassador Hill is here!" People yelled at each other in Albanian, "The Americans! Ambassador Hill!" Hill raised his arms for quiet and people began to shout, "Quiet! Everyone sit down!" Astoundingly, hundreds of men all around us began to sit on the ground so everyone could see and hear the ambassador.

Hill started to speak, and bit by bit, word by word, proceeded to transform the mob into an audience. He announced that NATO had just presented Milosevic with its non-negotiable plan to enter Kosovo. He told them how close Milosevic was to giving in, how close they were to being able to go back home. He said he knew they had suffered grievously and knew they thought the people in the building were guilty of atrocities, but they would bring no honor to themselves by taking matters into their own hands. "You know me," he said. "Give me the chance to take custody of these people and determine their guilt or innocence. I will do right by you. We have been through too much together to shame ourselves by making a horrible mistake." People listened, whispering among themselves. The whole crowd was now quiet, a mass of half-seen faces disappearing off into the darkness all around us.

As Hill spoke, I moved back toward the gate, using my awkward Albanian to ask people to clear a way for "the cars Ambassador Hill wants." This did not result in anyone actually moving—I was no Hill!—but at least they knew that vehicles were going to head that way. Two vans were waiting, and we inched them through the crowd and up to the building. The staff inside quickly loaded the battered Roma into the vans as hundreds of still surly but now quiet men stood packed against the building, glaring. We drove out fast. I jumped out at the gate and the vans tore off for a hospital. Ambassador Hill was thanking the crowd and urging everyone to return to their tents. He was given a loud ovation and, amazingly, people started to drift off into the darkness. It was over.

Within a few days we confirmed from records that these particular Roma had all been in Macedonia during the time they were accused of having committed war crimes in Kosovo. Tension, rumor, and mass hysteria had created the mob that had come so close to killing them. Within weeks, Stenkovac Camp was virtually empty, its former residents back in Kosovo trying to pick up the pieces of their lives. The beaten men recovered, and those families, too, went their own ways.

We never talked much about that night again—each day at Embassy Skopje brought too many new problems and issues connected with the Kosovo crisis. But I've come to realize that night was characteristic of much of our work in the Foreign Service: We confront so many unknowns, we have so little time, and— on scales large and small—the consequences of our actions and inactions can be so extraordinarily profound.

Charles A. Stonecipher was the political officer in Skopje from 1998 to 2001. He joined the Foreign Service in 1989. Other postings have included Bissau, Guinea-Bissau; Calgary, Canada; Washington, D.C.; Tirana, Albania; Geneva, Switzerland; and Gaborone, Botswana. His most recent assignment was to the State Department's Bureau of Political-Military Affairs in Washington, D.C.

ANATOMY OF AN EVACUATION

GUINEA, 2007
By Rosemary Motisi

For our first Foreign Service assignment, my husband and I were posted to Conakry, Guinea—one of the most corrupt, poverty-stricken, and poorly governed countries in the world. I was an office management specialist in the front office (where the ambassador and deputy chief of mission work), and my husband was an information management specialist. Within months of our arrival, civil disturbances erupted. The labor unions had called for a general strike over a series of demands, including new ministers for the government, and the country's civilian population was largely hunkered down, hoping for a peaceful resolution but preparing for the worst. The military dictator/president, Lasana Conté, had been in power since 1984.

Earlier strikes had elicited lukewarm concessions from the government, easily forgotten once the strikes ended. This time around, the organizers were hoping for a more permanent resolution, and the people of the country were desperate for any improvement. The idea was to shut the city down. Makeshift barricades materialized in the streets to halt traffic— piles of rocks, oil barrels with fires in them, whatever scraps were available. Occasionally, locals heading to work were

Gas lines in Conakry during the strikes.

attacked with rocks or sticks by strikers. For their own protection, most of our locally hired staff members were told to stay home.

As the strike lingered on, random violence began occurring, and we grew more worried. Some American citizens working for nongovernmental organizations searched for ways to leave the country safely. One friend's vehicle was attacked and the windshield broken by a big rock while en route to the airport. One of our officers received frantic calls from civil society leaders whose offices were being trashed by members of the army. And I was fielding calls from American missionaries who feared for their safety—sometimes I could hear gunshots in the background.

When the airport was officially shut down, it caused a panic in the expatriate and elite communities. We were taking calls from other embassies asking whether the United States was planning an evacuation. Americans were not being targeted, but you could easily find yourself in harm's way in a country on the verge of implosion.

Evacuations are delicate matters, however. Host country officials may take offense that their country is deemed unsafe, and other embassies may follow with their own evacuations. Also, evacuations are exceedingly expensive. Despite the complications, our embassy began quietly planning for a possible evacuation of family members and other American citizens. This involved much discussion among all sections of the embassy, calls to the State Department, talks with the Defense Department, and myriad other considerations.

The crisis peaked when a mass rally of Guineans headed to the downtown area to protest the high price of rice, horrible living standard, and the current regime. In response, in an effort to disperse the crowds, the military shot and killed many of the protesters, and the city was filled with fear. Rumors of more arrests and murders, conspiracies with neighboring countries, tribal alliances, and fighting ran rampant. It was terrifying.

The next day, the RSO arranged for all of us to be picked up by embassy vehicles and travel together to and from work. Making our way to the office that first morning after the rioting was an eerie experience. The streets were littered with rocks and small burning fires, but utterly deserted. The roving bands of street dogs were the only signs of life. At the embassy, we received word that the evacuation would take place the following day, triggering a flurry of activity to notify family members and the rest of the American community and organize safe passage to the airport.

Rosemary Motisi and her husband, Dan Malone, with a vegetable seller at a Conakry street market.

We spent that night in the embassy—my husband and I in the health unit, and everyone else scattered throughout the various offices—on mattresses that were on hand just in case this sort of event occurred. I was the officer on duty, so the Marine passed me a late-night call from a U.S. representative's office. He was calling about a constituent in Conakry who was refusing to be evacuated unless his co-worker (not an American citizen) was also evacuated. The congressional staffer needed to make sure the constituent got out safely and was calling to bring pressure to bear on the matter. I knocked on the door of the front office where my boss, the deputy chief of mission, was still awake, and transferred the call to him.

The next day, American family members, nongovernmental organization staff, and missionaries—as well as that constituent of concern and his colleague—flew out on a military plane. My husband and I were both designated "essential personnel," so we did not get on the plane. Those of us who remained behind held our breath for several days. Finally, with international pressure mounting and reports of the killing of unarmed civilians being broadcast worldwide, the government blinked and agreed to many of the demands. Unfortunately, the president succeeded in minimizing the influence of the new government, and the people of Guinea saw no significant improvements.

I have often thought since then that "the more things change, the more they stay the same." From 2007 through 2010, Guinea saw the death of one dictator, a nearly-successful assassination attempt on the next one, and a surge in ethnic-based violence. But then, in late 2010, the first democratic presidential election since independence was held, and reports were cautiously optimistic. All of us who have lived there and found so much to love in Guinea—especially in her people—are hoping for the best!

Rosemary Motisi joined the Foreign Service in 2005 as an office management specialist. Her first posting was to Embassy Conakry from 2005 to 2007; then Oslo, Norway; and

Geneva, Switzerland. Her earlier career included eight years as the judicial assistant to a Colorado State Supreme Court justice and more than a decade in the private sector. Rosemary is married to Dan Malone, an information management specialist. They have two young-adult children living in their hometown of Wheat Ridge, Colorado.

CYCLONE SIDR RELIEF

BANGLADESH, 2007
By Heather Variava

On November 15, 2007, Cyclone Sidr slammed into southwestern Bangladesh, killing thousands and leaving millions homeless. Bangladesh is an impoverished Muslim-majority nation that borders India. The fragile interim government in Dhaka had limited capacity to deliver water, food, and shelter to people devastated by the natural disaster, so the U.S. government stepped in to help.

The United States staged aerial relief efforts from an airfield in Barisal, a small city in southern Bangladesh, to deliver food and other supplies to remote villages further south. The local military and U.S. Marines jointly set up an operations center to stage the drop-off and pick-up of relief supplies. Colleagues from USAID Bangladesh and I, representing the embassy's political/economic section, established a liaison office at this forward operating base to coordinate military and civilian relief activities.

Thanks to combined U.S.-Bangladeshi efforts, we delivered literally tons of relief materials to the cyclone victims. As relief supplies from around the world poured into Dhaka, C-130 cargo planes from the U.S. Marine Corps, the U.S. Air Force, and the Bangladesh Air Force ferried the supplies down to Barisal. The USS *Kearsarge* and the USS *Tarawa*, anchored off the coast in the Bay of Bengal, sent U.S. Navy and Marine helicopters to pick up the food, blankets, and household items dropped off by the C-130s and deliver them to remote areas that could not be reached by road.

Meanwhile, my USAID colleagues fanned out from Barisal to assess the damage. Food, health, and shelter specialists visited villages and outlying areas to evaluate what people needed immediately and in the long run. I met with government officials to brief them on our work, helped obtain supplies for the operations center, coordinated communications with the command center in Dhaka, and escorted visitors and media, highlighting U.S.-Bangladesh cooperation during the crisis.

Despite the tragedy, it was inspiring to see U.S. diplomacy, development, and defense (the "three Ds") coming together to help a country in need. One afternoon stands out in my mind. We had four U.S. CH-46 helicopters on the apron of the airfield. Privates from the Bangladesh Army, as well as U.S. Marines, were running with bags of clothing and boxes of wheat, rice, and sugar, loading the supplies into the helicopters. At the same time, a U.S. C-130 was on the runway, and our

U.S. and Bangladeshi servicemen load relief supplies onto a U.S. Marine helicopter.

U.S. ground crew was off-loading more boxes of food with a forklift. And I was arranging the delivery of a water purification unit donated by USAID to a nongovernmental organization working in the region. It was windy, noisy, chaotic—and exhilarating.

A little more than a year later, in January 2008, the "three Ds" came back to Barisal, this time to spread good news rather than respond to bad. Led by our ambassador, we hosted "America Week in Barisal," highlighting all the ways the U.S. government works to help Bangladesh. USAID's NGO partners showed off their projects in the region—everything from solar energy and tuberculosis prevention to fish cultivation and literacy programs. U.S. military representatives organized a cricket tournament, involving local school children and police, to help build police-community relations.

My colleagues and I met with local officials and business representatives to learn about the political and economic challenges facing one of the poorest regions of Bangladesh. We promoted U.S. business by introducing American products to the local market, and we sponsored concerts of American jazz and a biographic film about President Barack Obama. Most rewarding of all, however, was seeing the Barisal region largely recovered from the cyclone and able to welcome us back.

Heather Roach Variava was deputy chief of the political/economic section of Embassy Dhaka, Bangladesh from 2007 to 2011. She joined the Foreign Service in 1996 and has also served in India, Mauritius, Vietnam, and Washington, D.C. She and her husband have two sons.

A HOT AUGUST IN KIRKUK

IRAQ, 2008
By Jeffrey Ashley

The sun's yellow-white heat burns, roasts, and blisters relentlessly all organisms that struggle under its blasting inferno. Out in the sand-swept plains surrounding the compound where I live, the gas flares in the desert oilfields erupt like a Vesuvius tantrum on the sun-baked, lonesome terrain. In temperatures that soar over 120 degrees, I feel my lungs screaming for relief as I inhale particles of dust, sand, and residue emanating from the sprawling oil fields of this ravaged, war-torn land. My clothes are worn-out and my skin is rubbed raw with grit and dirt. Hell hath no fury like an August day in Kirkuk.

A Foreign Service officer with the U.S. Agency for International Development for 14 years, I am serving as the USAID representative on the Kirkuk Provincial Reconstruction Team. The PRT sits in a compound located on a large U.S. military base with thousands of troops from various Army units and fancy, high-tech military machinery. We are surrounded by a jungle of imposing concrete T-walls (blast walls), sandbags, and bunkers.

I am sun-, heat-, and wind-burned, and I am exhausted. But, ironically, I have never felt more personally and professionally exhilarated than I do here, serving on a PRT in a theater of war. USAID/Iraq implements humanitarian and development assistance programs throughout war-ravaged areas of the country. In Kirkuk, USAID has implemented hundreds of projects assisting hundreds of thousands of people. My job is to ensure that the programs and projects are managed and implemented efficiently and that the Iraqi people gain access to these programs and services as quickly as possible.

When I visit projects in our area of operations, I don 40 pounds of protective body armor and a Kevlar helmet, and travel in heavy armored military vehicles, called MRAPs because they are "Mine Resistant Ambush Protected." Accompanied by a contingent of courageous U.S. soldiers for protection, I meet with local Iraqis to discuss the progress of various projects that address water and hygiene issues, education, health, microfinance, agribusiness, economic development, youth, conflict mitigation, and training and capacity-building for local district and subdistrict government councils, as well as nongovernmental and civil society sectors. In partnership with expatriate and local Iraqi professionals, these programs help restore essential services and employ thousands of people.

On any given day, I sit in a poorly furnished and sparsely decorated room of a heavily fortified government building in downtown Kirkuk, with security surrounding all corridors and entrances inside the building. PRT, Iraqi, and U.S. military colleagues and I talk over steaming, sugary tea. We discuss how best to implement our programs: a rapid-response project to create a shelter for battered women; a new well for a community; a law library for young lawyers starting out in their practices. We spend hours discussing how best to equip a burn unit in a hospital or a mobile trauma team to assist patients and victims of war-related casualties. During these meetings, we laugh, we sometimes tear up, and we recognize the strengths and hopes we all bring to the table in our shared aim to help the Iraqi people who are often the innocent victims of this tragic war.

On my way to one local council meeting in a high-risk security area of the province, I was whisked by foot through "Sniper Alley." Zigzagging quickly through the alley under the protection of Army infantry soldiers was a rather surreal G.I.-Joe experience. But the dangers are real and the soldiers' protection allows me to do my job as safely as possible every time I go "outside the wire."

Although the repercussions of war will be felt for many years to come, I whole-heartedly believe that our collective work, commitment, and passion for excellence in Iraq will establish the foundations for a strong democracy and a capable sovereign state.

Jeffrey Ashley served as the USAID representative in Kirkuk from 2008 to 2009. From there, he went on to an assignment as USAID mission director in Sana'a, Yemen. He joined USAID as a Foreign Service officer in 1995 and has also served in Indonesia, Angola, Cambodia, and Tanzania, as well as Washington, D.C.

IN THE WAKE OF TERRORIST ATTACKS

EGYPT, 2005
By Jacqueline Deley

On July 23, 2005, I was a first-tour officer about halfway through my two-year consular assignment at Embassy Cairo. In the wee hours of the night I received a phone call from the consul general summoning me to the embassy. There I learned that three coordinated terrorist bombings had occurred in a resort town in the Sinai between 1:15 and 1:20 a.m. that morning. After attending an emergency meeting with the ambassador and other section heads, the consul general asked me to go to the scene to determine if any of the casualties were American citizens and, if so, to render all necessary consular assistance. I rushed home, packed a small bag, and well before dawn was travelling across the Sinai in a motor pool vehicle heading for Sharm el-Sheikh.

When I arrived six hours later, I connected with colleagues from the regional security office and the legal attaché's office who had also been sent to investigate the bombings and liaise with Egyptian officials. There were no initial reports of American casualties, although the son of one of our Egyptian colleagues, a boy named Ahmed*, was reported missing. That first day, we visited the bomb sites, hospitals, and morgue looking for him.

I had never before been in a morgue. Thanks to the other, more experienced officers, we came prepared with masks, gloves, and moist towelettes—items that turned out to be absolutely necessary. I entered with trepidation, and while it was an extremely unpleasant experience, I found I was able to remain calm and focused as I looked at the bodies of the victims and noted their physical characteristics and clothing—in case any Americans were reported missing after the fact.

After working through the day without a break, my embassy colleagues and I gathered for dinner that evening, exhausted. There had been no sign of Ahmed among the casualties. Halfway through dinner, my cell phone rang. It was the consul general, telling me a hotel manager had called to report that two guests, an American girl and her British boyfriend, were missing. We went to the hotel immediately to talk to the manager and inspect their room.

The couple had left the hotel a few hours before the attacks and hadn't been seen since. Based on the items in their room—passports, money, and other valuables—they had intended to return. They had left behind their digital camera, and by reviewing their photos on the memory card, we were able to learn a great deal more about their physical characteristics than we could have from their passport photos alone. For example, Sarah*, the American, had several distinctive tattoos on her arms and back.

The other officers returned to Cairo the next day, leaving me with an embassy local employee security investigator and driver. I spent that day visiting hospitals and police stations, looking for Sarah and Ahmed. During these rounds, I heard that some remains had been taken to the morgue in El Tur, a small town about an hour away. I went there that afternoon and spoke to the director. We began looking through the freezer units.

One of them contained the remains of a man in his twenties—I recognized him immediately as the American woman's British boyfriend. The unit next to his held a woman, still beautiful in death, and I knew straight away who it was. From her face and her tattoos, I was sure I had found Sarah. I called the consul general to let him know, so her parents could be notified. I also called the British consular official onsite in Sharm el-Sheikh, saying I believed at least one British citizen was in the El Tur morgue.

The following day, I made a formal identification of the American woman's body and coordinated with my colleagues in Cairo to arrange for her remains to be transported there and then repatriated to the U.S., according to her parents' wishes. I also went back to her hotel room to pack up her belongings, which I brought with me when I returned to Cairo on July 26 and then forwarded to her parents. Ahmed's body was never found—it is assumed that he perished in the attacks, but was among the victims who were unidentifiable.

During those extraordinary four days, I came to understand the immense responsibility placed on consular officers in times of crisis. As emotionally wrenching as it was, I found the work incredibly meaningful. I am a career public diplomacy officer, but my experience in Egypt led me to seriously consider changing to the consular track. I deeply respect the vital work performed by consular officers every day of the week throughout the world.

*The names have been changed out of respect for privacy.

Jacqueline Deley served as a consular officer at Embassy Cairo from 2004 to 2006. She joined the Foreign Service in 2004 as a public diplomacy officer. In addition to Cairo, she has served in Jerusalem, Baghdad, and most recently, as deputy public affairs officer at Embassy Brussels. Before joining the Foreign Service, Jacqueline served as a Peace Corps Volunteer in Morocco (where she met her husband, fellow Volunteer Jeffrey Hobbs), and also taught English in both Hong Kong and Paris.

DISARMING IRAN'S NUCLEAR CAMPAIGN

AUSTRIA, 2005
By Matthew Boland

Matt Boland gives a speech on Radio Free Europe/Radio Liberty.

In July 2005, shortly after the election of hardline Iranian President Mahmoud Ahmadinejad, I arrived at the U.S. Mission to International Organizations in Vienna (UNVIE) as a brand-new Foreign Service officer and was promptly confronted with one of the greatest foreign policy challenges facing the United States: Iran's nuclear ambitions. The International Atomic Energy Agency (IAEA) is one of the most important organizations in UNVIE's portfolio, and strengthening international efforts to prevent the spread of nuclear weapons is a priority.

Just two weeks after U.S. Ambassador Gregory Schulte arrived in Vienna as head of UNVIE, Iran unexpectedly rejected a European proposal to resolve the nuclear issue. Tehran then cut the IAEA seals at its nuclear facility and began feeding 37 tons of yellowcake uranium into the process line of the Isfahan Uranium Conversion Facility. By breaking the seals, Tehran also broke the Paris Agreement, a pact with Europe committing Iran to suspend its nuclear activities while negotiations were ongoing. Countries around the world were shocked. Tensions skyrocketed within the IAEA. Global media focused on this saga, and it was now my job—as the new press spokesman and public affairs officer for UNVIE—to manage public diplomacy for the mission.

UNVIE offices are on the top floor of a skyscraper overlooking Vienna, one of Europe's most beautiful cities, nestled between the Danube River and the majestic green Alps. "Are you the new public affairs officer?" Ambassador Schulte asked when we ran into each other in the lobby on my first day on the job.

"Yes," I admitted.

"Well," he said with a smile as he got into the elevator, "I'm Ambassador Schulte, and I'm going to make you the busiest person in the mission!"

This energetic ambassador was intent on engaging in intense public diplomacy, and I was about to be charged with quickly launching a global campaign to help counter the threat posed by Iran's nuclear program.

Iran had signed the Nuclear Non-Proliferation Treaty in 1968, promising to put any nuclear program under IAEA safeguards—safeguards to assure the world that no nuclear material is being diverted for weapons. By 2005, IAEA reports indicated that Tehran had a hidden nuclear program and was refusing to cooperate with IAEA inspectors. The White House launched a major push to isolate Iran diplomatically and apply U.N. sanctions if Tehran refused to give up its efforts to develop its own nuclear technology. In June the United States had pressed its case on the fringes of the United Nations' General Assembly in New York, where 150 world leaders gathered to mark the 60th anniversary of the U.N.

Ambassador Schulte organized a flurry of meetings with groups of ambassadors who represent their countries on the IAEA Board of Governors. There he outlined U.S. views on the threat posed by Iran and asked each ambassador to support reporting Iran to the Security Council. I was thrilled to be invited to these meetings, which felt historic.

From the outset, however, we faced a huge challenge: U.S. credibility had been shattered when no weapons of mass destruction were found in Iraq. International public opinion was divided. "The potential for diplomatic solutions to all these questions is far from exhausted," Russia's ambassador said. India's ambassador made the same point. While the United States and some European countries believed Tehran was intent on developing nuclear weapons, many other countries remained sympathetic to its claim that it was merely trying to pursue a peaceful nuclear energy program.

But with Iran proceeding with enrichment—a critical step toward developing nuclear weapons—we faced a ticking clock. An emergency IAEA Board meeting was called, and Ambassador Schulte asked me to launch an active and global public diplomacy campaign focused on uniting the international community around reporting Iran to the Security Council. He expected several events each week aimed at Europe and pivotal countries on the IAEA Board: Russia, China, India, South Africa, Brazil, Colombia, Japan, and Egypt. With no prior experience, no staff and no time to waste, I felt like I was building an airplane while it was taking off.

I teamed up with Foreign Service officers in 16 other countries to launch a blizzard of events, including speeches by Ambassador Schulte, digital video conferences, press events, speaker programs, and travel by the ambassador to critical countries on the IAEA Board. Our message was clear: "Nuclear proliferation is a threat to all countries, and global threats require a global response. Iran must suspend its nuclear activities and return to the negotiating table or get reported to the Security Council."

In what one newspaper called satellite diplomacy, we set up digital video conferences between Ambassador Schulte and opinion leaders in 12 key countries. We collaborated with U.S. embassies to organize visits by the ambassador to Egypt, South Africa, Italy, the United Kingdom, Belgium, and Germany. Each visit included a dinner with a select group of nuclear experts, diplomats, and members of parliament; an on-the-record lecture at a prestigious venue; roundtable discussions with think-tanks; and interviews with major media outlets.

Thanks to the intensive diplomatic push from the White House and the State Department in Washington, combined with outstanding support from our embassies around the world, this public diplomacy campaign achieved several significant results.

On February 4, 2006, a majority of the IAEA Board, including the critical swing-vote countries (China, Russia, India, Brazil, and Egypt), voted to report Iran to the U.N. Security Council. The campaign generated thousands of news stories conveying why the United States and many in the international community believe that Iran's nuclear program poses a grave threat to international peace and security. And the campaign allowed us to personally engage, inform, and influence hundreds of diplomats, opinion leaders, and foreign citizens who attended our events. Finally, it enabled us to move beyond monologues and foster dialogues with people around the world to instill a sense of common interests, common values, and a shared commitment to solving global challenges.

Matt Boland served as a public affairs officer in Vienna from 2005 to 2007, his first Foreign Service assignment. He joined the Foreign Service in 2005 after 10 years in marketing. Following his Vienna tour, he was assigned to the State Department in Washington, D.C., as a public diplomacy desk officer for Western Europe. He and his wife, Emily, have three children.

A NEW COUNTRY IS BORN

Kosovo, 2008
By Christopher Midura

It was a chilly Sunday morning, and all was quiet as usual on Dragodan Hill, our residential perch above Pristina. But this Sunday—February 17, 2008—had a different feel: Pristina was about to become the world's newest capital city.

I did a quick morning workout at the compound of the "U.S. Office," soon to be upgraded to an embassy. I showered, pulled on some winter togs, and prepared to head downtown. Although the regional security officer had encouraged official Americans to steer clear of the street festivities, I wasn't going to miss them for anything. How many times in a career do you get the opportunity to witness the birth of a new nation?

International critics of Kosovo's secession from Serbia complained that independence was "rushed." But the speed of events is relative to where you are sitting as they proceed. For the Kosovars (ethnic Albanians who make up about 90 percent of Kosovo's population), nine years of U.N. administration could not end soon enough. For me, arriving as negotiations in the Security Council over the future of Kosovo were coming apart, the first few months of my tour were similarly marked by uncertainty and frustration.

I had been seconded from the State Department to the International Civilian Office Preparation Team (ICO-PT) to head its community affairs unit (European Union parlance for "minority rights"). The ICO-PT was established by the E.U. and other concerned nations to monitor implementation of a comprehensive proposal for the future of Kosovo drafted by U.N. Special Envoy and former Finnish President Marti Ahtisaari.

Much of the "Ahtisaari Plan" was focused on protection of the rights of minority communities in an independent Kosovo. But Kosovo Serbs, seeing themselves as part of the majority within Serbia proper, wanted no part of it. Admonished by the Serbian government to

Christopher Midura in Kosovo.

avoid any action that might make Kosovo independence more likely, few Kosovo Serbs would speak with us. Those who did anticipated violence and an exodus of Serbs once the Albanians took power. The one bright spot in this bleak scenario: while Serbian contacts were predicting that other Serbs would leave an independent Kosovo, few flatly stated they themselves would leave (and as it turned out, few did).

Cooped up in hot, dusty converted apartments in a shabby corner of Pristina, my ICO-PT colleagues and I spent most of the summer of 2007 drafting detailed plans for the day—the arrival of which was by no means assured—that the Ahtisaari Plan would form the constitutional basis for an independent Kosovo. We could then move to our shining new headquarters on Dragodan Hill and finally drop "Preparation Team" from our official name.

And so, on February 17, I took my usual route to central Pristina, down 200 stairs from Dragodan, and along the thoroughfare alternately known as "Beach Street" for its many outdoor cafés and bars, or "Bird (Crap) Street" for the thousands of crows that pack its curbside trees. It was lined with honking cars, most decorated with Albanian and American flags, some with photos of U.S. Presidents Bill Clinton and George W. Bush, or Gen. Wesley Clark, who led the NATO bombing campaign that chased Serbian forces from Kosovo in 1999.

I joined the crowd gathered outside the parliament for the formal announcement of independence, and then walked over to Mother Teresa Street, which was packed with revelers. There I found musicians in traditional Albanian dress, college students cheering, young boys flinging firecrackers in all directions, a giant cake shaped like a map of Kosovo, and flags fluttering everywhere. The two-headed Albanian eagle and our stars and stripes were ubiquitous; but also waving above the crowd were flags of the E.U., U.K., Germany, France, and Italy. I was also surprised to see T-shirts and printed copies of the new Kosovo national flag, the design of which had been announced only a few days earlier.

That evening, we watched fireworks from the apartment of the deputy head of the ICO, a fellow officer on detail from State. His apartment was one of the highest

Kosovo flags fly on independence day, 2008.

points in Dragodan, and its balcony offered a panoramic view. After the show, I dashed off a quick e-mail to my wife back in Washington: "Fireworks were spectacular, but lines of tracer bullets in the sky were definitely unsettling."

After independence, with the appointment of the International Civilian Representative, the pace of our work in the community affairs unit increased markedly. Attempted outreach to Serb communities continued to meet with resistance, slowing implementation of decentralization measures intended to give more local autonomy to minorities. But the participation of a Serb coalition in the Kosovo government provided us with a group of official interlocutors and grounds for hope.

Working with the newly renamed U.S. embassy in Pristina, we helped ensure that Kosovo's new constitution met Ahtisaari Plan requirements for protecting minority rights. We worked with government ministries and representatives of minority groups and international organizations to draft basic laws on local administration, education, and health.

As I prepared to depart in May 2008, my friends held a farewell dinner for me at a Serbian family-run restaurant we frequented on the outskirts of Pristina. We noted that the lone waitress, who had left Kosovo immediately following independence, had returned to work. We took this as a hopeful sign for Kosovo's future.

Christopher Midura served in Kosovo from 2007 to 2008. He joined the Foreign Service in 1988 as a public diplomacy officer. He has served in Bolivia, Guatemala, Zambia, El Salvador, the Czech Republic, and Kosovo. He and his wife, Kelly Bembry Midura, have two children.

WATCHING YOUR EMBASSY BURN

SERBIA, 2008
By Rian Harker Harris

Kosovo, once a province in the southern part of Serbia, declared itself an independent state on February 17, 2008. Though the historical tides of the Balkans had long been leading to this moment, the citizens of Serbia reacted with shock, anger, and genuine sadness.

Over President's Day weekend, on a snowboarding trip to Austria, I watched on CNN as rioters—fueled by nationalist rhetoric that blamed the United States for Kosovo's unwillingness to submit to Serbian rule—tried to attack Embassy Belgrade. I say "tried" because on that day the local police performed admirably, standing in an arc behind their plastic shields in front of the main door as rioters threw whatever they could find at them. When I started to get calls on my cell phone from local media in Serbia, asking for a reaction to what was happening, it was with emotion that I told them, "We genuinely appreciate the courage and professionalism of the Serbian police." The images were ugly, but the damage was minimal. Nothing could have prepared us for what was still to come.

Washington informed the embassy that U.S. recognition of the state of Kosovo would take place on February 18. My husband and I cut short our trip and sped down the Balkan highway as the appointed hour approached, hoping not to be told by an angry border guard that we were no longer welcome in Serbia.

During the next two days, the press section was eerily quiet. We spent our time circulating statements by Serbian government officials that said official relations with the United States were being broken, that the Serbian ambassador to the U.S. was being recalled, and that Serbia would fight Kosovo's independence to the end. I arranged for the ambassador to give an interview to a news agency to explain to the Serbian people why Washington had made the decision to recognize Kosovo, but few media outlets picked it up.

On February 21, the prime minister called for a national rally "to show the world that 'Kosovo is Serbia.'" The embassy closed at noon to allow staff to get home before the rally began. By the time I reached my apartment downtown, the buses had already started to arrive. The Serbian government had opened its coffers to bring in nationalist supporters from all over the country. As the bus doors opened, thousands of people, mostly young men, were disgorged, waving nationalist flags and toting half-empty two-liter bottles of beer. I took that as a sign to get off the street.

It is estimated that up to two million people attended the protest and listened to fiery speeches given from a stage set up in front of Parliament. The protesters then marched to the National Cathedral for a service to pray for the return of Kosovo. When the service broke up, the trouble started. Groups of young men began attacking diplomatic installations and looting both local and international businesses. The largest group headed toward the U.S. embassy.

As they approached, someone in the Serbian government gave the order for the police—who up to that point had stood decked out in full riot gear in a human wall around our building—to withdraw. Windows, doors, and security equipment were smashed. One of the protesters threw a Molotov cocktail into a second-story opening, where it burst into flames. Demonstrators used the flagpole to climb inside the upper floor of the chancery.

As soon as television crews began feeding images over the wires of an unprotected U.S. embassy being set afire by hooligans, the press phone began to ring. I took more than 75 calls that night, not just from Serb media, but from the United States, all over Europe, and even China. Miraculously, the cell-phone network in Belgrade did not collapse, and I was able to gather information from my colleagues and pass on accurate information to the press.

One of the rioters who had made it into an embassy building was overcome by smoke inhalation from the fire, lost consciousness and, tragically, died. With little solid information to go on, the local media reported a rumor that one of the U.S. Marine guards had shot the protester. Never had rumor control been as important to my job as it was that evening. I worked late into the night to set the story straight, and fortunately, that false representation of events dropped from the press reports, replaced by the sad truth.

The next morning, several officers gathered at the ambassador's residence to talk through our next steps and plan the evacuation of non-essential staff. Surfing the news sites at the dining room table, I found a series of photos taken by Reuters showing someone rehanging the American flag on the front of the building. The management counselor said it was a local staff member in the maintenance section, acting of his own volition.

Tear gas, dispersed by the special police unit that finally showed up to remove the rioters, had permeated everything, and it was difficult to go anywhere near the chancery without your chest burning and nose running. When we were able to return to the building, which our local staff had heroically cleaned and repaired, it was with a heavy heart. Steel plates were now being mounted on all the exterior windows of the building, blocking out the light and stifling the air flow to our offices. Several of our colleagues and all of our family members had been forced to leave on an ordered departure.

Many of us, however, were most upset by the realization that the images of the U.S. embassy being set on fire, now seen around the world, would hurt Serbia far more than the protestors had hurt the United States. Those of us, Serb and American, committed to rebuilding a partnership with Serbia—a partnership that had been broken after years of war and political upheaval—knew that this image of a pariah state once again thumbing its nose at the West did not truly represent the Serbian people, for whom the path to stability and prosperity seemed to have just become longer and more arduous.

Rian Harker Harris served as press officer in Belgrade from 2007 to 2009. She joined the Foreign Service in 2000 and has also served in Guatemala, Russia, Armenia, and Afghanistan. From Serbia, she went on to complete a master's degree in public policy at Princeton University's Woodrow Wilson School of Public and International Affairs and then to the State Department as special assistant to the assistant secretary for European and Eurasian affairs. Her husband, Christopher Harris, is also a Foreign Service officer.

U.S. SECURITY FOR THE BEIJING OLYMPICS

CHINA, 2008
By Sean O'Brien

An estimated one billion people watched the 2008 Beijing Olympic Summer Games. China put on a spellbinding show: against a backdrop of ancient and modern architectural wonders, a cast of thousands celebrated Chinese culture and played host to 10,500 international athletes in 37 venues spread over seven cities, from Shenyang to Hong Kong (almost equal to the distance from Boston to Miami).

My two-year-long, behind-the-scenes experience as the United States Olympic security coordinator in Beijing felt almost as complicated and daunting as hosting the games themselves. Given China's historic mistrust of foreign powers, foreign officials were regularly reminded that we were simply "guests." We possessed no authority in what was in any case a non-permissive environment.

As a diplomatic security agent thrust into this world of high-level international diplomacy, my watchwords were: be patient, show up every day to meet your counterparts, and respectfully stay on message. And do all that without, regrettably, speaking a lick of Mandarin or Cantonese.

Our job was, first, to convince our Chinese hosts that cooperating with us was in the interest of both countries. We gained access to the venues in all seven cities, ensuring that our security agents could fulfill their missions there. We also obtained unclassified communication access in China. We drafted operations plans and contingency plans, all within the framework of operating guidelines from the Chinese government.

It was a proud "coming of age" moment for China, opening the country up to the world while also playing to its historic moniker as the "Middle Kingdom," center of the universe. To host close to 200 countries sending thousands of athletes, along with 22,000 media representatives, Beijing was obliged to become less opaque. With a standing army of about three million, China would have no problem securing any major athletic event. But the country had to meet requirements established by the International Olympic Committee (IOC) for infrastructure, transportation (airports, highways, trains, and buses), security (police, military, and border control), hotel accommodations, athlete food quality, air quality, and more—all in an open and transparent fashion for the IOC to assess.

Three months prior to the games, 70,000 Chinese citizens lost their lives in the devastating Sichuan earthquake. That tragedy, combined with the televised protests over China's Tibet policy that accompanied many of the Olympic Torch Runs held around the world, put Beijing on the defensive. It was our good fortune that the San Francisco Police Department, along with the Diplomatic Security Service and Federal Bureau of Investigation's field offices, did a superb job during the San Francisco Torch Run. They were able to balance freedom of speech for protesters with unimpeded passage of the torch through the city. This had a positive impact on our daily negotiations in Beijing.

The United States can at times be the proverbial 800-pound gorilla, creating a huge "footprint" with every step, and Olympic participation is no exception. The unprecedented visit of a U.S. president, George W. Bush, along with his father—himself a past president and former U.S. ambassador to China—required a substantial Secret Service presence. But any overseas Olympics creates its own sizable security footprint with the need to protect, in this case, a 1,250-member U.S. Olympic team, visiting Cabinet-level officials, 20,000 U.S. corporate sponsors and tens of thousands of U.S. citizen spectators. The Olympic coordination office and Embassy Beijing had to accommodate hundreds of temporary staff involved in the Olympic visit.

The Diplomatic Security Bureau, working with the FBI and Secret Service, under the leadership of Embassy Beijing's senior management, achieved an unprecedented level of cooperation with our Chinese hosts. We created a 24-hour joint operations center in the embassy comprised of representatives from a dozen federal agencies—including the National Geospatial Agency, the Department of Defense, and the Federal Aviation Administration, among others—and various embassy offices, including public affairs, the American citizen services unit of the consular section, medical, and translation—all to act in concert to protect Americans.

In short, two years of give-and-take negotiations yielded the cooperation necessary for U.S. participation in a successful Olympic Games. Only government service overseas could provide such a unique experience, and the teamwork of outstanding public servants from various federal agencies made it a success.

Sean O'Brien served as United States Olympic security coordinator in Beijing from 2006 to 2008. He has served for 23 years as a diplomatic security special agent, with tours of duty in Latin America, the Middle East, Asia, and the United States.

AL-QAIDA ATTACK ON THE CONSULATE

SAUDI ARABIA, 2004
By Heather E. Kalmbach

Crouching beneath my desk as gunfire flew past my office window at U.S. Consulate General Jeddah was, without a doubt, the most terrifying moment of my life. The al-Qaida attack on our consulate on December 6, 2004, will remain forever imprinted on my mind as a day when five brave souls from the countries of Yemen, Sudan, India, Sri Lanka, and the Philippines lost their lives as they stood steadfast in the face of terrorism. During the attack, 10 staff members were injured so gravely that years later, many continue to suffer daily as a result of the bullet wounds. The U.S. Marine Corps house was burnt to ashes, car windows were shattered, and most debilitating of all, the consulate spirit took a serious blow.

That day began like every other in Jeddah: at six o'clock sharp, the muezzin's voice echoed throughout the city, calling Saudis to the dawn prayer. By eight, the streets were packed with honking cars and buses heading to work; and by nine, we were settling into our work day at the consulate. Then, at 11:15 a.m., the high-pitched duck-and-cover alarm rang out across the chancery building, jarring my ears and shaking me out of my chair. At first I thought it was a drill and, taking my time, locked up my office. Moments later, the whistle of bullets just outside my window told me this was no drill. A security officer ran in and escorted me quickly down the hallway where I joined my colleagues in a safe room, tiny and windowless. There we waited tensely for the next few hours, as a fight ensued outside the walls of the building.

Much of that day is still a blur for me, but on piecing the events together, a frightening story emerges. Mid-morning, a local al-Qaida cell from the Hejaz region attacked the consulate with the goal of killing American diplomats. The incident started when five men in a sedan tailed a diplomatic vehicle into the compound. Although the terrorists' car was stopped by a gate at the entrance, the men climbed out and fired on Saudi soldiers and local guards who stood along the wall's perimeter. The attackers penetrated the compound and, for the next two hours, took control of the grounds.

Although they did not breach the chancery building, the five men wandered the consulate grounds, firing at parked cars, and blowing up the Marine Corps house with a pipe bomb. They tore down the American flag that stood tall on the front lawn. And, most horrifying of all, they killed five local employees and wounded 10 local staff members, including consulate drivers, gardeners, and technicians.

During those seemingly interminable hours inside the chancery, consulate staff banded together to help one another, regardless of job title or nationality. The Marine security guard on duty at the front door bravely guarded the building as the attackers tried to destroy the main entrance with explosives. Other guards escorted more employees to the safe room. The consul general worked the phones to ensure that, even in the middle of the night, Washington knew what was happening. We made calls from our cell phones to reassure those stranded outside the chancery.

In the hot, cramped room, we tried to make sense of what was going on outside. Rumors flew as staff called petrified family members at home who were watching the events unfold on television. *Eighteen terrorists gained entry to the compound. They are on the roof now. Now they are inside the building.* Trying to ease our fears, we talked in small groups, shared water, said prayers, and comforted each other. A remarkably strong sense of community and solidarity developed in those few hours.

By mid-afternoon, Saudi forces had gained control of the compound. Four terrorists had been killed and one was taken into Saudi custody. As we stumbled out of the safe room, I walked gingerly down the hallway. My office was untouched, but my neighbor's office was riddled with bullet holes—the windows, couch, and even the television had been shot up. Gunshots had made spider-web cracks in the glass of the lobby door.

Despite our shock, we knew there was work to be done. The security officer teamed up with Saudi police to sweep the compound grounds for explosives. The nurse and general services officer delivered the heartbreaking news to families who had lost loved ones. I accompanied the ambassador to the hospital to visit a local guard who was shot in the shoulder and another employee who suffered nerve damage.

Returning home late that night, I turned on the television and found the CNN headline news: "Militants attack U.S. consulate in Jeddah, killing five employees. Group called al-Qaida in Arabian Peninsula claims responsibility." It was a stark reminder of the perils that Foreign Service members and local staff face around the world.

Despite our grief, every American and local employee returned to work following the attack. Together, we picked up the pieces and moved forward, step by step, determined to carry with us the bravery demonstrated by all on that day. I still hear from colleagues on the December 6 anniversary. Today we are serving in different parts of the world, but we are bound together by those terrible hours, the pain of losing friends and colleagues, and our strengthened commitment to the Foreign Service.

Heather Kalmbach served as a political officer in Saudi Arabia from 2004 to 2005. She joined the Foreign Service in 2004 and has also served in Jerusalem and Washington, D.C.

A PRAYER FOR DEMOCRACY

BURMA, 1998

By Andrew R. Young

Down Rangoon's Merchant Street, past trees that offered scant protection to democracy activists shot by soldiers in 1988, I walk to the Supreme Court on a spring day 10 long years after those killings. Easy to find, the halls of justice are surrounded by troops and barbed wire. Burma's junta sealed off the court's front entrance, so now one enters via the back door—a fitting metaphor for a once-proud judicial system reduced to a mere adjunct of the military dictatorship.

A hundred National League for Democracy (NLD) supporters have gathered to support Nobel Laureate Aung San Suu Kyi's attempt to end the illegal detention of about 50 parliamentarians. Elected in the NLD's 1990 landslide victory, but not permitted to take office, the political leaders have been harassed for most of the past decade. The regime has detained them for a year now without charge in the latest effort to break their spirit.

These years have been rough on NLD supporters. Jailed in record numbers, they have lost jobs and family members, and seen a decade pass without freedom. Aung San Suu Kyi arrives to cheers of "Long Live the NLD!" She and the elderly party leaders (the younger leaders are in prison) know the outcome of

Women and children from the Pa-o ethnic minority in Burma.

the case in advance—just as I do. Aung San Suu Kyi persists in a nonviolent struggle that inspires people to action, armed only with the conviction that they are right and protected only by party uniforms of homespun cloth.

Today's court date is a cynical ploy to suggest that the rule of law prevails. But no witnesses are allowed into the court. In fact, I'm the only diplomat who even tries to enter. Did the others give up? Or worse, have they begun to believe the lies put out by the regime. A Burmese bureaucrat backed by gun-toting soldiers tells me I must leave. My refusal is tolerated. In an attempt to reason with the junta, I explain on camera to the regime's videographer that this charade of judicial freedom is both obvious and pointless. Their attempt to force me to leave only ensures that I will stay. I wait and observe.

Later, I must return to the embassy, after surreptitiously indicating to NLD supporters that the United States is watching, that they are not alone in their struggle for freedom. Within 15 minutes, riot police clear the street using truncheons. Such is the duality of a diplomat's power and impotence. I can prevent violence against democracy activists only as long as I can witness regime actions.

Weeks earlier, a parliamentarian visited me. I suggested he not tarry, as covert operatives certainly saw him enter the embassy. He chastised me, saying, "I have a right to be here. A right to talk to anyone. I know what will happen to me. But before it does, I want to earn the trust of the people who elected me. I want to do something." Six months later, he was sentenced to 21 years in prison. He did nothing more than talk. But talk is dangerous in Burma. A monk once invited me into a monastery, through a locked door and down into a cave cut 35 feet into a granite hillside. At last he said, "Now, we can talk." How courageous the Burmese are, even when informants seem everywhere.

I've met the bravest people in my life here. The Burmese struggle on for democracy despite the repression, despite setbacks. Here the State Department wages a righteous fight for justice. Some day, the Burmese people will win their freedom. I pray that change comes soon, comes peacefully, and comes before more lives are destroyed.

Postscript: Over the past decade, democracy activists in Burma suffered continued oppression. Many lives were frozen in time, exiles unable to return to their homeland. On November 13, 2010, Aung San Suu Kyi was released from house arrest, once again able to share her message of nonviolence in the struggle to bring democracy and prosperity to Burma. The military regime in Burma is unpredictable, but perhaps with the right amount of determination and support, Burma will one day join the community of democratic nations. Until then, U.S. diplomats will do their best to bring attention to the struggle of the Burmese people.

Andrew R. Young was political officer in Rangoon from 1997 to 2000. He has also served in Hong Kong, China; Washington, D.C.; Mumbai, India; Auckland, New Zealand; Paris, France; and Seoul, Korea.

PART V

So You Want to Join the Foreign Service?

By Shawn Dorman

A GUIDE TO STATE DEPARTMENT GENERALIST (FSO) HIRING

The United States Foreign Service carries a reputation as an elite and prestigious profession. This cachet has endured through the generations in part because of the mystique surrounding the difficult process candidates must traverse to gain entry to the career. There is strong attachment inside the Foreign Service to keeping this gateway challenging and meritocratic, so that passing the exams continues to be seen as a badge of honor for those who make it through.

Over the past several decades, of the thousands who applied each year, only 2 to 3 percent have been offered a position, averaging 200 to 300 officers a year. There have been lean years—the early 1990s, for example—and then years of increased hiring to replenish the ranks. Secretary of State Colin Powell's Diplomatic Readiness Initiative (DRI) from 2001 through 2004, in part a response to the depleted numbers at State, brought in several thousand new Foreign Service officers and specialists. But soon after DRI hiring was completed, shortages emerged again due to staffing demands for new U.S. missions in Iraq and Afghanistan.

The most recent hiring increase began in 2009 with funding initially requested by Secretary of State Condoleezza Rice. It was accomplished under Secretary of State Hillary Rodham Clinton's Diplomacy 3.0—Diplomacy, Development and Defense—primarily a hiring initiative designed to bulk up the strength and numbers for diplomacy and development. Her goal was to increase the ranks of the State Foreign Service by 25 percent by 2013 and to double the size of USAID's depleted Foreign Service ranks by 2012. The State Department hiring target for 2009 was met, with 1,350 Foreign Service officers and specialists hired; for 2010 the hiring goal was 1,425; and for 2011, numbers were predicted to be slightly lower, about 800 or 900. The number of applicants has changed over time, but in 2010 and in 2011, more than 25,000 people per year were competing for State FSO positions.

For many years, State management has been concerned about the extremely long time it takes to hire a new Foreign Service officer. Over the last 20 years, the average wait between taking the written exam, the first step in the process, and the job offer has been 12 to 24 months. Until 2007, the written exam was typically given only once a year. This meant that even the perfect diplomat might have to wait up to 11 months just to take that first step. After the written exam, candidates waited three months for their results. Those who passed would be invited to take the Oral Assessment—at some future date.

Then, another long wait followed while the required medical and security clearances were processed. Only after those clearances were given would a candidate be placed on a register. Even that achievement was (and still is) no guarantee of a job, just a promise that if the needs of the Service reach as far as that candidate's number on the register before 18 months elapse, an offer will be made to join an A-100 training class for new diplomats. Not everyone could afford to wait that long.

A SHORTER, BETTER-FOCUSED PROCESS. For years, State flirted with the possibility of changing the exam process, making marginal adjustments every so often. In 1997, aiming to better compete in the so-called "War for Talent," the department hired the management consulting firm McKinsey & Company to evaluate State Department Foreign Service recruitment and retention. At the time, the dot.com boom had federal managers worried. Later it was higher salaries and quicker intake for jobs in the private sector that created a reasonable concern among State recruiters. During his tenure, Secretary Powell succeeded in reducing the amount of time it took to process security clearances, but the total hiring process still averaged more than a year.

In 2006, then-Director General of the Foreign Service George Staples ordered a comprehensive review and improvement of the entry process, with the aim of making it faster and more candidate-friendly. State again enlisted McKinsey, this time to evaluate its assessment and hiring process. Certain best practices were already in place—namely, the Foreign Service Written Exam and the Oral Assessment, both of which McKinsey considered the "gold standard." According to McKinsey, the one significant missing element, routine in the private sector, was a long, close look at experience and background early in the hiring process. The consultant recommended, and the State Department adopted, a "Total Candidate" approach that would take into account experience as well as exam scores.

For many years, the hiring process had been almost entirely "blind," in the sense that a look at the candidate's experience—work history, languages, education—was one of the last steps. From the mid-1980s until about 2001, examiners did not see candidates' files until they succeeded in reaching what was essentially the exit interview, having passed through the daylong oral assessment. Only then could a candidate wow the examiners with fluent Arabic, a Ph.D. in international relations, Peace Corps experience, or years working for a nonprofit in Latin America. If they happened to have useful experience, great. But they had to get over most of the hurdles before that could be considered. The practice created a level playing field for candidates, but maybe it was *too* level. Maybe experience mattered and should be counted much earlier.

In addition, the Secretary of State and human resources officials increasingly sought diversity in the applicant pool. "We want the Foreign Service to look like America" became a common refrain. And State has reached out to talented minority students to increase awareness of the Foreign Service career option. Once an individual applies to join the Foreign Service, however, there is no special preference; all compete on merit and now, to a greater extent than ever before, on experience.

DISABLED AND IN THE FOREIGN SERVICE
By Avraham Rabby

It was once unheard of for people with disabilities to work in the Foreign Service, representing the interests, democratic values, and multicultural society of the United States around the world. Prior to 1990, the policy of the Department of State was to retain in employment, as a humanitarian gesture, Foreign Service employees who had become disabled while on active duty, but to reject applications from candidates who were already disabled.

The thinking was that people with disabilities would only be able to serve in a limited range of postings and therefore unable to comply with the department's fundamental principle of worldwide availability. In my own case, the department further argued that, given my total blindness, I would not be able to handle the massive amounts of paperwork involved, would not be able to observe the facial expressions of foreign diplomats seated across the negotiating table from me, and would not be able to cope with the changing environments and cultures typical of the average Foreign Service career.

However, ever since the department, to its credit, reversed its policy in 1990, it has not only welcomed candidates with disabilities into the Foreign Service ranks, but has done its utmost to provide disabled recruits with all the accommodations necessary to enable them to maximize their productivity and compete on an equal footing with their non-disabled peers. These accommodations have included the removal of architectural barriers to the physically disabled, the purchase of specialized access technology to enable the visually impaired to read their computer screens by means of speech software, Braille displays or screen magnification, and the provision of human assistants, such as readers and sign-language interpreters for blind and deaf officers respectively. As was the case in all my postings, the State Department hired a reader (usually a Foreign Service spouse with a security clearance) who would read the daily newspapers and incoming classified cables to me, format my response cables as instructed, conduct Internet research, and accompany me to meetings and receptions in order to read name tags and let me know who else was in attendance.

Although my basic career path was that of a political officer, my aim was not to focus exclusively on political reporting but to experience the Foreign Service in all its variety and richness. And, in fact, by the time I retired, I had completed seven assignments on five continents, and what an incredibly fulfilling ride it was!

At the American embassies in London, Pretoria, Lima, and Port of Spain, I carried out the normal responsibilities of a political officer: presenting the U.S. position to the host country's foreign ministry, receiving the host government's response, reporting on discussions with contacts, analyzing the latest political developments in the country, drafting speeches for the ambassador, and briefing congressional and other delegations on the local political scene. Perhaps my most moving experience as a political officer occurred on April 27, 1994, when I served as an official international observer during South Africa's first post-apartheid election, which brought Nelson Mandela to power. Following Mandela's inauguration, I remained at the embassy late into the evening drafting a reporting cable on that historic event.

Negotiating the precise texts of United Nations (U.N.) resolutions during an assignment to the U.S. Mission to the United Nations in New York City presented unique challenges to me, since my reader continually had to print out Braille versions of the ever-changing drafts of resolutions and rush them to me in the negotiating rooms. In addition, I would often ask her to accompany me through the halls and corridors of U.N. headquarters, in order to spot other-country delegates whose support for the U.S. position on this or that resolution I needed to secure.

The only time I strayed from the political track was to serve in a public diplomacy position at Embassy New Delhi. Responsible for the electronic media unit, I supervised eight local Indian employees, arranging TV and radio coverage for embassy events, overseeing the screening of educational videos about the United States, and moderating people-to-people dialogues between Indian and American grassroots citizen groups through digital video conferences.

Today, people with all kinds of disabilities carry out Foreign Service assignments that are as diverse as those of their non-disabled peers, including at hardship and danger posts. Although the State Department must be commended for the enormous progress it has made since 1990, Foreign Service officers and staff with disabilities still face obstacles and challenges—some procedural, others attitudinal. The Bureau of Diplomatic Security still takes a long time to issue security clearances for individuals hired to assist officers with disabilities and to certify the specialized computer access technology to be used by these officers. Such delays make it impossible for new employees with disabilities to become fully and immediately productive.

Although I was fortunate enough to have had a most rewarding career, I always had to be on my guard, during each assignment bidding cycle, to ensure that prospective hiring managers did not rule me out of consideration simply because I was blind. Hiring managers clearly did that on two occasions in my career. On a more subtle level, what I encountered among my superiors, co-workers, and those reporting to me was the same range of attitudes and behaviors toward my disability—both positive and negative, both socially accepting and socially distant—as I would expect to find at any other place of work. As more and more people with disabilities join the Foreign Service, such wariness and discomfort will gradually disappear.

One promising development has come with President Obama's July 2010 directive, Executive Order 13548, calling for an additional 100,000 individuals with disabilities to be employed by the federal government. The order gives specific performance targets and deadlines for each federal agency to meet, and includes the State Department Civil Service and Foreign Service.

It is interesting to note that foreign diplomats never once referred to my disability and invariably treated me as their absolute equal. When disabled American diplomats deliver the U.S. foreign policy message to host-country governments, when disabled American diplomats negotiate resolutions with delegates from the 191 other member states of the United Nations, or when disabled American diplomats speak to civil society groups around the world about U.S. culture and values, they are living proof, more convincing than anything else could be, of the openness, pluralism, and vibrancy of American society.

Avraham Rabby joined the Foreign Service in 1991 and served for 16 years, in London, Pretoria, Lima, Port of Spain, New Delhi, at the U.S. Mission to the United Nations in New York City, and in Washington, D.C.

By government standards, the resulting changes to the Foreign Service hiring system were implemented at warp speed. The review began during the summer of 2006, and the first new Foreign Service Officer Test—formerly called the Foreign Service Written Exam—was given in the fall of 2007. In 2010, the FSOT was being offered more often and in more places than ever before.

While standards remain high, State is seeking a slightly different diplomat today, someone who might be described as the "perfect diplomat plus." It used to be acceptable to "just be brilliant." But now, as one senior official from the Bureau of Human Resources explained, "brilliant is good, but we want people who know how to be practical and solve problems, how to work well with people."

CHANGED WORLD, NEW NEEDS. The world in which diplomats operate has changed dramatically in the past several decades since the end of the Cold War.

Bipolarity and the predominance of state-to-state relations, while still key, are giving way to multipolarity and the interaction of a wider variety of state and non-state actors, presenting new opportunities along with new dangers and challenges.

The number of unaccompanied postings—to places including Iraq, Afghanistan, and Pakistan—has tripled in the last decade, from a couple of hundred in the 2000s, to more than 900 by 2010 (generalist and specialist positions combined). Today, incoming FSOs should expect to serve in an unaccompanied post at some point in their careers.

The State Department is seeking candidates who not only have intellectual abilities, but real-world skills. The diplomat's traditional reporting function is now combined with, and sometimes overtaken by, more action-oriented pursuits. This shift began with Secretary Powell and became more pronounced during Secretary Rice's tenure, from 2005 to 2009, as part of her Transformational Diplomacy initiative.

As Secretary Rice explained in a February 2008 speech at Georgetown University: "America must recruit and train a new generation of Foreign Service professionals with new expectations of what life as a diplomat will be. ... We see it in the jungles of Colombia, where our diplomats are helping old guerrilla fighters become new democratic citizens. We see it in Zimbabwe, where our diplomats are taking up the just and peaceful cause of a tyrannized people." The concept of diplomats out in the field helping build democracy was not new—but it was becoming a broader policy priority.

THE UPDATED HIRING PROCESS. The basic structure of the Foreign Service assessment process remains intact, but has been expanded. Candidates still have to pass "the written exam"—now called the Foreign Service Officer Test, or FSOT—to be invited to take the Oral Assessment. But in order to have a shot at the orals, the candidate now must pass another significant hurdle first—the Qualifications Evaluation Panel (QEP). This panel reviews the complete file of each applicant who passes the FSOT, taking the measure of what is called the "Total Candidate"—including education, work and overseas experience, and foreign languages spoken.

There have been other changes, as well. The State Department has come a long way from the predominantly male Foreign Service of the past. A gender discrimination class-action suit, known as the Palmer case, that wound its way through the legal system for over a decade was resolved in 1989 in favor of the plaintiffs, leading to the cancellation of that year's FS written exam, because it had been found to be biased against women and minorities. The written exam was changed and, in recent years, most A-100 classes have been about half female. The State Department has made it a priority to increase minority hiring, though achieving this goal is tied to outreach—casting a wider net and letting more people know about the career options—and not to the exam process.

Processing time from test to job offer has been steadily improving under the new system. "I am aware of at least one person who took the written exam in

SAMPLE QUESTIONS FROM THE NEW FOREIGN SERVICE EXAM

By Brian Aggeler, FSO

September, passed the oral assessment in December, received his clearances by February, and started A-100 in May," said one new FSO in 2009. "There's your poster child for the improvement in the test-to-offer time."

The following pages will take you, step by step, through the Foreign Service generalist hiring process at the State Department.

Step One: Registration

American citizens between the ages of 21 and 59 are eligible to apply for generalist positions. A college degree is not required. The Foreign Service Officer Test is given three times a year, during one-week (eight-day) "windows." For 2007 and 2008, the Bureau of Human Resources set a maximum total pool of 15,000 applicants per year, with a maximum of 5,000 candidates taking the written exam during any given test period. In 2009, seats were quickly filled, and some candidates had to wait for the next window to get a spot. Due to the increasing interest in the Foreign Service career, and the hiring increase beginning in 2009, the number of seats available during each testing window was expanded to 9,000 in 2009—or 27,000 for the year. *Tip: Seats are allocated by date, location, and career track, and can fill up quickly, so sign up early.*

There is no paper in this process. The only way to register is online at www.careers. state.gov. Candidates can register at any time, but must schedule a testing "seat" within one year of registration and at least 48 hours prior to the opening of the window during which they want to test. Once the registration has been submitted successfully, candidates receive an e-mail authorizing them to sign up online for a seat at a particular testing center on a particular date within the testing window selected. Test seats are given out on a first-come, first-served basis. *Tip: Hold on to the personal login and password that you use to register; you'll need it later to download results and other information.*

The registration procedure has varied over time, so be sure to check the State Web site for current requirements. There was, and still is, no fee to take the test. For many years, signing up was about as simple as sending in your name, so the written exam could be taken on a whim. Some people have taken the exam, known as the ultimate "smarty-pants" test, without seriously considering the FS career, but just to see if they could pass. As not all who registered were serious candidates, the number of no-shows for the test was sometimes high. That number has dropped significantly since State began levying a $50 fee for those who do not appear for the test date they selected and do not give 48-hour notice of cancellation.

In 2007, State made registration much more labor-intensive, requiring six personal-narrative essays up front. Registration was taking candidates from three to six hours, or more. The heavy front-loading of the process was deterring applicants, and the registration process has since been streamlined—now the essays are not required until after the candidate passes the written test.

The registration process, as of 2011, takes about 40 minutes. It consists of three parts, described below. *Tip: Save and print the completed forms, because they cannot be opened again once you hit "submit."*

STRUCTURED RÉSUMÉ. Candidates fill out a "structured résumé" form, which asks for information on education, work history, overseas experience, and other background information. While extensive overseas experience is now a plus on the application, the security background check still takes longer because of it.

CAREER TRACK SELECTION. The five career tracks—still familiarly known as "cones"—from which all applicants must choose are: consular, political, economic, management, and public diplomacy. Though the political track continues to be the most sought-after, State has been hiring a roughly equal number of officers for each track in recent years. Hiring is based on the needs of the Service for officers in each category at any given time, and successful applicants are put on the register only for their selected career track—so selection can be a tricky exercise. While choosing a track that is less popular or has more current openings may seem to offer an advantage in terms of getting in, the numbers are always shifting. Moreover, candidates should not select a track in which they do not actually want to work. Though it can be done, switching tracks once you are in the system is not easy and is not a recommended strategy. See the box on this page for a detailed discussion of choosing a career track, and visit the State careers Web site for more information on each track.

WHICH CAREER TRACK IS RIGHT FOR ME?
By Kelly Adams-Smith

When registering to take the Foreign Service Officer Test, applicants are asked to make the first big decision of their Foreign Service careers—the choice of a career track. While all Foreign Service officers are technically termed "generalists," the choice of functional specialization will determine what type of work a Foreign Service officer will do for most of his or her career.

The five generalist career tracks, or "cones" as they were once officially and still commonly called, are Consular, Economic, Management, Political, and Public Diplomacy. Each career track is unique, with its own advantages and drawbacks. Talking with Foreign Service officers, you'll probably find there are some strong views and stereotypes about each of the cones, with everyone thinking his or her cone is "the best." To find out which track is right for you, potential FSOs should do their research, not just on paper, but preferably through conversations with officers currently working in each career track of interest.

When doing this research, it is important to keep an open mind. No matter what anyone tells you, no career track is a guaranteed ticket to the top. No one cone promises unconditional happiness or accelerated promotion. No cone is better or worse than any other. The trick is to decide which one is right for you, your personality, and your background. And it may not be the one you first thought you'd choose.

Consular Track

Consular officers are our face to the world. They are often the first and only American a foreign citizen will ever meet at an embassy. They may also be the only diplomat an American ever meets when traveling overseas. Being the face of America to the world and the face of the Foreign Service to the traveling American public is a privilege and responsibility. Deciding who does and does not get a visa, consular officers are also on the front lines promoting

U.S. business interests, tourism, and educational exchanges, while protecting American borders from those who seek to break U.S. immigration laws and perhaps do us harm.

Consular officers help Americans in distress. When a fellow citizen has been arrested, hospitalized, or has fallen victim to crime overseas, the consular officer is there to help, working with local authorities, calming nerves, and helping to make decisions. If a natural disaster, major accident, or civil unrest forces an evacuation from a foreign country, it is the consular officer who takes charge. Consular officers also perform notary services for fellow Americans, issue reports of birth and death abroad, and replace lost or stolen passports. They are witnesses to the happiest and saddest occasions in the lives of our fellow citizens overseas. They see the joy of the American parent who has just received an immigrant visa for the baby he has adopted. They may be the first to deliver the news that a loved one has died overseas.

Given these responsibilities, a consular officer is part attorney and part counselor. The work can be adrenaline-charged and stressful. Successful consular officers have good crisis management, foreign-language, and people skills. Of all our colleagues, it is often the consular officers who have the best Foreign Service stories.

Diplomats generally spend the first two to four years of their career doing consular work because the need is so great. A rite of passage for FSOs, the consular tour provides a common bonding experience. Many officers love the work so much that they never leave it.

Economic Track

Economic officers are at the forefront of the trends shaping our world and America's place in it. They identify the world's next economic trouble spots, as well as important opportunities overseas for U.S. companies. Their contacts include everyone from local government officials and business leaders to central bankers and representatives of the big international financial institutions. Economic officers must be comfortable conversing with all of them.

Like political officers, economic officers have fewer supervisory responsibilities early in their careers than consular and management FSOs. Instead, they focus on building subject-matter expertise in areas such as energy security and trade policy. They write congressionally mandated reports on a wide range of issues, from evaluating a country's level of intellectual property rights protection to reviewing investment disputes and market access concerns. They deliver economically focused messages from Washington to the host government and try to persuade local interlocutors to support U.S. policy positions.

Actually, "economic officer" is somewhat of a misnomer, for the issues handled in this career track go far beyond economics. These officers are responsible for all matters related to the environment, science, technology, health, and labor. They work closely with U.S. diplomats from the Foreign Commercial Service and the Foreign Agricultural Service, handling those issues fully at smaller posts where these departments may not be represented. Economic officers level the playing field for U.S. companies, promote U.S. exports abroad, and work closely with local American Chambers of Commerce.

Economic officers also advise the ambassador on all matters in their portfolio, often writing speeches on economic matters for embassy leadership or delivering them in person. They serve as control officers for high-level U.S. government visitors, devising agendas and arranging site visits to local ports or factories. As they rise through the ranks, economic officers may become lead U.S. negotiators for economically focused bilateral or multilateral treaties and agreements.

While the work in this career track requires a certain familiarity with economic, trade, and business principles, even the best economic officers spend very little time crunching numbers. While many enter with some background in economic and business affairs, the State Department also offers first-class training opportunities to those economic officers wanting or needing a skills upgrade. The best economic officers combine this technical expertise with analytical minds and excellent writing and people skills.

Management Track

Management officers run our embassies. Similar to managers in multinational firms, State Department management officers handle all of an embassy's human resources, budget and finance, real estate and property matters, in a multicultural, multilingual environment.

It is not necessary to come into the Foreign Service with previous management, human resources, or budget experience in order to be a successful management officer. What the State Department's extensive training program does not teach, the management officer learns on the job. More important, however, than technical skills is a management officer's ability to lead. The management cone is about supervising, mentoring, advising, and deciding.

Our managers often head large sections very early in their careers, directing the work of sometimes hundreds of local-hire staff. Some have been on the job for years. Others are new hires, completely unfamiliar with the embassy environment and American work culture. Some do not speak English well, so the management officer has to communicate with them using a language just learned. The officer needs to find ways to relate to all of these employees, finding different ways to motivate them.

The management officer's goal is to provide the best possible service to his or her colleagues—to ensure they have what they need to carry out the embassy's mission. Management officers oversee the technical staff providing our communications systems, direct the work of staff responsible for improving family member morale, and chair countless committees—from those ensuring mission resources are being utilized fairly among various U.S. government offices represented at the embassy, to those assigning housing to incoming officers and those giving awards to employees.

Being privy to just about everything that is going on in a mission, the management officer is one of the ambassador's closest advisers, keeping the executive office informed on everything from morale issues to the embassy's obligations under U.S. and local laws.

In contrast to officers in some of the other career tracks, where the impact of a particular policy or program can take years or decades to materialize, management officers can point to tangible accomplishments every day. If you like to get things done, are comfortable making decisions, have good people skills and like being in charge, the management track may be right for you.

Political Track

Political work is what many think of when they think of diplomatic work. A political officer makes and maintains contacts in the national and local governments and keeps in close touch with political parties, think-tanks, nongovernmental organizations, activists, and journalists. He or she delivers official messages, called démarches, from the U.S. government to the local government and reports the response to those messages. A political officer will use the insight gained from local contacts and experiences to report on a variety of issues that may be of interest to Washington—from which party may win the next election to which indigenous group may be seeking greater political sway in the capital.

But good political officers do not just report on what they see or experience; their job is to analyze, advise, and influence. Political officers do not just deliver our message to the host government, but use their skills of persuasion to motivate a government to take a certain action or support a certain policy. A successful political officer analyzes trends and, using excellent writing skills, makes recommendations to Washington on opportunities to advance U.S. policy objectives in the country or region.

While colleagues in other career tracks often get significant management experience early on, political officers typically supervise fewer people early in their careers. Instead, they become subject-matter experts in areas such as human rights, trafficking in persons, fighting corruption, and electoral politics. They accompany the ambassador and other high-level officials to meetings, taking notes and reporting conversations. They serve as control officers for visiting U.S. officials and congressional delegations, designing their agendas, accompanying them to meetings, and managing logistics. They research and write numerous congressionally mandated reports on everything from human rights and religious freedom to narcotics trafficking and counterterrorism.

Political officers advise the ambassador and deputy chief of mission—the embassy's "front office"—on whom to meet and what to say. They must have excellent interpersonal skills and enjoy using foreign languages. The best political officers have a natural ability to earn the trust of their interlocutors. They are at ease in a variety of environments, from exchanging business cards at receptions and giving speeches at conferences to investigating conditions in refugee camps. They are patient, knowing that the results of their work may not be evident for years. The ability to write well is crucial. If this describes you, then political work may be the right choice.

Public Diplomacy Track

Public diplomacy (PD) officers are our public relations professionals. They shape and deliver our message to the world; handle our interaction with U.S. and foreign media; explain our history, culture, and the value of our diversity to foreign audiences; and promote educational and cultural exchange. This career track involves tremendous contact work: meeting with and developing close ties to foreign journalists, government officials, educators, nongovernmental organizations, think-tanks, and those in the arts.

Public diplomacy work also requires close interaction with colleagues and knowledge of all the issues they handle—from political policies and economic programs to a controversial consular case or a complex legal issue being handled by the management section. The PD officer must keep on top of it all in order to explain it, if necessary, to the press and public.

PD officers usually get management experience early on. They are responsible for programmatic budgets and often supervise significant numbers of local staff. Information officers, or those PD officers in charge of press affairs, work closely with journalists, acting as a source of information, and promoting free speech and transparency. Cultural affairs officers, or those PD officers handling cultural and educational exchanges and programs, may spend their day chairing the local Fulbright Exchange Commission, managing grants to local arts groups, nongovernmental organizations, or think-tanks, or selecting noted American jazz musicians or hip-hop dancers for U.S.-sponsored local tours.

Public diplomacy officers advise the ambassador and other embassy leaders on what to say publicly and when to say it. They track local public opinion, and travel often to speak and provide U.S.-themed programming to regions far from the capital. They must have excellent foreign-language and public speaking skills. They should enjoy the spotlight and have grace under pressure. The most successful PD officers also have a passion for U.S. history and culture and enjoy explaining and sharing these with the world.

What If I Choose the "Wrong" Cone?

It does occasionally happen that a Foreign Service candidate will choose a career track only to find, after being in the Service for several years, that he or she is much more suited to another track. The good news is that it is possible to change. The process isn't quick or easy, and therefore shouldn't be undertaken lightly; but it can sometimes be done after you have completed several tours in another cone.

Switching tracks may not be necessary, however. You will have plenty of opportunities to work outside of your career track, and many Washington-based jobs are not defined by track, but are "multifunctional." Remember that to be a well-rounded officer, you should seek opportunities to work outside of your chosen career track from time to time. Being multifunctional gives you breadth of experience and knowledge that can help at promotion time. It also makes an already exciting career all the more interesting.

Kelly Adams-Smith is a Foreign Service officer who has served in Moscow, Tallinn, and Sofia. She currently lives and works in Washington, D.C., with her Foreign Service officer husband Steve and their two children. While she is an economic-coned officer, Kelly has officially or unofficially spent time working in all five Foreign Service career tracks.

LANGUAGE ABILITY SELF-ASSESSMENT. The registration form also asks candidates to list their foreign languages and assess their own competence in speaking/listening and reading/writing on the State Department's scale of 1 to 5, with 5 being the level of a college-educated native speaker, 3 being general professional proficiency and 2 being minimal professional proficiency. Speaking/listening and reading/writing skills are rated separately, so a score of 2/2 represents minimal professional proficiency in Speaking/Reading. Reading proficiency is not tested prior to entry into the Foreign Service; but speaking ability is tested at different points of the application process, depending on the language.

The State Department divides languages into three groups: world languages (e.g., French, Spanish, German), Critical Needs Languages (CNL), and Super Critical Needs Languages (SCNL). The two latter categories change periodically depending on the needs of the Service. In 2011, the Critical Needs Languages were: Arabic (forms other than Modern Standard, Egyptian, and Iraqi), Azerbaijani, Bengali, Chinese [Cantonese], Kazakh, Korean, Kurdish, Kyrgyz, Nepali, Pashto, Punjabi, Russian, Tajik, Turkish, Turkmen, and Uzbek. In 2011, the Super Critical Needs Languages were: Arabic (Modern Standard, Egyptian, and Iraqi), Mandarin Chinese, Dari, Farsi, Hindi, and Urdu. Refer to the State Department careers Web site for more information and to check for any changes.

Any candidate who claims a working-level speaking ability (2/0 or higher) in one of the SCNLs will be instructed to take a telephone test given by instructors from the State Department Foreign Service Institute immediately after passing the written exam. These are pass/fail tests, with a level 2 score required to pass. Competency in the CNLs and world languages is considered, and tested, later in the process.

To help determine what your language proficiency level is, visit www.govtilt.org and click "speaking" under skill-level descriptions. There is also a speaking self-assessment tool on the site. For further information on the role of languages in the hiring process, see p. 231.

Step Two: Taking the Foreign Service Officer Test

After candidates submit their registration package, they are notified by e-mail when testing windows open for scheduling the Foreign Service Officer Test. Seats for specific dates and locations then fill up on a first-come, first-served basis.

As part of the effort to streamline and speed up the hiring process, State tossed out the old blue books and pencils, opting instead for an entirely online FSOT. The test now takes three hours, as opposed to the previous five. The first online exam was given in September 2007 at more than 200 centers in the United States. Dozens of overseas testing sites, many of them at U.S. embassies, have since been added.

Candidates report to their designated testing center and log on to a computer terminal to take the online test. The FSOT includes four sections: Job Knowledge, English Expression and Usage, Biographic Information, and the Written Essay. The aim of the FSOT is to test the candidate on areas of knowledge that have been determined to be critical for successful performance as an FSO in any of the five career tracks. Though the test no longer contains separate career track sections, there are career-specific questions in the job knowledge section that all candidates must answer. *Tips: Questions are not grouped or identified according to career track. Because there is no penalty for wrong answers, it is advisable to answer all questions.*

SECTION 1: JOB KNOWLEDGE. This is the section that presents the biggest challenge for most applicants, because it covers the widest variety of topics. There will be topics that surprise even the most well-prepared applicants, for the exam is designed to test an impossibly broad range of knowledge.

In 2010, this section consisted of 60 multiple choice questions and the time allowed was 40 minutes. Some clues to the types of questions that will be asked can be found in the list of topics provided by the State Department in the *Guide to the FSO Selection Process*. The basic topics are:

- **Communication.** A general understanding of principles of effective communication and public speaking techniques, as well as general knowledge of the common sources of information, public media, and media relations.
- **Computers.** A general understanding of basic operations such as word processing, databases, spreadsheets, and preparing and using e-mail.
- **English Language.** Ability to use correct grammar, organization, writing strategy, sentence structure, and punctuation required for writing or editing reports.

- **Economics.** An understanding of basic economic principles, as well as a general understanding of those issues and the U.S. economic system.
- **Management.** A general understanding of basic supervisory techniques and methods, including knowledge of human psychology, leadership, motivational strategies, and equal employment practices.
- **Mathematics and Statistics.** A general understanding of basic mathematical and statistical procedures.
- **U.S. Government.** A general understanding of the composition and functioning of the federal government, the Constitution and its history, the structure of Congress and its role in foreign affairs, as well as the U.S. political system and its role in governmental structure, formulation of policies, and foreign affairs.
- **U.S. Society and Culture.** An understanding of major events, institutions, and movements in U.S. history, including political and economic history, as well as national customs and culture, social issues and trends, and the influence of U.S. society and culture on foreign policy and foreign affairs.
- **World History and Geography.** A general understanding of significant events, issues, and developments in world history, including their impact on U.S. foreign policy, as well as knowledge of world geography and its relationship to U.S. foreign policy.

SECTION 2: ENGLISH EXPRESSION AND USAGE. The English expression and usage section of the FSOT is designed to test the candidate's use of the English language, from grammar, spelling, punctuation, and usage to organizational skills related to writing and editing. In 2010, this section consisted of 65 multiple choice questions and the time allowed was 50 minutes. *Tip: Review* The Elements of Style, *by Strunk and White.*

SECTION 3: BIOGRAPHIC INFORMATION. The biographic section of the test is designed to evaluate the candidate's prior experience—both work and life—that may relate to the ability to perform successfully as an FSO. It aims to elicit information that can show how well the candidate resolves conflicts, interacts with others, adapts to other cultures, and sets priorities. This section consists of about 75 questions to be answered in 40 minutes. Most questions are multiple choice, but some are followed by a space for details or examples to back up the answer.

SECTION 4: THE STRUCTURED ESSAY. The structured essay section is where candidates show their ability to write clearly and concisely under time pressure by writing either one or two essays on assigned topics. The essay is only evaluated if the candidate gets a passing score on the multiple-choice sections. Essays are evaluated based on the quality of the writing rather than the opinions expressed. There are no "right" answers. On exams with two essays, only one actually counts, but the candidate will not know which one.

With the implementation of online testing, the allotted time to write each essay was cut from 50 minutes to 30. The fact that candidates use the computer rather than write longhand clearly saves time for most, but many candidates still find the time allocated to go very quickly.

Foreign Service work often requires rapid drafting under deadline—the senator's plane is departing in one hour and the report on his meeting with the president must be signed off on before he goes to the airport; the ambassador has a meeting with the foreign minister, and she needs talking points in 20 minutes—so this part of the assessment can help show how well the candidate writes under time pressure.

ACRONYMS AND TERMS FOR THE ASSESSMENT PROCESS

13 Ds:	Thirteen Dimensions, criteria used in QEP and FSOA to evaluate candidates	**FSR:**	Final Suitability Review, after the FSOA and clearances
A 100:	Orientation course for all new FSOs	**FSWE:**	Foreign Service Written Exam (old name for FSOT)
BEX:	Board of Examiners	**GE:**	Group Exercise portion of FSOA
BIO:	Biographical portion of FSOT	**ICO:**	Immediate Conditional Offer
CM:	Case Management portion of FSOA	**JK:**	Job Knowledge portion of FSOT
CNL:	Critical Needs Language	**LEH:**	List of Eligible Hires
CO:	Conditional Offer	**NDA:**	Non-Disclosure Agreement
Cone:	Career Track	**NFATC:**	National Foreign Affairs Training Center
EE:	English Expression portion of FSOT	**PNQ:**	Personal Narrative Questions, "mini-essays" (for QEP)
EQIP:	Electronic Questionnaires for Investigative Processing, online version of the SF-86, for the security clearance	**QEP:**	Qualifications Evaluations Panel (between FSOT and FSOA)
FSI:	Foreign Service Institute (now named NFATC)	**SCNL:**	Super Critical Needs Language
		SI:	Structured Interview portion of FSOA
FSOA:	Foreign Service Oral Assessment (the oral exam)	**SOI:**	Statement of Interest: why you want to be an FSO, due at FSOA
FSOT:	Foreign Service Officer Test (the written exam)		

HOW TO PREPARE FOR THE FSOT. There are sample multiple choice and essay questions in the State Department's *Guide to the Foreign Service Officer Selection Process*, which can be downloaded for free from the State Web site at careers.state.gov. Also helpful is the study guide from ACT, the company that holds the State Department contract to administer the test. The ACT guide can be purchased for $23 through the State careers Web site. These two guides provide an informed look at the types of questions to expect on the test, because they are produced by the organizations that actually give the exam and thus accurately reflect the true format.

Most insiders do not recommend months of study for the FSOT, because the test is designed to measure the breadth of knowledge a candidate has acquired naturally through education, work, and life experience. More than a few people describe the FSOT as a bit of a crap shoot. But the best advice probably falls somewhere in between full-time devotion to studying and no studying at all. Former State Department Diplomat in Residence Robert Dry advises applicants to address areas in which they are not strong, suggesting reviews of high school texts as refreshers or quick reads of "Dummy" types of books on history, government, etc. Advanced Placement books can also be helpful.

The structured essay is designed to test how well a candidate can write under pressure, so it can't hurt to practice timed essay writing to get comfortable with that type of task. It is important to pay attention to the time and aim to save a few minutes at the end to review and clean up the essay. "Think about the structure of your essay from the beginning," Robert Dry advises. "A short outline can help, but remember that the clock is running. The essay should have a clearly articulated thesis, backed up by substantive statements in supporting paragraphs, and a conclusion. Remember that you are writing against a standard and not competing with other candidates."

WEEDING OUT THE DUMMIES
By Anonymous

This unofficial take on the Foreign Service assessment has circulated for years.

THE NEW STATE DEPARTMENT ENTRANCE EXAM FOR PROSPECTIVE FOREIGN SERVICE OFFICERS

INSTRUCTIONS: Read each question carefully. Answer all questions. Time limit: four hours. Begin immediately.

HISTORY: Describe the history of the papacy from its origins to the present day, concentrating especially, but not exclusively, on its social, political, economic, and philosophical impact on Europe, Asia, America, and Africa. Be brief and specific.

MEDICINE: You have been provided with a razor blade, a piece of gauze, and a bottle of Scotch. Remove your appendix. Do not suture until your work has been inspected. You have 15 minutes.

PUBLIC SPEAKING: Twenty-five hundred riot-crazed guerrillas are storming the classroom. Calm them. You may use any ancient language except Latin or Greek.

BIOLOGY: Create life. Estimate the difference in subsequent human culture if this form had developed 500 million years earlier, with special attention to its probable effects on the English parliamentary system. Prove your thesis.

MUSIC: Write a piano concerto. Orchestrate and perform it with flute and drum. You will find a piano under your seat.

PSYCHOLOGY: Based on your knowledge of their works, evaluate the emotional stability, degree of adjustment, and repressed frustrations of each of the following: Ramesses II, Gregory of Nyssa, William of Ockham, and Hammurabi. Support your evaluations with quotes from each man's work, making approximate references. It is not necessary to translate.

PHILOSOPHY: Sketch the development of human thought; estimate its significance. Compare with the development of any other kind of thought.

SOCIOLOGY: Estimate the sociological problems which might accompany the end of the world. Construct an experiment to test your theory.

ENGINEERING: The disassembled parts of a high-powered rifle have been placed on your desk. You will also find an instruction manual printed in Swahili. In 10 minutes a hungry Bengal tiger will enter the room. Take whatever action you feel to be appropriate. Be prepared to justify your decision.

ECONOMICS: Develop a realistic plan for refinancing the national debt. Trace the possible effects of your plan in the following areas: Cubism, the wave theory of light, the Sonatist controversy. Criticize this method from all possible viewpoints. Point out the deficiencies in your point of view.

POLITICAL SCIENCE: Start and end World War III. Report its sociopolitical effects, if any.

EPISTEMOLOGY: Take a position for or against truth. Prove the validity of your stand.

PHYSICS: Explain the nature of matter. Include in the answer an evaluation of the impact of the development of mathematics on science.

GENERAL KNOWLEDGE: Describe in detail. Be objective and specific.

There are Yahoo groups devoted to preparing for the Foreign Service Officer Test and the Oral Assessment, called "fswe" and "fsoa." Each group has more than 8,000 members who sign up to be part of an ongoing discussion related to getting into the Foreign Service. The discussions offer a tremendous amount of information about the process and individuals' experiences with it. Those posting to the group are aware of non-disclosure rules all candidates must follow, but there is still a lot that can be shared. For candidates who want to be in the loop and in the conversation about the process, the Yahoo groups are a valuable resource. But be advised, this community can be intimidating to some who might not be spending as much time focused on and preparing for the exams as many members of this group. And be cautious, because not all of the information posted is accurate. Still, the Yahoo groups are a great resource for those trying to get a handle on a complex process and highly recommended as a place to connect with other candidates.

Step Three: The Mysterious QEP Process

You passed the FSOT! Now what? As always, there is a cutoff passing score for the FSOT that varies depending on the numbers of applicants for each career track and the needs of the Service at the time. In 2010, about 40 percent of candidates were passing the FSOT.

Candidates are notified by e-mail when the test results are available, and can then log on to download the "results letter" that indicates whether they are invited to the next phase of the process, the Qualifications Evaluation Panel, known as the QEP. Those who pass are given instructions for writing five personal narrative essays at this time.

The State Department Human Resources Bureau has made it a priority to find ways to reduce the time it takes to send out results following the FSOT. In 2008, three months was the wait time for FSOT results. Though this may change, in 2010 results were being made available after approximately three weeks. Candidates can request a breakdown of their scores by contacting ACT directly, and many do.

THE PERSONAL NARRATIVE QUESTIONS. Those who pass the written exam are given three weeks from notification of their score to submit five 200-word "mini-essays," answers to Personal Narrative Questions that are designed to evaluate six core competencies sought in successful candidates. The essays should present evidence of the following six competencies:

- leadership skills
- managerial skills
- interpersonal skills
- communication and foreign language skills
- intellectual skills
- substantive knowledge.

These short essays—200 words is not much space—need to pack a lot of real substance into an extremely limited space.

To deter misrepresentation by applicants on the extensive application forms and essays, HR instituted a verification process. Each mini-essay must include a contact person who can verify the events described, and some references are contacted. However, verification at this early stage in the hiring process, long before it's clear if a Foreign Service job offer will be forthcoming, has raised concerns among some candidates, especially when a current supervisor is contacted.

Many candidates do not realize that they are not required to put a current supervisor down as one of the contacts, and will not be penalized for such an omission. Previous supervisors or alternative contacts at a current job can be offered as references instead.

CAN YOU SAY SUPER CRITICAL NEEDS LANGUAGE? Those candidates who passed the FSOT and claimed proficiency in one of the super-critical languages noted previously (see p. 220) are invited to take a telephone language test at this point, before the next stage of the assessment process. The results from this language test are noted in the candidate's file, which is then passed on to the Qualifications Evaluation Panel that reviews all candidates who pass the FSOT.

THE PANEL REVIEW. Before the assessment process was updated in 2007, every candidate who passed the written test was invited to the Oral Assessment. Not any more. Now each candidate must successfully pass through another gate to be invited to the orals: the Qualifications Evaluation Panel.

Sometimes called the Screening Panel, the QEP comprises three Foreign Service officers serving on the Board of Examiners, the division of the Human Resources Bureau that manages the assessment process. Candidate files are divided up by career tracks, and each panel reviews candidates from a particular track.

The QEP lens is primarily focused on the six core competencies that help identify people who will make successful FSOs. These are the same metrics used to evaluate and promote FSOs throughout their careers, and the State Department views them as proven measures of success.

The QEP examines each part of the candidate's application: the structured résumé application form, especially educational and work background; the responses to the personal narrative questions; written test and structured essay scores; and relevant Super Critical Needs Language scores. Candidates are ranked using a point system. Then management—not the examiners—sets the cutoff numbers according to hiring needs at that time, and those above the cutoff line are invited to the Oral Assessment.

The Yahoo e-mail groups devoted to the written exam and oral assessment have swirled with commentary and concern about the QEP. Candidate concerns tend to focus not so much on whether the QEP is a valid screening process (no one seems sure), but on what is seen as a lack of transparency. Many candidates feel that this part of the hiring process is a mystery. One reason may be that those who get turned down by the QEP are not told why. This is in contrast to the availability of score breakdowns for the written test, which some candidates try to use to determine what areas to strengthen for a subsequent application attempt. (Candidates can keep taking the Foreign Service exam over and over again—although only once a year—until they pass, and many do keep trying.)

State human resources officials contend that there is no great mystery to the QEP, explaining that the panels operate under strict guidelines and procedures based on specific criteria, and examiners go through extensive training. HR calls the QEP a "closed loop, an insular process" with no room for political influence or outside interference. Candidates are not asked for their political affiliation, and never have been. No inquiries are accepted from outside. Not only are Board of Examiners staff prohibited from accepting any inquiries about a particular applicant; they are required to report any approach to the director of the board.

As another type of protection against possible bias, the sections of the application form that capture information about age, gender, race, ethnicity, or other personal traits that are not relevant to this review are electronically purged before a candidate's file reaches the QEP panelists. Officials from the American Foreign Service Association were briefed regularly by State HR about changes to the assessment process and were satisfied that adequate precautions against bias and politicization were being taken.

Step Four: The Oral Assessment—Mind Your 13 Ds

Once candidates pass the QEP, they receive an invitation to the Oral Assessment. QEP results letters are usually posted about four months after the FSOT date. The delay between the written exam and the invitation to the orals is a source of stress for some candidates. However, today the wait is shorter than it has ever been, and State is working to speed up the processing time even further.

Under the updated hiring process, the average number of candidates invited to the Oral Assessment each year has been approximately 1,800, about half the number invited under the old process when anyone who passed the FSOT was automatically invited to the Oral Assessment. "By evaluating more information about the candidates based on the identified core competencies, we are finding that we invite a much more competitive group to the oral assessment," explained one HR official. "In fact, the pass rate for candidates in the Oral Assessment has markedly increased."

The Oral Assessment focuses on testing for what are known as the "13 Dimensions" (see box), which are components of the six competencies. The six competencies (see p. 226) and the 13 Dimensions all help assess the candidate's "KSAs"—knowledge, skills, and abilities. While that sounds wildly bureaucratic, anyone applying to the Foreign Service would be well advised to become familiar with the 13 Dimensions.

The basic format of the Oral Assessment has remained essentially unchanged since the assessment process review began. On any given testing day, the number of candidates going through the Oral Assessment process, which lasts six or more

THE THIRTEEN DIMENSIONS OF FOREIGN SERVICE WORK

COMPOSURE. To stay calm, poised, and effective in stressful or difficult situations; to think on one's feet, adjusting quickly to changing situations; to maintain self-control.

CULTURAL ADAPTABILITY. To work and communicate effectively and harmoniously with persons of other cultures, value systems, political beliefs, and economic circumstances; to recognize and respect differences in new and different cultural environments.

EXPERIENCE AND MOTIVATION. To demonstrate knowledge, skills, or other attributes gained from previous experience of relevance to the Foreign Service; to articulate appropriate motivation for joining the Foreign Service.

INFORMATION INTEGRATION AND ANALYSIS. To absorb and retain complex information drawn from a variety of sources; to draw reasoned conclusions from analysis and synthesis of available information; to evaluate the importance, reliability, and usefulness of information; to remember details of a meeting or event without the benefit of notes.

INITIATIVE AND LEADERSHIP. To recognize and assume responsibility for work that needs to be done; to persist in the completion of a task; to influence significantly a group's activity, direction, or opinion; to motivate others to participate in the activity one is leading.

JUDGMENT. To discern what is appropriate, practical, and realistic in a given situation; to weigh relative merits of competing demands.

OBJECTIVITY AND INTEGRITY. To be fair and honest; to avoid deceit, favoritism, and discrimination; to present issues frankly and fully, without injecting subjective bias; to work without letting personal bias prejudice actions.

ORAL COMMUNICATION. To speak fluently in a concise, grammatically correct, organized, precise, and persuasive manner; to convey nuances of meaning accurately; to use appropriate styles of communication to fit the audience and purpose.

PLANNING AND ORGANIZING. To prioritize and order tasks effectively; to employ a systematic approach to achieving objectives; to make appropriate use of limited resources.

QUANTITATIVE ANALYSIS. To identify, compile, analyze, and draw correct conclusions from pertinent data; to recognize patterns or trends in numerical data; to perform simple mathematical operations.

RESOURCEFULNESS. To formulate creative alternatives or solutions to resolve problems; to show flexibility in response to unanticipated circumstances.

WORKING WITH OTHERS. To interact in a constructive, cooperative, and harmonious manner; to work effectively as a team player; to establish positive relationships and gain the confidence of others; to use humor as appropriate.

WRITTEN COMMUNICATION. To write concise, well organized, grammatically correct, effective, and persuasive English in a limited amount of time.

hours (including a break for lunch), is usually about a dozen at any given testing site. There are three parts to the assessment: the Group Exercise, the Case Management Exercise, and the Structured Interview.

Candidates should keep in mind that they are competing against set standards and not directly against each other. There is no quota on how many people within one group at an oral assessment can pass, so it is best to look at the oral assessment as a collegial rather than competitive exercise.

WHAT TO BRING. Candidates need to bring the *Statement of Interest,* Form DS-4017, to the Oral Assessment. The statement answers this question: Why do you want to become a Foreign Service officer? Also bring copies of the SF-86, *Questionnaire for National Security Positions.* The form should be filled out online, certified, and saved. Then it should be printed along with release forms and brought to the assessment.

Other useful items to bring to the Oral Assessment include a valid photo ID (this is required to get in the door); a favorite pen; a snack (something to share can win you friends); and a watch (you will want to keep track of the time during each part of the assessment, although the rooms do have clocks). Wear comfortable, but professional, clothing.

THE GROUP EXERCISE. Candidates are assigned to a group of five or six people who must negotiate the funding for various projects. Each member of the group is given a different project to study and then present, following a set amount of time to review a packet of materials. Each member of the group gets a different packet. The group will have limited funding and not all projects will be funded fully. Each group member is given a limited time (six minutes) to present his or her project. There are examiners in the room watching the group come to agreement on what to fund.

The group exercise portion of the Oral Assessment is "blind"—the examiners do not know who the candidates are. On this level playing field, the candidates interact, negotiate with each other, and solve problems, while the examiners observe.

Scores are not based on whether a candidate's project gets funded but on how each candidate works in the group. *Tips: Present well, be an active and attentive listener, and make a positive contribution to the discussion. Play well with others.*

THE CASE MANAGEMENT EXERCISE. Each candidate is given a binder of material on a particular topic, and the task is to write a memo. This section is designed to test how well a candidate can process and assimilate information and then write about it clearly. Anything that is asked for in the directions needs to be specifically addressed in the memo. *Tip: Follow the directions!*

THE STRUCTURED INTERVIEW. This is a personal interview, where the examiners will get to know the candidate as an individual. Candidates are asked questions about motivation and experience. In addition, the examiners will ask "hypotheticals" to gauge how well the candidate might respond to various challenging situations. During the structured interview part of the orals, examiners *do* have the candidate's file, and at this time can discuss experience, background, and the *Statement of Interest* with the candidate.

Step Five: Languages and Clearances

You passed the orals! What's next? Candidates leave the Oral Assessment knowing whether they have passed. At the end of the day candidates are called one by one, given their scores and told whether they will move on to the next stage of the process. The FSOA is scored on a seven-point scale, and scores are given for each of the 13 dimensions. A 5.25 minimum overall average score is required to pass. Those who make it over this hurdle move on to the clearance process and other language tests.

LANGUAGES: TAKE TWO. At this stage, successful candidates are invited to take telephone tests with the Foreign Service Institute for Critical Needs Languages and world languages that they claimed on their registration forms (Super Critical Needs Languages were tested *before* the QEP).

Bonus points are offered for a passing score in any language, but the size of the bonus depends on the category of the language: the more "critical" the language, the bigger the point bonus. Extra language points can boost a candidate's placement on a register.

Working knowledge (a speaking score of 2 or above) of a Super Critical Needs Language or a Critical Needs Language will result in a boost of 0.4 points in the candidate's ranking on the register. Arabic offers a 0.5 point bump.

Other languages will raise your score by 0.17 points, though world languages require a speaking level of 3 to qualify, while the CNL and SCNLs require only a speaking level of 2 to be counted. Visit the State careers Web site to find the current requirements.

By accepting the extra points for a CNL or an SCNL to move up on the register, a candidate agrees to serve in a country where that language is spoken at least twice: once during the first two tours and again after reaching the mid-level ranks of the Service.

SECURITY CLEARANCE. All incoming Foreign Service officers must obtain a top-secret clearance from the Department of State. The vetting process now averages about three months, though it can take longer depending on the candidate's background.

Before the Oral Assessment, candidates complete the SF-86, *Questionnaire for National Security Positions*, which serves as the basis for the background investigation. Information required on the questionnaire covers the candidate's basic life history, including all former residences and jobs. References provided by the candidate may be interviewed during this process, as well as people not listed as references.

The security investigation also considers financial history—for example, whether the candidate has defaulted on any loans or has had problems with credit or bankruptcy—as well as employment records, any history of drug or alcohol abuse, and criminal records. A candidate who cannot obtain a security clearance will not be eligible for appointment as an FSO. *Tip: Get your financial house in order before going through the process. Past financial difficulties are much less likely to cause a problem in the clearance process if you can show they have been successfully overcome.*

MEDICAL CLEARANCE. The medical clearance process is based on the completion of a physical exam paid for by the Department of State. Candidates living within 50 miles of Washington, D.C., must have their medical exams performed by the State Department's Office of Medical Services. Others can go to their local physicians. Candidates must receive an "unlimited" clearance for worldwide assignment.

Medical clearances for family members must be obtained before an overseas posting, but are no longer required for pre-employment. (Family members who cannot travel to a post of assignment for medical reasons may be eligible for a "separate maintenance allowance" to remain behind.)

WORLDWIDE AVAILABILITY. One requirement for employment as a Foreign Service officer is to agree to worldwide availability and sign a document to that effect. In other words, you will go anywhere that the Service needs you. In today's Foreign Service, almost all employees will be required to serve in at least one unaccompanied assignment—a post is deemed too difficult, unstable, or dangerous for family members—during the course of a career, and some will serve in unaccompanied posts more than once. Most unaccompanied postings are for one year.

The number of unaccompanied positions—in places like Iraq, Afghanistan, and Pakistan—has more than tripled during the last decade to about 900 in 2010 (including both generalist and specialist positions).

FINAL REVIEW PANEL: SUITABILITY CLEARANCE. Once the medical and security clearance process is done, the last step is the Final Review Panel convened by the Board of Examiners. This panel reviews the complete file for the candidate, confirms that all information is in order, and makes a final determination of suitability.

Step Six: On to the Register

Once candidates successfully pass the final suitability review, they are placed on a register to wait for an actual job offer—the invitation to join an upcoming A-100 class. Candidates are considered only for the career track they selected when they registered for the exam, and are placed on that particular register. When and if that invitation ever comes depends, in part, on where each candidate's name is on the priority ranked list, and also on the needs of the Service for new hires from the particular career track the candidate selected.

The State Department is working to speed up the time between placement on the register and the job offer and, indeed, some candidates are getting "the call" soon after being placed on the list. The maximum time a candidate can remain in contention is 18 months, at which point the candidacy expires. To try again, the candidate must start back at the beginning. Some candidates actually go through the entire application process again while they are waiting on a register, hoping to get a higher score and thus a higher place on the register that will make a job offer more likely.

The number of candidates hired each year varies. The State Department is making every effort not to leave candidates hanging until their eligibility expires; they aim to add to the lists close to the same number of people who will actually be offered positions in the Foreign Service.

For the most up-to-date information on the application and hiring process, go to the State Department careers Web site at www.careers.state.gov. State's *Guide to the Foreign Service Officer Selection Process* can be downloaded for free from the site. Other resources on the Web site include a multiple-choice questionnaire to help determine which career track is the best fit, descriptions of each career track, videos of active-duty officers talking about their work, as well as details on the application process.

Last Step: The Call

The entry process is complete when the candidate gets the call and is offered a job by the Department of State. Soon after, the new FSO heads to Washington for the A-100 orientation. That is where the Foreign Service career officially begins.

PREPARING FOR A CAREER IN THE FOREIGN SERVICE:
WHAT TO READ, STUDY, AND DO
By Mark Palermo

Yes, it is true. Only a small percentage of initial applicants succeed at joining the Foreign Service each year. That begs the question, "What sets those successful candidates apart?"

The main hurdles in the hiring process are the Foreign Service Officer Test (FSOT), the Qualifications Evaluation Panel (QEP), and the Foreign Service Oral Assessment (FSOA). The FSOT is a general knowledge exam tailored for entrance to the Foreign Service. The QEP is an evaluation of a personal narrative and written responses to several questions designed to elicit more information about one's suitability for this career. The FSOA is an assessment of a candidate's capabilities in the so-called "13 Dimensions" deemed necessary to succeed in the Service: from composure and cultural adaptability to working with others and written communication.

Here are some tips based on what I learned from my own experience.

The Obvious

Education is key. It does not matter what you studied or where you went to college (technically, it does not matter if you went to college at all), but to survive the exams and thrive in the career, you will need to have a broad academic foundation, intellectual curiosity, good study habits, and strong research and writing skills.

Live overseas if you can. In my A-100 class, 85 percent had previously lived overseas either for school, volunteer service, or work. Going abroad is a good gut-check for anyone thinking about a career in the Foreign Service, and provides ample anecdotes to demonstrate the 13 Dimensions.

Know what you are getting into. Review everything about joining the Foreign Service that is available on the State Department Web site. It really provides an excellent overview of the selection process and the career. Then follow up on some of the additional resources and references. The fact that you are reading this book is already a great sign!

Prepare for the FSOT, QEP, and FSOA. Take all the practice exams you can in order to get a feel for the content of the FSOT. I found a prep book for the high school Advanced Placement U.S. History test to be an especially helpful refresher. Try writing FSOT-like five-paragraph essays and FSOA-like case study memoranda under the relevant time constraints. Think of the QEP as a written version of the FSOA personal interview and, like the FSOA, prepare for the QEP well before you are asked to do it. Read *The Economist* and the U.S. Constitution. Think of examples from your own experience that demonstrate the 13 Dimensions, and learn to deliver them as a quick "elevator pitch."

What Might Surprise You

You do not need to know a foreign language. You do not need to be fluent in any language other than English to enter the Foreign Service. The State Department will train you in languages as required. However, knowing a language certainly helps. Quite literally, a passing language score can boost your position on the hiring register.

Prior work experience in foreign affairs is not necessary. Before joining the Foreign Service, I was the chief operating officer of a commercial architecture firm. Among my A-100 classmates, recent careers included: stage drama director, design/color coordinator for animated television, full-time mom, coffee shop owner, real estate market analyst, tour guide company owner, town planner, IT professional, elementary school teacher, fishmonger, and freelance writer. While the vast majority of my classmates had lived overseas, less than 40 percent of us had any direct experience in traditional international affairs jobs.

Life is the best experience. The value of maturity may be reflected in the typical age of entry-level officers. Fully half of my classmates were in their 30s. Another 20 percent of us were 40 or older. Your nonprofessional experience is a rich trove of stories that can illustrate any or all of the 13 Dimensions and genuinely prepares you to deal with a career in the Foreign Service.

The Importance of Reaching Out

Your Foreign Service relationships start long before you enter. The process of joining the Service can be grueling, and connecting with other people who are going through that process can help you maintain balance while you continue to live your current, "real" life. Reaching out through the Yahoo groups for the FSOT and FSOA, or attending study sessions and public information meetings, can help you prepare for the process and start friendships that will be valuable once you join the Service. Almost every member of an FSOA study group I was in is now in the Foreign Service, and several of us are still in touch.

This is a family affair. The Foreign Service is your career, but the life that comes with it has a profound impact on your loved ones. You will move every few years. You will miss some big family events and important milestones. Of course you will gain uniquely meaningful moments as well, but you need to talk with your family and friends about the tradeoffs. Do not be surprised if other people are not as excited as you are about your pursuit of this career. If they seem excited at first, do not be surprised if their disposition changes once you are actually offered a place in A-100. That is particularly true if you have a partner and/or children. This is no ordinary job; your whole family has to commit to it, and you have to negotiate it with them.

Last word: patience. Some people move straight through the process on the first try, but it is not uncommon to find extraordinary officers who struggled to get hired. Many people do not pass the FSOT the first time through. During my first Oral Assessment I sat with someone who was taking her fifth FSOA (her perseverance paid off—she passed). Even if you survive the screening process, your candidacy is only valid for 18 months.

In years past, successful candidates far outnumbered hiring authorization, and thus many qualified applicants were not offered jobs. I was on my third candidacy before finally getting "the call," an odyssey that lasted three-and-a-half years from the time I passed my first FSOT to when I started A-100.

In the end, I am actually glad it worked out that way. I was able to test my interest in the Foreign Service against myriad changing circumstances. My wife and I had two children, and my career was never better. Through it all, I remained committed to serving my country, and absolutely certain that the best place for me to do so was the U.S. Foreign Service.

Mark Palermo joined the Foreign Service in November 2008. His first tour was as an economic officer in Lahore, Pakistan. He is now serving in the consular section in Paris, France. Mark and his wife, Kirsten, have two young children.

A GUIDE TO STATE DEPARTMENT SPECIALIST (FSS) HIRING

Working alongside Foreign Service generalists are State Department Foreign Service specialists who provide a wide variety of management, administrative, technical, and healthcare services at overseas posts and in State Department offices in the United States. Specialist positions fall into seven major categories: Administration, Construction Engineering, Information Technology, International Information and English Language Programs, Medical and Health, Office Management, and Diplomatic Security.

The selection process is competitive. Positions for each specialist track are advertised separately online, and applications must be tied to particular openings. Descriptions of each career track, and tools for determining if one is a good fit, are on the State careers Web site at www.careers.state.gov/specialist. Because specialist jobs open up at different times, some infrequently and only briefly, it is easy to miss an opportunity to apply. Once you have found a specialist track that looks like a good fit for your background, education, skills, and experience, it is a good idea to select the option on the Web site to be notified by e-mail when a vacancy announcement is posted for open positions in particular tracks (click on the red envelope).

State looks for three essential commitments from specialist candidates. The first is flexibility, which means being a team player willing to perform work outside of your functional field whenever necessary. The second is that all Foreign Service employees must show public support for U.S. government policies no matter what their personal views may be. The third is worldwide availability: all Foreign Service specialists must be willing to serve wherever they are needed. Individual and family preferences and personal situations are taken into account in the bidding process, but the final decision on assignments rests with the State Department.

The First Step

In considering a job as a Foreign Service specialist, the first question to answer is: which career track would be a good fit? There are 20 career tracks for State Department specialists, listed here under the seven major categories.

Administration
Facility Manager
Financial Management Officer
General Services Officer
Human Resources Officer

Construction Engineering

Information Technology
Information Management Specialist
Information Management Technical Specialist (Digital, Radio, or Telephone)

English Language Programs
English Language Officer
Information Resource Officer

Medical and Health
Regional Medical Officer (primary care doctor)
Regional Medical Officer/Psychiatrist
Health Practitioner
Regional Medical Technologist

Office Management Specialist

Security
Diplomatic Security Special Agent
Diplomatic Courier
Security Engineering Officer
Security Technical Specialist
Security Protective Specialist
Supervisory Protective Specialist

Candidates apply for a particular specialist opening. Each track requires particular skills. To determine whether you qualify for a specialist track, visit the State careers Web site and select "Specialist" under the "Work" tab. Then click on "Vacancy Announcements" to find out which specialist tracks have openings. Information on specialist openings can also be found through the USA Jobs Web site at www.usajobs.gov.

The Application and Initial Review

To be eligible to apply for a specialist position, a candidate must be a U.S. citizen between the ages of 21 and 59 (hired before age 60) for all positions except Diplomatic Security agents, who must be between 21 and 36 (hired before 37th birthday); and must be available for worldwide assignment. Qualified veterans should check the State Web site for specific guidance tied to the Veterans Employment Initiative of 2009 designed to help those who have served in the military obtain federal government jobs. Questions can be sent to vets@state.gov.

Most application forms for specialist positions are posted online along with the vacancy announcement for that position. Some openings require a hard copy of the *Application for Federal Employment*, DS-1950, along with supporting documents. Others can only be submitted online. Because each specialist track requires particular skills, the application materials for each vary. The vacancy announcement will contain a list of all the material required for the application. Once you submit your application, the State Department will conduct an initial review to confirm your eligibility.

The Qualifications Evaluation Panel

Once a candidate passes the initial review, the application goes to a Qualifications Evaluation Panel. This panel is similar to the QEP for generalists, except that members of the specialist panels have subject-matter expertise for the specialist position being sought. The QEP reviews the application file looking at the candidate's skills, expertise, and professional experience, as well as motivation for joining the Foreign Service.

The Oral Assessment and Writing Exercise

The most competitive candidates in the QEP process are invited to an Oral Assessment in Washington, D.C. The specific nature of the assessment varies depending on the career track, but you can expect a writing exercise and a structured interview, and possibly a timed online job knowledge test.

The Oral Assessment is evaluated on the basis of 12 Dimensions (See box, next page.) that the State Department has determined represent the skills and qualities essential for successful performance as a Foreign Service specialist. The writing exercise is designed to assess writing ability, not personal views on a topic. Key elements for successful writing in this exercise are that the essay be concise, well-organized, grammatically correct, effective, and persuasive.

For the writing exercise, candidates will either write an essay on an assigned topic or a memo describing how to solve a particular hypothetical problem in an embassy. The hypothetical problem will be related to the particular area of specialization for which the candidate is applying. The time allotted for the exercise is 45 minutes.

For certain specialties, candidates then take a job knowledge written exam, or competency exam. These exams last about 45 minutes. After that, the candidate is interviewed by two examiners for about an hour and 15 minutes. One examiner is from the special-

THE 12 DIMENSIONS FOR SPECIALISTS

Composure
Cultural Adaptability
Experience and Motivation
Information Integration and Analysis
Initiative and Leadership
Judgment
Objectivity and Integrity
Oral Communication
Planning and Organizing
Resourcefulness
Working with Others
Written Communication

ist track for which the candidate has applied, and the other is a Foreign Service generalist. Candidates are asked to explain why they want to join the Foreign Service and are given a chance to discuss relevant background and experience. The interview may also cover technical areas related to the chosen field, and the examiners may pose hypothetical issues for the candidate to resolve. *Tip: Become familiar with the 12 Dimensions and think about personal examples from your experience to illustrate those characteristics.*

The final part of the Oral Assessment is the exit interview, during which you learn whether you scored high enough to move on to the next step in the process.

Placement on Register

Those who pass the Oral Assessment are immediately given a conditional offer of employment and placed on the register for their particular career track. This does not guarantee a job, however. Clearances and language tests come next.

Foreign Language Assessments

Those candidates who claim proficiency in any foreign language will test for that language after passing the Oral Assessment. Telephone tests are conducted by teachers from the Foreign Service Institute. Language testing is done at the same time as the background investigation and medical clearance process. Proficiency in a language is not required, but will enhance your competitiveness through bonus points that can boost your overall score and place on the register.

Bonus points are offered for a passing score in any one language, but the size of the bonus depends on the category of the language: world language (e.g., French, Spanish, German), Critical Needs Language, or Super Critical Needs Language.

The more "critical" the language, the more points it adds to the score. The Super Critical Needs Languages, in 2011, were Arabic (Modern Standard, Egyptian, and Iraqi), Mandarin Chinese, Dari, Farsi, Hindi, and Urdu. The Critical Needs Languages were Arabic (forms other than Modern Standard, Egyptian, and Iraqi), Azerbaijani, Bengali, Chinese (Cantonese), Kazakh, Korean, Kurdish, Kyrgyz, Nepali, Pashto, Punjabi, Russian, Tajik, Turkish, Turkmen, and Uzbek.

Those who take advantage of the score boost for a critical language agree to serve in a country where that language is spoken. Be sure to visit the State careers Web site for current language classifications.

Medical Clearance

Candidates who pass the Oral Assessment go through a medical and security clearance process. For a medical clearance, a physical examination is required. It can be done at the State Department if you live in the Washington, D.C., area, or by your local physician if not. Then State's Office of Medical Services will review your medical history and the results from the physical exam and determine whether you can be medically cleared. Medical clearances for family members are also conducted at this time but do not affect your candidacy.

Security Clearance

Candidates must obtain a top secret security clearance in order to be hired, and the State Department begins a comprehensive background investigation once they pass the Oral Assessment. The SF-86 form, *Questionnaire for National Security Positions*, serves as the basis for the investigation. Information required on the questionnaire covers the candidate's basic life history, including all former residences and jobs. References provided by the candidate may be interviewed during this process, as well as people not listed as references. The background check can take several months or more.

The Final Review

Once a candidate obtains a the security clearance, a Final Review Panel will look over the entire file for instances that would affect his or her suitability for the Foreign Service, such as: misconduct in prior employment; criminal, dishonest, or disgraceful conduct; misrepresentation in the application process; repeated or habitual use of alcohol to excess without rehabilitation; trafficking in or abuse of narcotics; conduct that shows poor judgment; disloyalty to the United States; or financial irresponsibility.

Registers of Cleared Candidates

Once a candidate has obtained security and medical clearances, and passed the final review, he or she is placed on one of the Registers of Cleared Candidates to await a job offer. Each register is for a separate specialist track, and the lists are rank-ordered by score and the date you were placed on the register. A candidacy expires after 18 months on the list. The State Department does not prohibit multiple candidacies at one time, so there are candidates who apply for more than one specialist track at the same time. There are also some who, while waiting on the register, begin the application process again to see if they can get a higher score and thus boost their place on the list. Veterans can qualify for additional point boosts for military service. If you accept a job offer in any one candidacy, however, your other applications will be terminated.

The Offer

When your name comes up on the list, you will receive an actual job offer. Study the offer carefully and make sure that all your qualifications and experience have been taken into account in setting your entry grade and step. If you feel they have not, inform the State Department hiring office right away. With few exceptions, this will be your last chance to influence your entry salary. At that point, you will be invited to report to Washington, D.C., to join an upcoming training class for specialists, called, no surprise here, "Orientation for Foreign Service Specialists." All new hires from the various specialist career tracks attend the same three-week orientation and then go on to skills-specific training.

JOINING THE U.S. AGENCY FOR INTERNATIONAL DEVELOPMENT

"Whatever it is we're trying to do in the world—whether it's lowering the number of women who die in childbirth, or eradicating a disease, or trying to bring democratic governance to parts of the world that are in transition—it takes staff who are smart and optimistic, and who understand how to invest in people. USAID should be a 'mixing pot' of people with backgrounds in banking, health, education, engineering, energy, and consulting, so the agency can incorporate best practices from industry into its operations. We're looking for people who are fundamentally entrepreneurial, and who can bring a 'Yes, we can' approach to USAID."
—Dr. Rajiv Shah, USAID Administrator

The U.S. Agency for International Development (USAID) provides economic, development, and humanitarian assistance around the world in support of the foreign policy goals of the United States. Headed by an administrator, USAID receives foreign policy guidance from the Secretary of State. USAID Foreign Service officers serve in Washington, D.C., and overseas at USAID missions, which are often housed in their own buildings, sometimes on the embassy compound and sometimes out in the city. The USAID mission director is part of the embassy country team.

USAID's key program areas are agriculture and the environment; education and training; democracy and governance; global health; economic growth and trade; and humanitarian assistance. USAID hires candidates with professional backgrounds in agriculture, economics, environment, administration, contracting, financial management, health, political science, business, engineering, and legal services.

In 2009 and 2010, USAID was in hiring mode, looking for the right people to fill critical development jobs around the world, especially in Afghanistan and Pakistan. The ranks of USAID FSOs were depleted over the last two decades, from about 1,750 in 1992 to fewer than 1,000 in 2001. More of the technical work that had previously been done by USAID staff was turned over to contractors, and USAID Foreign Service officers managed more contracts.

Priorities began to shift following 9/11, and the number of USAID Foreign Service officers has risen in recent years, to about 1,400 as of early 2010. In 2008, with the goal of re-establishing the U.S. government's leadership role in the development arena, the agency embarked on a hiring initiative. The Development Leadership Initiative (DLI) aimed to rebuild the permanent USAID Foreign Service work force. The DLI set out to double the number of USAID Foreign Service officers from 1,100 to 2,200 by the year 2012. Hiring in 2009 and 2010 was robust, but budget constraints in 2011 were raising questions about whether the goal would be met by 2012.

Subject to continued funding, USAID plans to continue bringing in new officer classes up to six times a year. USAID brings in career professionals primarily through the junior officer (JO) program. The program seeks qualified professional candidates willing to make a long-term commitment to the Foreign Service and international development. Most new hires enter through the JO program, although a limited number of mid-career positions in selected technical and support areas are also available.

Openings for the JO program are advertised on a continuing basis, and applicants must apply for openings in their particular area of expertise. To qualify, candidates need an advanced degree in a relevant technical area. Prior professional experience overseas or relevant domestic experience makes an applicant more competitive.

USAID candidates must be at least 18 years of age and not more than 59 at the time of application. Candidates must be U.S. citizens, available for worldwide assignment, and able to obtain a medical clearance to serve anywhere in the world. Male applicants must be registered with the Selective Service, and all applicants are subject to drug testing.

Information about USAID hiring, career track descriptions, and a link to job openings can be found on the USAID careers site at www.usaid.gov/careers. USAID job listings are posted on the USAID careers site as well as at www.usajobs. opm.gov.

The USAID Hiring Process

Candidates begin the hiring process by submitting an online application for an open position. Applications are reviewed by a Technical Selection Panel, and those candidates the panel finds qualified are then rated and ranked. The highest-ranking applicants are then invited to an onsite assessment that includes a written exercise, a group discussion exercise, and a personal interview conducted by the panel. The panel then evaluates the candidates and recommends the highest-ranked for hiring. Those successful candidates must then pass through security, medical, and other pre-employment checks.

Successful applicants are brought into USAID through career-conditional appointments. Once hired, they enter a three-year training program. Each new officer will have an Individual Development Plan (IDP) that serves as the framework for the training period. After a five-week orientation in Washington, D.C., new officers move on to specialized backstop (career track) training and meeting language requirements for tenure prior to their first assignments. The initial training phase in Washington before the first assignment can last from four to 12 months or more, depending on the job and whether or not language studies are required. New USAID officers spend their first overseas tour in on-the-job training, rotating through various USAID offices at a mission and completing required training.

Each new USAID FSO has five years to become tenured. For tenure, officers must have achieved proficiency in at least one language and have at least three years of service, of which 18 months must have been in an overseas assignment. New officers will be eligible for tenure after completion of 24 months at a USAID mission overseas, or at their three-year anniversary, whichever comes first.

USAID FSO Career Tracks/Backstops

The following descriptions of each type of USAID technical and administrative position are based on information from the agency. These career tracks are also known as backstops.

POPULATION/HEALTH/NUTRITION OFFICER. Known as PHN officers, Population/Health/Nutrition officers have responsibility for development, oversight, management, and evaluation of USAID programs in the following areas: population, family planning, and reproductive health; child survival; maternal health; HIV/AIDS and sexually transmitted infections; infectious diseases; nutrition; social marketing and behavior-change endeavors; population, health, and nutrition policy reform; operations and programmatic research, and biomedical and clinical research; commodity and pharmaceutical logistics and supply chain management; and health systems strengthening and health economics. An example of the kind of project a PHN officer might design or manage is the Pakistan Initiative for Mothers and Newborns, in which USAID collaborates with community-based organizations to transform traditional birthing practices around the country.

ECONOMIST. USAID economists provide technical expertise to country, regional, and agency-wide programs, as well as to the governments of developing countries. They analyze current trends and emerging opportunities and challenges to provide input for strategic planning. They also apply economic analysis and insight to help guide decisions concerning the allocation of resources among sectors, program design within sectors, and programs affecting cross-cutting issues such as environment or gender.

In addition, USAID economists help design and implement programs with the host country directed at achieving more rapid, sustained, and broad-based economic growth. They develop project proposals, prepare technical project specifications and related analyses, and initiate procurement actions. Programs typically emphasize technical assistance and support for capacity-building among the host country government's key economic policy agencies, as well as among private nongovernmental organizations, business associations, think tanks, and academic institutions.

AGRICULTURE OFFICER. USAID's agriculture officers analyze constraints on agricultural development in their host country and recommend action to overcome them. They design, manage, and evaluate a wide variety of interventions—in the areas of crop and livestock production and marketing, agribusiness development and trade, farm-to-market roads, irrigation systems, human and institutional capacity development, innovation systems, and agricultural policy—to enhance food security and enhance rural livelihoods.

EDUCATION OFFICER. USAID education officers provide advice on education issues and leadership in the review, evaluation, and analysis of education sector data. They conduct research and assessments and establish programs in the education sector. For example, in Liberia, USAID education officers developed a program that helps war-affected students complete their elementary school education by allowing those who missed out on schooling due to the collapse of the system to complete six grades in three years. There are nearly 30,000 students nationwide enrolled in these accelerated classes. As education ambassadors, USAID education officers meet frequently with high-ranking local officials and advocate for sound education policies, programs, and interventions in their country of assignment.

ENVIRONMENT OFFICER. USAID environment officers serve as technical leaders in strategic planning exercises and the design and management of programs across a wide range of development issues, including climate change, natural resource management (forests, wetlands, wildlife, and coastal and marine zones), biodiversity, water, energy, pollution prevention, environmental law, tourism, and urban programs. Officers analyze the status of environmental threats, environmental policy, and governance, and evaluate their environmental impact. They coordinate and negotiate with host-country and U.S. government officials, community organizations, universities, nongovernmental organizations, corporations, other donors, and other USAID partners on what needs to be done and how best to accomplish it within the framework of the U.S. foreign assistance program and American foreign policy.

PRIVATE ENTERPRISE OFFICER. USAID private enterprise officers work across the public and private sectors to stimulate economic growth and create an environment in which private enterprise can flourish. They serve as a technical resource for the mission, assessing data and providing assistance and advice on economic growth issues. They help develop and manage strategies, policies, plans, procedures, and guidelines for a wide array of private enterprise programs in the economic growth sector.

CRISIS, STABILIZATION, AND GOVERNANCE OFFICER. USAID crisis, stabilization, and governance (CSG) officers—previously known as democracy officers—research, plan, negotiate, implement, and evaluate emergency, crisis, transition, humanitarian assistance, food assistance, and democracy and governance programs. Democracy and governance programs address the rule of law, electoral and political processes, civil society and media, and good governance. CSG officers develop requirements and manage financial instruments (contracts, cooperative agreements, and grants) with agency partners.

For example, in the Philippines, CSG officers carried out a program to strengthen the capacity of the country's Human Rights Commission to investigate and prosecute human rights abuses. The program contributed to a significant drop in extra-judicial killings of political activists and journalists. In Ethiopia, CSG officers working for USAID's Food for Peace Office arranged to move U.S.-donated food to feed chronically malnourished children, while officers working for the Office of Foreign Disaster Assistance directed the U.S. government's response to the 2004 tsunami in Indonesia.

ENGINEERING OFFICER. Engineering officers with USAID provide technical expertise in design, construction, and maintenance of infrastructure facilities and other construction projects, including water and sanitation infrastructure, roads and transportation, energy, hospitals, clinics, schools and other public facilities, and housing. Officers research and analyze data, and provide construction management advice and services using advanced engineering techniques that support lower costs, shorter construction time, and better products. Officers are knowledgeable about the requirements for constructing and designing any project under host-country standards and laws. In Egypt, for example, USAID engineers have advised on projects from renovated classrooms in the country's most remote regions to Cairo's main power stations and water treatment facilities.

EXECUTIVE OFFICER. USAID executive officers serve as primary advisers to the country director on administrative matters. They provide overall direction for general service operations, facilities management, information technology and security, occupational safety and health programs, and construction management. These officers possess strong knowledge of federal rules, regulations, and guidelines concerning management issues and develop and monitor internal systems and procedures ensuring efficient and proper use of government resources within the mission.

Executive officers represent USAID on numerous interagency committees at overseas posts, such as the post Housing Board, the Interagency Administrative Council, and the Post Employment Committee. They interact regularly with members of the embassy's management office and collaborate with the regional security office and USAID's Office of Security to ensure compliance with and implementation of all security programs. In addition, executive officers are responsible for the administrative budget for the mission in coordination with the controller, and provide regular advice to USAID implementing partners on administrative issues.

CONTRACTING OFFICER. Contracting officers serve as business advisers for overseas USAID missions. Responsibilities include the negotiation, award, and administration of both acquisition and assistance contracts; accordingly, these officers must possess detailed knowledge of federal and agency acquisition and assistance laws, regulations, and policies. Contracting officers train and support technical staff in the implementation and monitoring of sound development programs while ensuring compliance with award terms and conditions.

PROGRAM/PROJECT DEVELOPMENT OFFICER. Program/project development officers play a critical role in planning and managing USAID programs worldwide. They are responsible for country strategy development, policy formulation, performance reporting, programming/budgeting of resources, coordination with other donors and U.S. government agencies, and public communications and outreach. Program/project officers also ensure sound planning, design, and implementation of a wide variety of international development programs by providing policy guidance, advice, and support to technical program teams in the overseas field missions. They make sure that cross-cutting issues such as gender, climate change, food security, and youth are included in projects, as appropriate, and that programs comply with federal law and agency policy. They also prepare and negotiate program agreements with host-country governments.

FINANCIAL MANAGEMENT OFFICER. USAID financial management officers work as members of the controller's team. The controller is the member of the USAID mission's senior management team charged with the responsibility of accounting and budgeting for mission operations and conducting a broad range of financial analyses on agency programs and local implementing partners, including host-country financial systems. Financial management officers assist the controller to provide advice and assistance to all components of the mission regarding financial practices and procedures applicable to USAID program implementation.

JOINING THE FOREIGN AGRICULTURAL SERVICE

If your special interest is agriculture or, more specifically, linking U.S. agriculture to the world, you may want to consider a career with the Foreign Agricultural Service (FAS), the foreign affairs agency of the U.S. Department of Agriculture (USDA). Established in 1930 and headed by an administrator, the agency has primary responsibility for the international activities of the USDA. FAS works to improve foreign market access for U.S. products, build new markets, improve the competitive position of U.S. agriculture in the global marketplace, and provide non-emergency food aid, as well as technical assistance, to foreign countries.

An agricultural attaché is a diplomat who collects, analyzes, and acts on information concerning agriculture, food, and agribusiness in foreign countries. The work of the agricultural attaché includes reporting on host-country crop conditions, food availability, and domestic agricultural policy; negotiating food aid agreements and agricultural credit lines, as well as bilateral and multilateral trade agreements; and implementing agricultural technical assistance programs. In many countries, agricultural attachés also work on issues such as environmental protection, food security, and food safety.

The FAS is the "eyes and ears" of U.S. agriculture abroad. Their main clients are American farmers, American agricultural exporters, and USDA policymakers. They monitor how trade policies, multilateral trade agreements, and developments in the international arena affect U.S. exporters. They also assess marketing opportunities abroad for those exporters and monitor crop developments in major producing countries.

USAID agricultural officers, on the other hand, help foster development in the agricultural sector of the country in which they work. Their main clients are the local community, host government, and USAID officials. They support country-driven strategies and invest in strengthening both public and private institutions that underpin growth of the agricultural sector of the host country.

FAS is one of the smallest of the five foreign affairs agencies established by the Foreign Service Act of 1980, with only about 180 Foreign Service officers, including those in Washington, overseas, and on details to other federal agencies. FAS has a total of about 1,200 employees, including Civil Service, temporary contract (Schedule B), and Foreign Service employees. Another several hundred work as locally employed staff in the more than 100 FAS offices overseas.

Unlike the other Foreign Service agencies, FAS appoints Foreign Service officers through a lateral-entry process. The key requirement for becoming an FSO with FAS that differs from the other agencies is that you must be a Civil Service employee at the U.S. Department of Agriculture in order to apply.

The lateral-entry application process takes place just once a year. Converting to the Foreign Service is competitive and openings are limited, but new FAS officers are selected every year. In order to apply for the FAS Foreign Service, you must first have 18 months of experience in the Civil Service of USDA, 12 of which must be with FAS. Time spent in the Career Internship Program or the Cooperative Education Program counts toward the 18 months.

By only allowing candidates who have experience working for the Foreign Agricultural Service, the agency ensures that they come to the process with a solid understanding of the work of the USDA and the role of FAS. Applicants come from a variety of Civil Service positions within FAS—economists, trade specialists, and international specialists, among others.

Candidates must apply in response to a specific vacancy announcement. The required documents include: a résumé, a statement addressing the specific evaluation criteria in the job announcement; a supervisory appraisal form; a current performance appraisal (no more than 15 months old); a narrative statement; certification of worldwide availability; and any other information related to the particular vacancy announcement.

Following the written application submission, candidates are screened by a Qualifications Review and Evaluation Panel that prepares a rank-ordered list of applicants determined to be qualified for successful performance as FAS officers. The list is presented to the FAS administrator, who reviews it and refers qualified applicants on to the next step.

Successful candidates are then scheduled for a written and oral assessment conducted by a panel of three FSOs, two from FAS and one from another foreign affairs agency. The assessment consists of a written exam and an oral exam. The written exam tests how well the candidate can produce written work and measures the candidate's understanding of the FAS mission and programs. The oral exam seeks to determine the candidate's skill in oral communication, focusing on the ability to present positions and arguments related to FAS work overseas.

Candidates are notified of their results on the examination day. Successful candidates are given a "conditional offer" to convert to the Foreign Service, contingent on the ability to obtain a security clearance and a medical clearance, and to pass a final suitability review at the end of the process—a review of the whole application file including all background information.

Once candidates obtain medical and security clearances, and pass the final suitability review, they are offered a five-year limited appointment in the Foreign Service. In order to be commissioned as a career FSO, candidates must achieve proficiency in a foreign language within these five years. In most cases, candidates are reviewed for career status after three years of service in a limited appointment.

FAS officers spend approximately two-thirds of their careers overseas, working at U.S. embassies and consulates as part of the Office of Agricultural Affairs or in an Agricultural Trade Office. They are required to serve at least one hardship tour.

More information on joining the Foreign Agricultural Service is online at www.fas.usda.gov/admin/newjobs/foreignservice.asp.

JOINING THE FOREIGN COMMERCIAL SERVICE

The United States and Foreign Commercial Service (U.S. Commercial Service) is one of the smallest of the foreign affairs agencies. The Commercial Service is the trade promotion arm of the U.S. Department of Commerce's International Trade Administration. Commercial Service officers represent U.S. businesses overseas, helping them find international partners. They promote the export of U.S. goods and services and defend U.S. commercial interests overseas. The Commercial Service offers market intelligence (helping U.S. exporters find the right markets overseas); trade counseling for U.S. businesses; business matchmaking services to connect U.S. businesses with partners and prospects; and trade advocacy for U.S. companies to level the international playing field.

Commercial Service officers work in U.S. missions overseas as well as in Washington, D.C., and in more than 100 domestic field offices around the United States. The Commercial Service entry process is highly competitive. Candidates must be U.S. citizens between the ages of 21 and 59, available for worldwide assignment, and with either three years of specialized experience or a graduate degree and two years of specialized experience.

Applications are accepted online—at www.trade.gov/cs/employment.asp—and those candidates who make it through the initial screening are invited to a one-day oral assessment.

Because the Commercial Service Assessment evaluates skills and abilities rather than knowledge, it tends not to require a lot of study time. In addition to becoming more familiar with the Commercial Service role and mission, qualified candidates should find that their relevant experience has prepared them well for the assessment.

The Commercial Service Assessment is only offered every two years, so joining can take a long time. The assessment is designed to evaluate written and oral communication, problem-solving and decision-making, the ability to achieve results, skills working with and leading others (including negotiation, consensus building), cultural skills, and capacity for personal and professional growth.

The Commercial Service Assessment has five parts, outlined below:

The Structured Interview

This part of the assessment consists of two interviews. During the Hypothetical Interview, job-related situations are described and the candidate explains how he or she would handle particular problems. During the Behavior Interview, candidates describe how they have actually performed in situations that are similar to those they could expect as commercial officers.

The Group Exercise

Up to six candidates, observed by CS examiners, work in a group to resolve an issue of the type that would come up on the job. Each member of the group gives a presentation, and then the group debates and reaches a decision.

The Advocacy Exercise

Candidates role-play as commercial officers, advocating on behalf of a U.S. company. They give a presentation, respond to questions, and compose a memo to summarize the presentation and offer suggestions for next steps.

The In-Box Exercise

Candidates are given papers that resemble what they might find in their in-box working in the field as a commercial officer. Papers are of various types, some requiring action and response. The task is to respond as appropriate and to identify the three most urgent items. Some background information and instructions are given to guide the process.

The Editing Exercise

Candidates edit typical reports written by staff who do not speak English as their native language.

Those who pass the assessment are placed on a list called the Rank Order Register. As vacancies become available, top candidates are called off the list and given conditional offers of employment, pending the completion of a background check and acquisition of a security clearance and a medical clearance. If a candidate on the register is not called within two years, the candidacy expires.

JOINING THE INTERNATIONAL BROADCASTING BUREAU

The International Broadcasting Bureau is the smallest of the foreign affairs agencies. Overseen by the Broadcasting Board of Governors, the IBB supports U.S. broadcasting to the world in 59 languages. The IBB provides the program placement and transmission services for all the BBG broadcast organizations, including the Voice of America. Today there are two types of Foreign Service members at IBB—radio broadcast technicians, who maintain and manage transmitter sites around the world, and VOA News Foreign Correspondents, who cover the news and manage bureaus in more than a dozen countries. These positions require specific technical or journalistic skills. More information can be found at www.bbg.gov and www.voanews.com.

INTERNSHIPS AND FELLOWSHIPS:
A CHANCE TO "LEASE BEFORE BUYING"
By Scott Kofmehl and Danielle Derbes

State Department Internships. One of the best ways to get a sense of the State Department is actually getting inside the "belly of the beast" by doing an internship. Interns collaborate on projects, gain a sense of how the organization works, and learn about career options. You can apply to work in Washington or overseas at an embassy or consulate. State has a wide range of internships—chances are, there is one that is perfect for you. Deadlines are early, several months before the internship start date. The process is quite competitive, so do not be discouraged if you are not chosen. Most State internships are unpaid, but some overseas posts provide housing if available. You must be an undergraduate or graduate student to apply.

Some tips:

- The summer internship is the most competitive. Consider applying for a fall or spring semester internship.

- If interning abroad, find out whether the post provides housing for interns. If the internship is in Washington or at a post without intern housing, begin the housing search early.

- If interning abroad, ask about visa regulations for the country where you are heading early as well.

- Get to know your fellow interns and take advantage of the city you're in, whether it be Washington, D.C., or a post abroad.

To learn more about internships and other student programs, go to: www.careers.state.gov/students.

Virtual Student Foreign Service (VSFS) eInterns: Announced by Secretary of State Hillary Rodham Clinton in 2009, this program provides the opportunity for students to participate in Web-based internships. The eIntern is partnered with either a post abroad or an office in Washington with which they communicate via the Internet. VSFS eInterns can participate in their internships from their college campus and are expected to commit five to 10 hours per week to the internship. VSFS internships can include a variety of tasks, such as: managing social media projects, producing videos, helping to produce electronic journals, and researching economic, human rights, or environmental issues. All VSFS eInterns are unpaid. For more information, visit: www.state.gov/vsfs.

American Association for the Advancement of Science Fellowship. AAAS selects 30 to 40 accomplished scientists and engineers as Diplomacy, Development, and Security Fellows each year. Fellows contribute to the federal policymaking process while learning firsthand about the intersection of science and policy. Fellowships are for one year with a possible one-year extension. Applicants must have a Ph.D. or an equivalent doctoral-level degree at the time of application. Applications are due in December. Go to http://fellowships.aaas.org for details.

Council of American Ambassadors International Affairs Fellowship. This fellowship is a summer program that combines mentoring by former U.S. ambassadors, a State Department internship, and international affairs courses at Georgetown. Apply during your junior year in college; six fellows are selected annually. More information at www.americanambassadors.org.

Diplomacy Fellows Program. This program offers participants from a range of scholarship and fellowship programs the opportunity to advance directly to the Foreign Service Oral Assessment. Eligible programs include: AAAS Diplomacy Fellows, Boren Fellows, Fascell Fellows, Institute for International Public Policy Fellows, Pickering Fellows, Presidential Management Fellows, Truman Scholars, and Jack Kent Cooke Graduate Scholars. This program is not offered every year. For the latest information, visit www.careers.state.gov/grad-postgrad.

Franklin Fellows Program. This fellowship is designed to bring mid- and upper-level professionals (five or more years of experience) from academia and the private and nonprofit sectors to work on critical foreign policy and international development issues at the State Department and USAID. Franklin Fellows work as consultants and senior advisers, contributing their knowledge and expertise to policymakers. Fellowships are for one year, with a possible one-year extension. Each Fellow's home organization is responsible for paying the salary, as the program is unfunded. Candidates without an organizational sponsor may self-nominate. There is no application deadline, as the FFP is a rolling program. Visit www.careers.state.gov/FF.

Jefferson Science Fellowship. This fellowship establishes a new model for engaging the American academic science, technology, and engineering communities in the formulation and implementation of U.S. foreign policy. Tenured academic scientists and engineers from U.S. institutions of higher learning are eligible for this fellowship. Fellows spend one year at the State Department or USAID in Washington, D.C., and may coordinate extended stays at U.S. embassies abroad. The fellows' home institutions must cover the salary, but the State Department provides per diem up to $50,000. Application deadline is January 14. More information at http://sites.nationalacademies.org/PGA/Jefferson.

National Security Education Program Boren Awards for International Study. Boren Scholarships provide up to $20,000 to undergraduate students to study abroad in areas of the world that are critical to U.S. interests. Boren Fellowships provide up to $30,000 to graduate students to add an important international and language component to their graduate education. Scholarship and fellowship applicants should identify how their studies, as well as future academic and career goals, will contribute to U.S. national security, broadly defined. All award recipients commit to one year of federal government service. Many Boren Scholars and Fellows have found job opportunities at the State Department. Details at www.borenawards.org.

Pamela Harriman Foreign Service Fellowship. Sponsored by the College of William and Mary, this fellowship provides $5,000 to two college students pursuing summer internships in Embassy London and Embassy Paris and to one college student pursuing a summer internship in a component of the Office of the Secretary. Undergraduate students entering their junior or senior year are eligible. Details at www.careers.state.gov/students.

Pickering Foreign Affairs Fellowship. Applications are accepted during the junior year of an undergraduate degree program (usually a February deadline)—20 fellowships are awarded annually. The fellowship provides funding for the senior year and the first year of a master's degree—tuition, room & board, books, and fees. Many graduate schools will assist with a financial aid package for the second year. Also, the fellowship arranges both Washington, D.C., and overseas internships. The best part is a three-year service commitment, which provides a conditional offer of employment to join the Foreign Service. However, Fellows still have to pass both the Foreign Service Officer Test and the Oral Assessment to make a career of it. More information at www.woodrow.org/higher-education-fellowships.

Pickering Graduate Foreign Affairs Fellowship. Similar to the above program, but for those applying for graduate school—20 fellowships are awarded annually. This program pays for a full two-year master's program—tuition, room & board, books, and fees. It offers Washington, D.C., and overseas internships. The three-year service commitment comes with a conditional offer to join the Foreign Service, subject to passing the FSOT and

FSOA. For both Pickering fellowships, women, members of minority groups historically underrepresented in the Foreign Service, and students with financial need are encouraged to apply. Find out more at www.woodrow.org/higher-education-fellowships.

Presidential Management Fellowship. Designed to develop the next generation of government leaders, the PMF is a two-year program that offers rotational assignments and professional development in addition to a full-time position in the U.S. government. The PMF application process occurs during the final year of a graduate degree program. One caveat: as a PMF finalist, you are not guaranteed a job at the department of your choice. The State Department does have positions for PMFs, but they are particularly competitive. Find out more at www.pmf.gov.

Rangel International Affairs Summer Enrichment Program. This six-week summer program for undergraduate students provides academic and professional development opportunities to prepare Rangel Scholars for careers in international affairs. Applications are due in February, and 15 to 20 scholars are selected annually. Students live at Howard University, attend classes, and participate in a variety of programs with foreign affairs professionals at Howard and at several locations around Washington, D.C. More information at www.rangelprogram.org.

Rangel International Affairs Graduate Fellowship Program. The Rangel Fellowship provides significant financial support for a two-year master's degree, internships (on Capitol Hill and at a U.S. embassy), and other professional development. Fellows have a three-year service commitment with the Foreign Service, and those who successfully complete the Rangel Program and Foreign Service entry requirements will receive appointments as FSOs. Both Rangel programs encourage members of minority groups historically underrepresented in the Foreign Service and those with financial need to apply. Applications are due in January; 20 fellowships are awarded annually. More information at www.rangelprogram.org.

BEYOND STATE

U.S. Agency for International Development Internships. USAID offers numerous internship programs, from the paid student intern program throughout USAID to internships offered by specific offices, such as the Bureau of Legislative and Public Affairs and the Office of Transition Initiatives. Internships in Washington and overseas missions are available. USAID seeks applicants from a wide range of academic backgrounds.

Check www.usaid.gov/careers/studentprograms.html for the latest updates and vacancies.

Foreign Commercial Service Internships. The Overseas Work-Study Internship Program provides college juniors, seniors, and graduate students of economics, business administration and related fields with "hands-on" (unpaid) experience working in the commercial section of a U.S. embassy. These interns typically serve for one semester during their academic year or for at least 10 weeks in the summer. Interested students should correspond directly with the senior commercial officer in the particular country in which they would like to work. Find details at http://trade.gov/cs/employment.asp.

Foreign Agricultural Service Summer Internship Program. The Foreign Agricultural Service offers 15 to 20 paid summer internships in Washington, D.C., for college students with skills, interests, and backgrounds in a variety of areas, including economics, trade, biotechnology, criminal justice, public affairs, information technology, and program analysis. Students gain a broader view of U.S. agricultural interests through interaction with other USDA agencies. A broader perspective on U.S. international trade and development interests is achieved through interaction with overseas offices and other federal agencies such as the State Department, U.S. Agency for International Development, the Department of Commerce, and the U.S. Trade Representative. The SIP also functions as an entry into internship programs potentially leading to permanent employment. More information at www.fas.usda.gov/admin/student/program.asp.

International Agricultural Internship Program. This program provides international agricultural trade experience to undergraduates and graduate students. Interns are placed in the 90 overseas offices of the Foreign Agricultural Service. Find out more at www.fas.usda.gov/admin/student/iaip/index.asp.

Appendix

ACRONYMS AND ABBREVIATIONS

Agencies and Organizations

ADB	Asian Development Bank
AFRICOM	United States African Command
AFSA	American Foreign Service Association
APEC	Asia Pacific Economic Cooperation
APSA	American Political Science Association
ASEAN	Association of Southeast Asian Nations
AU	African Union
BBG	Broadcasting Board of Governors
CDC	Centers for Disease Control and Prevention
CENTCOM	United States Central Command
CFE	Treaty on Conventional Armed Forces in Europe
CIA	Central Intelligence Agency
DEA	Drug Enforcement Administration
DHS	Department of Homeland Security
DOD	Department of Defense
DPKO	United Nations Department for Peace Keeping Operations
EPA	Environmental Protection Agency
EU	European Union
EUCOM	United States European Command
FAA	Federal Aviation Administration
FAO	Food and Agricultural Organization
FAS	Foreign Agricultural Service
FBI	Federal Bureau of Investigation

Agencies and Organizations *(continued)*

FBIS	Foreign Broadcast Information Service
FCS	Foreign Commercial Service
FS	Foreign Service
FSI	Foreign Service Institute
GAO	Government Accountability Office
GLIFAA	Gays and Lesbians in the Foreign Affairs Agencies
HHS	Department of Health and Human Services
IAEA	International Atomic Energy Agency
IBB	International Broadcasting Bureau
ICC	International Criminal Court
ICJ	International Court of Justice
ILO	International Labor Organization
IOC	International Olympic Committee
IOM	International Organization for Migration
IMET	International Military Education and Training
IMF	International Monetary Fund
IRS	Internal Revenue Service
JCS	Joint Chiefs of Staff
NATO	North Atlantic Treaty Organization
NFATC	National Foreign Affairs Training Center (known as Foreign Service Institute)
NGA	National Geospatial Agency
NGO	Nongovernmental Organization
NSA	National Security Agency
NSC	National Security Council
OAS	Organization of American States
OECD	Organization for Economic Cooperation and Development
OFDA	Office of Foreign Disaster Assistance
OPEC	Organization of Petroleum Exporting Countries
OPIC	Overseas Private Investment Corporation

OSCE	Organization for Security and Cooperation in Europe
SSA	Social Security Administration
UN	United Nations
UNDP	United Nations Development Program
UNESCO	United Nations Educational, Scientific, and Cultural Organization
UNHCR	United Nations High Commissioner for Refugees
UNICEF	United Nations Children's Fund
UNSC	United Nations Security Council
UNVIE	U.S. Mission to International Organizations in Vienna
USAF	U.S. Air Force
USAID	U.S. Agency for International Development
USCIS	U.S. Citizenship and Immigration Service
USDA	U.S. Department of Agriculture
USEU	U.S. Mission to the European Union
USMC	U.S. Marine Corps
USPACOM	U.S. Pacific Command
USSOUTHCOM	United States Southern Command
USTR	U.S. Trade Representative's Office
USUN	U.S. Mission to the United Nations
VA	Veterans Administration
VOA	Voice of America
WHO	World Health Organization
WTO	World Trade Organization

Embassy Offices, Positions, and Related Terms

ACS	American Citizen Services Section
AGR	Office of Agricultural Affairs (FAS)
AMB	Ambassador
APP	American Presence Post
CAO	Cultural Affairs Office

Embassy Offices, Positions, and Related Terms *(continued)*

CG	Consul General and Consulate General
CIO	Chief Information Officer
CLO	Community Liaison Office
COM	Chief of Mission
CON	Consular Section
CPO	Communications Program Office
CSG	Crisis, Stabilization, and Governance Office (USAID)
DAO	Defense Attaché Office
DATT	Defense Attaché
DCM	Deputy Chief of Mission
DLI	Development Leadership Initiative (USAID)
DRI	Diplomatic Readiness Initiative
DS	Diplomatic Security
ECON	Economic Section
EER	Employee Evaluation Review
EFM	Eligible Family Member
ELO	Entry-Level Officer and English Language Officer
EPAP	Expanded Professional Associates Program
ESTH	Environment, Science, Technology, and Health Section
FAMER	Family Member Employment Report
FMA	Family Member Appointment
FM	Facility Manager
FMO	Financial Management Officer
FSN	Foreign Service National (now Locally Employed Staff)
FSO	Foreign Service Officer
GEI	Global Employment Initiative
GSO	General Services Office
HTF	Hard to Fill
IDP	Individual Development Plan (USAID)

IIP	International Information Program
IO	Information Officer
IMO	Information Management Office
IMS	Information Management Specialist
IMTS	Information Management Technical Specialist
IRM	Information Resources Management
ISU	Iraq Support Unit
IV	Immigrant Visa
JO	Junior Officer (now Entry-Level Officer)
LABATT	Labor Attaché
LEC	Law Enforcement Coordinator
LES	Locally Employed Staff, also Locally Engaged Staff (formerly Foreign Service National)
MOH	Member of Household
MSG	Marine Security Guard
NEP	New Entry Professional Program (USAID)
NIV	Nonimmigrant Visa
OMS	Office Management Specialist
PAO	Public Affairs Officer
PD	Public Diplomacy
PHN	Population, Health, and Nutrition (USAID)
PMF	Presidential Management Fellowship
POL	Political Section
POLAD	Political Adviser
PRM	Bureau of Population, Refugees, and Migration
PRT	Provincial Reconstruction Team
PSC	Personal Service Contract
REO	Regional Environment Office
RMO	Regional Medical Office
RSO	Regional Security Office
VPP	Virtual Presence Post

FOREIGN AFFAIRS ONLINE RESOURCES

American Foreign Service Association	www.afsa.org
U.S. Department of State	www.state.gov
State Department Careers	www.careers.state.gov
U.S. Agency for International Development	www.usaid.gov
Foreign Agricultural Service	www.fas.usda.gov
Foreign Commercial Service	www.trade.gov/cs
International Broadcasting Bureau	www.bbg.gov
American Academy of Diplomacy	www.academyofdiplomacy.org
American Diplomacy	www.americandiplomacy.org
Amnesty International	www.amnesty.org
Associates of the American Foreign Service Worldwide	www.aafsw.org
Association of Diplomatic Studies and Training	www.adst.org
Atlantic Community	www.atlantic-community.org
CIA World Factbook	www.cia.gov/cia/publications/factbook
U.S. Department of Agriculture	www.usda.gov
U.S. Department of Commerce	www.commerce.gov
Embassy World Website	www.embassyworld.com
European Union	http://europa.eu
Foreign Affairs Magazine	www.foreignaffairs.org
Foreign Policy Association	www.fpa.org
Foreign Policy Magazine	www.foreignpolicy.com
Foreign Service Journal	www.afsa.org/fsj
Foreign Service Youth Foundation	www.fsyf.org
The Globalist	www.theglobalist.com
InterAction	www.interaction.org
National Security Education Program	www.nsep.gov

North Atlantic Treaty Organization   www.nato.int

Organization of American States   www.oas.org

Organization for Security and
Cooperation in Europe   www.osce.org

Peace Corps   www.peacecorps.gov

State Department Dipnote   www.blogs.state.gov

State Department Family Liaison Office www.state.gov/m/dghr/flo

Tales from a Small Planet
("Real Post Reports")   www.talesmag.com

United Nations   www.un.org

U.S. Diplomacy   www.usdiplomacy.org

United States Embassies   www.usembassy.state.gov

World Bank   www.worldbank.org

SELECTED READINGS

Berridge, G.R. *Diplomacy: Theory and Practice, Fourth Edition*. Palgrave Macmillan, 2010.

Freeman, Chas. W. *Arts of Power: Statecraft and Diplomacy*. U.S. Institute of Peace, 1997.

Gilbert, Martin. *A History of the Twentieth Century*. Harper Perennial, 2002.

Kiesling, John Brady. *Diplomacy Lessons: Realism for an Unloved Superpower*. Potomac Books, 2007.

Kennan, George. *Memoirs 1925-1950*. Random House, 1983.

Kennedy, Stuart C., and William D. Morgan. *American Diplomats: The Foreign Service at Work*. iUniverse, 2004.

Kissinger, Henry. *Diplomacy*. Simon & Schuster, 1994.

Kopp, Harry W. and Charles A. Gillespie. *Career Diplomacy: Life and Work in the U.S. Foreign Service, Second Edition*. Georgetown University Press, 2011.

Linderman, Patricia and Melissa Brayer-Hess, Editors. *Realities of Foreign Service Life, Volumes 1 and 2*. iUniverse, 2002 and 2007.

O'Brien, Patrick, Editor. *Atlas of World History, Second Edition*. Oxford University Press, 2010.

Rosati, Jerel A. and James M. Scott. *The Politics of United States Foreign Policy, Fifth Edition.* Wadsworth Publishing, 2010.

Ross, Dennis. *Statecraft: And How to Restore America's Standing in the World.* Farrar, Straus and Giroux, 2008.

Shultz, George P. and Kenneth W. Dam. *Economic Policy Beyond the Headlines.* University of Chicago Press, 1998.

Zakaria, Fareed. *The Post-American World.* W.W. Norton & Company, 2009.

STUDY RESOURCES FOR THE FOREIGN SERVICE OFFICER TEST

Guide to the Foreign Service Officer Selection Process. Department of State, 2011. www.careers.state.gov/resources

The Foreign Service Officer Test Study Guide. ACT, 2009. www.careers.state.gov (under "take the FSOT" then "test prep resources")

Davis, Kenneth C. *Don't Know Much About History: Everything You Need to Know About American History but Never Learned.* Harper Collins, 2004.

Hirsch, E.D., et. al. *The New Dictionary of Cultural Literacy: What Every American Needs to Know.* Houghton Mifflin Harcourt, 2002.

Jordan, Terry L. *The U.S. Constitution and Fascinating Facts About It, Seventh Edition.* Oak Hill Publishing Company, 1999.

Strunk, William and E.B. White. *The Elements of Style: 50th Anniversary Edition.* Longman, 2008.

For refreshers on management, economics, or history, check out the *Dummies* guides, the *Cliffs Quick Reviews*, or any Advanced Placement Test study guides.

Useful Web Sites

Association for Diplomatic Studies and Training, *Foreign Affairs Oral History Collection*: http://www.adst.org/Oral_History.htm

Foreign Service Officer Test Yahoo Group: http://groups.yahoo.com/group/fswe

Foreign Service Officer Assessment Yahoo Group: http://groups.yahoo.com/group/fsoa

Foreign Service Officer Test Essay Prep Yahoo Group: http://groups.yahoo.com/group/fswe_essayprep

Foreign Service Officer Test Online Course: http://testprepreview.com/fsot_practice.htm

Foreign Service Officer Test Wiki: http://fsot.wikidot.com/start

U.S. Department of State Web site: http://careers.state.gov

DipNote: U.S. Department of State Official Blog: http://blogs.state.gov/

U.S. Department of State's Office of the Historian: http://history.state.gov

U.S. Department of State YouTube Channel: http://youtube.com/user/statevideo

I'm passionate
about green initiatives.

This is my life trip.

I've worked as an Action Officer for science, technology and health issues abroad.

I worked on coordinating Palestinian participation in multilateral water talks and regional programs.

I've had the opportunity to work with USAID in monitoring and responding to a humanitarian crisis.

Miriam, U.S. Diplomat, Economic Career Track

★ CAREERS REPRESENTING AMERICA ★

careers.state.gov/AFSA

My career path isn't what you'd expect. I started out in investment banking and then became a diplomat with the U.S. Department of State. Working as a Foreign Service Officer in the Economic career track, I've been able to focus on something that means a great deal to me – environmental issues. Partnering with local officials in the Middle East and the Mediterranean, I've utilized my business and communication skills to promote renewable energy and negotiate water rights. And in my role, over the past six years, I haven't just had an impact on the world economy, I've also positively affected the global ecology. Now how many careers allow you to do that?

U.S. citizenship is required. An equal opportunity employer.

To start your own journey, visit careers.state.gov/AFSA

Foreign Affairs from an Insider's Perspective

Articles cover hot topics, from global economics and politics
to American foreign policy and the practice of diplomacy.

Subscribe now to the
Foreign Service Journal
www.fsjournal.org

BOOKS

Foreign Service Books
American Foreign Service Association
2101 E Street, N.W.
Washington, DC 20037
Telephone: (800) 704-2372 or (202) 338-4045
Fax: (202) 338-8244
E-mail: embassybook@afsa.org
Web site: www.afsa.org